T0304089

Published 2023 by River Publishers
River Publishers
Alsbjergvej 10, 9260 Gistrup, Denmark
www.riverpublishers.com

Distributed exclusively by Routledge
605 Third Avenue, New York, NY 10017, USA
4 Park Square, Milton Park, Abingdon, Oxon OX14 4RN

*Disruptive Artificial Intelligence and Sustainable Human Resource Management: Impacts and Innovations – The Future of HR /
Anamika Pandey, Balamurugan Balusamy and Naveen Chilamkurti.*

Routledge is an imprint of the Taylor & Francis Group, an informa business

ISBN 978-87-7022-991-3 (hardback)
ISBN 978-87-7004-044-0 (paperback)
ISBN 978-10-0380-687-5 (online)
ISBN 978-1-032-62274-3 (ebook master)

While every effort is made to provide dependable information, the publisher, authors, and editors cannot be held responsible for any errors or omissions.

Disruptive Artificial Intelligence and Sustainable Human Resource Management: Impacts and Innovations – The Future of HR

Editors

Anamika Pandey
Associate Dean, School of Business, Galgotias University,
Delhi-NCR, India

Balamurugan Balusamy
Associate Dean (Student), Shiv Nadar University,
Delhi-NCR, India

Naveen Chilamkurti
Associate Dean (International Partnerships),
Head of Cybersecurity Discipline, School of Computing,
Engineering and Mathematical Sciences, La Trobe University,
Melbourne, Australia

River Publishers

Routledge
Taylor & Francis Group
NEW YORK AND LONDON

RIVER PUBLISHERS SERIES IN COMPUTING AND INFORMATION SCIENCE AND TECHNOLOGY

Series Editors

K.C. CHEN
National Taiwan University,
Taipei, Taiwan

University of South Florida,
USA

SANDEEP SHUKLA
Virginia Tech,
USA

Indian Institute of Technology Kanpur,
India

The "River Publishers Series in Computing and Information Science and Technology" covers research which ushers the 21st Century into an Internet and multimedia era. Networking suggests transportation of such multimedia contents among nodes in communication and/or computer networks, to facilitate the ultimate Internet.

Theory, technologies, protocols and standards, applications/services, practice and implementation of wired/wireless

The "River Publishers Series in Computing and Information Science and Technology" covers research which ushers the 21st Century into an Internet and multimedia era. Networking suggests transportation of such multimedia contents among nodes in communication and/or computer networks, to facilitate the ultimate Internet.

Theory, technologies, protocols and standards, applications/services, practice and implementation of wired/wireless networking are all within the scope of this series. Based on network and communication science, we further extend the scope for 21st Century life through the knowledge in machine learning, embedded systems, cognitive science, pattern recognition, quantum/biological/molecular computation and information processing, user behaviors and interface, and applications across healthcare and society.

Books published in the series include research monographs, edited volumes, handbooks and textbooks. The books provide professionals, researchers, educators, and advanced students in the field with an invaluable insight into the latest research and developments.

Topics included in the series are as follows:-

- Artificial Intelligence
- Cognitive Science and Brian Science
- Communication/Computer Networking Technologies and Applications
- Computation and Information Processing
- Computer Architectures
- Computer Networks
- Computer Science
- Embedded Systems
- Evolutionary Computation
- Information Modelling
- Information Theory
- Machine Intelligence
- Neural Computing and Machine Learning
- Parallel and Distributed Systems
- Programming Languages
- Reconfigurable Computing
- Research Informatics
- Soft Computing Techniques
- Software Development
- Software Engineering
- Software Maintenance

For a list of other books in this series, visit www.riverpublishers.com

Disruptive Artificial Intelligence and Sustainable Human Resource Management: Impacts and Innovations – The Future of HR

Contents

List of Contributors

A. Rajeswari, *Research Scholar, VIT Business School, Vellore Institute of Technology, Vellore, Tamil Nadu, India*

Agnihotri, Alka, *Assistant Professor (HR), School of Business, Galgotias University, India*

Arora, Richa, *Associate Professor, Delhi Metropolitan Education, Noida, India*

Asif, Mohammad, *Assistant Professor, College of Administrative and Financial Sciences, Saudi Electronic University, Riyadh, KSA*

Bali Kamra, Neetu, *Associate Professor (HR), Lloyd Business School, India*

Biswabhushan Behera, *Research Scholar, School of Business, Galgotias University, India*

Chakraborti, Jayanta, *Symbiosis Skills and Professional University, India*

Chandra Singh Negi, Harish, *Research Scholar, School of Business, Galgotias University, India*

Chilamkurti, Naveen, *Professor & Head of Cyber Security, La Trobe University, Australia*

Chinmayee, Abbey, *Research Scholar, School of Business, Galgotias University, India*

Demirkol, Ahmet Yasar, *Associate Professor of Educational Management and Planning, Final Educational Institutions (University and Secondary Schools), Türkiye*

Ganguly, Chandrani, *Associate Professor, School of Business, Galgotias University, India*

Gaur, Mamta, *Professor, School of Business, Galgotias University, India*

Gomathi, S., *Professor, VIT Business School, Vellore Institute of Technology, Vellore, Tamil Nadu, India*

Gupta, Sandeep Kumar, *Professor, AMET University, Chennai, India*

Jana, Bhaswati, *GD Goenka University, India*

Junaid, Abdullah Bin, *Associate Professor, American College of Dubai, UAE*

Kadry, Seifedine, *Professor, Noroff University College, Kristiansand, Norway*

Kant Pal, Surya, *Department of Mathematics, School of Basic Sciences and Research, Sharda University, India*

Kapoor, Shikha, *Professor, Amity University, India*

Khaskel, Priyadarshini, *SAP Consultant, Infosys, India*

Kishor, Amit, *Assistant Professor, Department of Computer Science & Engineering, S.I.T.E., Swami Vivekanand Subharti University, Meerut*

Kumar, Ankur, *M.Tech., Student, School of Computer Science and Engineering, Galgotias University, India*

Lenka, Reena, *Assistant Professor, Symbiosis Institute of Management Studies, Symbiosis International (Deemed University), Pune, India*

Mathad, Kavita, *Dean and Chief Growth Officer, GIBS Business School, Bangalore, India*

Mishra, Shimar, *Assistant Professor, Department of Food Technology, S.I.T.E., Swami Vivekanand Subharti University, Meerut*

Misra, Sumita, *Assistant VP, Credit Suisse, Singapore*

Mohan Baral, Manish, *Department of Operations, GITAM Institute of Management, India*

Mukherjee, Subhodeep, *Department of Operations, GITAM Institute of Management, India*

Mutsuddi, Indranil, *Head of Department and Associate Professor, School of Management Studies, JIS University, Kolkata, India*

Nangia, Richa, *Associate Professor, K. R. Mangalam University, Gurugram*

Nikylina, Olena, *Associate Professor, Department of Management, The University of Life and Environmental Sciences, Ukraine*

Pandey, Anamika, *Professor, School of Business, Galgotias University, India*

Pandey, Suruchi, *Professor, Symbiosis Institute of Management Studies, Symbiosis International (Deemed University), India*

Penava, Marija Benei, *Associate Professor, University of Dubrovnik, Department of Economics and Business, Lapadska, Croatia*

Pradhan, Indira Priyadarsani, *Assistant Professor, Institute of Management Studies, Ghaziabad (University Courses Campus), India*

Prasad, Lalit, *D. Y. Patil Institute of Management Studies, Pune, India*

Rana, Renu, *Assistant Professor, Department of Management, IIMT College of Engineering, India*

Recep, Yucel, *Professor, Kirikkale University, Turkiye*

Rendu, Chait, *Assistant Professor of Travel, Business and Health Department of Tourism, Events and Attractions, Rosen College of Hospitality Management, University of Boulevard, Orlando, Florida*

Sabale, Anjali, *Research Scholar, VIT Business School, Vellore Institute of Technology, Vellore, Tamil Nadu, India*

Sachar, Dimpy, *Assistant Professor, Maharaja Surajmal Institute of Technology, Janakpuri, Delhi, India*

Saxena, Parul, *Associate Professor, Sharda University, India*

Seifedine Kadry, *Professor, Noroff University College, Kristiansand, Norway*

Shankar Shyam, Hari, *School of Business Studies, Sharda University, India*

Sinha, Chandranshu, *Associate Professor, Department of Psychology, University of Allahabad, India*

Sinha, Ruchi, *Dean, Amity Global Business School, Noida (AUUP), India*

Yucel, Sebnem, *Professor & Head of Health Management Department, Selcuk University, Konya, Turkiye*

List of Figures

List of Tables

List of Abbreviations

AGFI	Adjusted goodness-of-fit index
AGI	Artificial general intelligence
AI	Artificial intelligence
AIML	Artificial intelligence and machine learning
ANI	Artificial narrow intelligence
ANN	Artificial neural network
ANOVA	Analysis of variance
AR	Augmented reality
ARIMA	Auto regressive integrated moving average
ASI	Artificial super intelligence
ATS	Applicant tracking system
AVE	Average variance extracted
AVI	Asynchronous video interviews
BFSI	Banking, financial services and insurance
BI	Business intelligence
BPO	Business process outsourcing
CFI	Comparative fit index
CNN	Convolutional neural networks
CRM	Customer relationship management
D&I	Diversity and inclusion
DL	Deep learning
EAP	Employee Assistance Programs
ETL	Extract, Transform, Load
FAQ	Frequently answered questions
GDPR	General Data Protection Regulation
GUI	Graphical user interface
HED	High energy detector
HP	Hewlett Packard
HR	Human Resource
HRA	Human resource analytics
HRIS	Human resource information system
HRM	Human resource management
HRMS	Human Resource Management Systems

HRPA	Human Resource Predictive Analytics
HT	Hyper Transport
HTMT	Heterotrait Monotrait
IJICC	International Journal of Innovation, Creativity and Change
IoT	Internet of Things
KPI	Key performance indicators
KRA	Key result areas
L&D	Learning & Development
ML	Machine learning
MOOC	Massive Open Online Courses
NLG	Natural Language Generation
NLP	Natural language processing
NSA	National Safety Apparel
PDM	Predictive decision-making
PLS	Partial least square
PwC	Pricewaterhouse Coopers
RMSEA	Root mean square error of approximation
ROI	Return on investment
RPA	Robotic process automation
SRMR	Standardized root mean square residual
SVM	Support vector machines
TA	Talent acquisition
TLI	Tucker-Lewis Index
TM	Talent management
TQM	Total quality management
TR	Talent retention
US	United States
VIF	Variance inflation factor
VIT	Vellore Institute of Technology
VOE	Voice of the employee
VR	Virtual reality

Introduction

Disruptive Artificial Intelligence Technology in Human Resource Management

Anamika Pandey[1], Balamurugan Balusamy[2] and Vandana Sharma[3]

[1]Associate Dean & Professor, School of Business, Galgotias University, India
[2]Associate Dean (Student Engagement), Shiv Nadar University, Delhi-NCR, India
[3]Amity Institute of Information Technology, Amity University, India

Email: anamika2005@gmail.com; kadavulai@gmail.com; vandana.juyal@gmail.com

Introduction

It is a well-established fact that every organization is established having certain purposes and goals and a longer vision to have sustainability of their organization. Virtually all business organizations regularly obtain measurements dealing with end results, such as production, sales, profits and percentages of net earnings to sales. But what is reflected on the balance sheet does not necessarily show the true worth of organizations and these profits do not ensure their survival. Thus, the question arises as to what exactly makes the organizations sustainable and successful in an ever-changing environment. Several companies at present have set examples globally having the existence of its business for more than 300–350 years successfully. These companies were able to sustain effectively because they have put their focus not only on gaining profits but also putting more emphasis on acquiring, developing and retaining human resources, adopting innovative practices and developing environment-fit culture at the workplace. The fact that companies seem to place a greater emphasis on their human resource development and management than on financial results which further indicates that the micro-level HR practices and processes can contribute largely to the sustainability and holistic development of the organizations. Thus, it can be referred that organizations are required to pay equal attention to three bottom lines, that is, people,

1

profits, and environment for its sustainability and success which should not only meet the needs of the present generation but should have a futuristic perspective as well.

With the amalgamation of technology in every aspect of human life, the adoption of technology is fast-paced and actively changing workplaces. One such technology is artificial intelligence (AI). It is one of the key components for which an organization needs to be innovative and adaptive to function effectively and can have a competitive advantage over others. AI can help HRM professionals to master newer skill sets and gain various horizons in the current practices. Such implementation will provide more strategic time for the policymakers within an organization. According to Barends et al. (2018), about 81% of HR found it challenging to keep pace with the technological aspect of today's time, and abridging the gap is difficult. At present, the technologies associated with AI are reshaping the entire HR practices and their related industry. Chapter 1 of this book covers the role of artificial intelligence in enhancing the efficiency of HR processes and how HR analytics can help to predict various data functions for effective people management at the workplace.

Role of AI in HRM

From a laymen's point of view, AI technology leverages the implementation of improvised actions based on decisions made in past. The decision is based on the recommended actions which are repetitive and follows a pattern in decision-making. Thus AI is important to streamline the HR processes and improve the efficacy of the organization. The process of making the machines intelligent enough to make a decision is done by feeding the right set of instruction set. Many useful insights can be drawn from the knowledge gained from the process. In LinkedIn et al. (2018), most organizations are now implementing technology it is indeed very important for HR professionals to embrace the technology and prepare themselves for the huge diversification. In Chapter 2 a new era of HRM in the World 2.0 is discussed which basically covers the technology-enabled HR practices adopted in the new normal.

AI encompasses a wide range of techniques, from algorithms and conversational AI to decisional AI and machine learning, to name a few. Moreover, the number of practical applications of AI is increasing rapidly. AI can be divided into weak AI and strong AI, with the latter also known as 'general artificial intelligence'. This type of AI refers to a machine that is endowed with consciousness, sensitivity and intellect and is capable of solving any problem, not just a specific one. Despite the advances being made in

AI, a project manager recently remarked that 'we do not yet have AI systems that are incredibly intelligent and that have left humans behind. It's more about how they can help and deputise for human beings'.

AI in Action

AI is not only an opportunity for HR managers to save time and increase productivity, but also enhance the employee experience. In Kumar et al., with 600 start-ups innovating in HR and digital technology, including 100 specifically in HR and AI, the HR function is a highly lucrative market for start-ups. It is crucial for each organization to not only adopt new technology and implement it successfully but also keep focusing on the sustainability of its existence. There are three pillars of sustainability viz., people, profit, and environment (planet). Thus, organization must meet not only the present needs but also have the capacity and ability to meet future needs. Here, the role of HR becomes crucial to support the organization in improving its effectiveness from the operational level to economic to cultural fit. Modern technology-equipped HR practices can provide leverage to this process and can have an efficient way of functioning. This book aims to explore the modern technology-based functioning of the organization for HR sustainability. For sustainable practices, it is crucial to have an effective implementation and follow-up of each process. Chapter 9 discusses the impact of the implementation of AI on human resource management functions and the feedback mechanisms for its sustainability. There are various applications of artificial intelligence in HR practices and functions which are discussed in this book along with the sustainability of its existence.

Applications of AI in HRM

Among the various implementation of AI in HRM the most promising and evolving application is employee recruitment and onboarding, and the second one is an overall improvement of processes and the automation of the administrative tasks related to HRM.

Recruitment and Onboarding

AI helps in phasing out the first step of recruitment like filtering out the job applications. In Banks et al., (2019), the HR process starts with calling out the right job applications. Chapter 8 of this book, it is discussed in detail how organizations have started embracing AI technology for smart recruitment where many mid-level sector organizations are still dependent on referrals. The percentage of the best-in-class recruitment process is less than 10% in the majority of companies. It elaborated on the use of AI for creating a job application process in a user-friendly manner to keep a check on the number of abandoned applications which are incomplete. With the implementation of AI in HRM, the recruitment process is easier and simpler giving more rationale to the user and all other stakeholders. This further helps in improving the application completion rates. Many follow-up emails and the discovery of the right candidate for a particular skill set can be set with the help of AI. AI helps in analysing the existing pool of campuses that fit the job role and soon triggers the advertisement as the requirement comes up. This helps in identification of the qualified prospective employees to the fullest and with one simple click as compared to the traditional way of hunting the candidate. Once the HR managers find the best out of the entire pool the next level of the recruitment process starts. The onboarding process starts and with the advent of AI, the process is not restricted to only the working hours of the organization. This is another big advantage of using technology in the recruitment process.

AI technology has integrated the chatbots with the application process allowing the candidate to understand the process and apply with ease. It has helped the candidate to remotely support the overall process at any time in the day and reduced the administrative burden and fastened the process.

Internal Assessment, Intra Mobility and Retention of Employees

Another feature of AI as discussed by Tambe et al. (2019), GRM is to boost internal employee assessment. This includes minor factors like attendance, leave pattern, employee punctuality, funds and benefits provided to improve employee retention. The process is automated with continuous feedback and for employee engagement to identify the employees for the higher and remote job roles for shorter- or long-term duration. Job satisfaction and employee engagement in the company process are more required in today's scenarios than ever. Continuous feedback helps the organization and the HRM to improve the process and match the right candidate with the right job profile. According to a recent study, AI-based software is a key indicator of employee success to identify the key indicators for the promotion and driving force for the employees and internal exchange programmes. This not only saves enormous time but also reduces the overall talent acquisition cost of the organization. AI has also helped in understanding the reason for employees quitting the job, as the indicators are well present with the software implementation, and having this information beforehand helps in deploying the retention benefits to the specific employees.

Automation of the HR Administrative Task

AI has key benefits of leveraging AI in various HR processes as it is in other sectors, automating low value, easily repeatable administrative tasks giving more time for strategic planning at other levels. Chapter 6 of this book covers the role of Artificial intelligence in reinventing strategic HR practices for creating and implementing HR sustainability. This enables HR to bridge the gap between the organizational strategic visions of the environment to people sustainability.

Dennis & M.J. (2018), Smart Technologies can automate the process of screening candidates, and scheduling the interviews and the focus can now be on the result rather than the process. Deploying AI can ease out many small and tedious tasks, say for instance as the study found that AI implementation has made the administrative process easier as compared to the non-implementation of automation.

Challenges Faced in Implementing AI in HR

Technology always has its merits but on the same side, they have its limitations also. One of the major concerns is the handling of data and keeping it private and secure. In a survey, 31% of the respondents expressed that it is difficult to interact with the automated system at times due to technical glitches faced during the process. Another prominent expression from HR leaders is that interaction with a human can never be replaced with HR. Technology somehow can never be ignored and at the same time, HR has to move forward and understand the implication, and be prepared for the change. Another important aspect involved with the HR process is the handling of the sensitive data of the company and employees. Here AI can be used to draw useful knowledge at the abstract level and also get data on various segments at the same time.

For example, the employee's personal information is vulnerable to data breaches and henceforth HR must initiate suitable action to involve security measures in the account. HR must be equipped with the tools and technology transfers as it lays a strong foundation for HR as a profession, as it evolves.

Significance of AI Technology in HR

According to a survey, 130 million jobs will emerge in various sectors with the dawn of AI. The major reason is the use of electronic gadgets and smart devices. The usage of the gadgets has made it more evident to improvise the HR process.

Integration of AI with HR Process

Most of the functioning of the organization is real-time based and needs real-time analysis and decision-making. AI makes it easier and real by implementing proven algorithms and other solutions using computing techniques. According to Kaplan & Haenlein(2019), the companies are open to adapting the AI within the existing infrastructure to undergo the influence of AI along with the implementation of IoT and Cloud infrastructure.

As AI is promising and capable of imitating human intelligence, the implementation of AI is more responsible and less prone to errors. The data so collected by these processes are more reliable.

Risks Associated with the Implementation of AI in HRM

The recent adoption of AI by human resources has been a big topic of discussion. While start-ups have been pushing the boundaries of innovation, and virtual reality is currently all the rage, the technology still faces many obstacles when it comes to HR. According to a survey of HR managers and digitization project managers in large companies, there are three main potential issues with AI in the HR field: the data used, the potential for the technology to become a gimmick, and algorithmic governance. Data is a major issue when it comes to AI. It is important to ensure that the data used to power AI is accurate and up-to-date, as this will be the basis for any decisions made by the technology. Chapter 5 discusses the effect of the implementation of artificial intelligence tools in Human Resource Analytics so that organization can have proactive approaches to human resource development and management. This is especially important in the HR field, where decisions about employees can have serious implications. The risk of AI becoming a gimmick is also a major concern. Companies may be tempted to use AI to give the appearance of being innovative, without really integrating it into the way they manage their employees. This could lead to the technology being used ineffectively, or not being taken seriously by employees.

Streamlining Operations and Maximizing Efficiency by providing Administrative and Legal Assistance

AI is revolutionizing the way HR teams handle their day-to-day tasks. By freeing up staff from mundane and repetitive tasks, HR teams can focus on more complex assignments. Vanet al. (2019) states that AI is also playing a major role in helping to automate questions asked by employees, such as those related to training applications, vacation days and more. For example, EDF has elected to create a legal chatbot to automatically respond to frequently asked questions and guide users to find the correct legal advice or an expert in the field. AI is just not needed to handle absenteeism and leaves or process expenditure reports and training but also look into the administrative and legal aspects of job roles, payroll and salary policies for each individual. Further, AI systems can be used to issue checks and balances for accurate calculations and consistency in all legal declarations. AI can also provide packages of personalized social benefits based on employee profiles. Overall, AI is streamlining the HR process, allowing for greater efficiency and accuracy with a smoother process. HR teams can be confident that their employees are getting the correct information and resources quickly and accurately.

Recruitment: Helping to Choose Candidates

AI is revolutionizing the recruitment process and is proving to be a great asset for companies with large volumes of applications. Chatbots are being implemented to replace first-level interactions between HR managers and candidates, allowing more time to focus on other important tasks. Algorithms can analyse job offers semantically, delivering the best candidates to the recruiter. Start-ups are now offering a service that does not even require CVs, diplomas, or experience, instead focusing on predictive matching based on affinities and smart data. However, it is important to note that AI has its limitations, particularly when it comes to complex positions that require high-level skills. There is also a divide among HR managers and project managers on the value of AI for recruitment, with some believing it is a great asset while others believe people are 'over-promising' what it can bring to the table. Nevertheless, AI is continuing to evolve, and new practical examples are emerging all the time.

Training and Skills: Personalized Career Paths

The use of AI in employee training is revolutionizing the way businesses acquire and develop skills. By utilizing learning analytics, companies can track and measure how quickly employees learn and the depth of their understanding. This data can then be used to customize career paths and training techniques for each individual. AI is also allowing for improved internal mobility, allowing employees to pursue their desired pathways, positions and programmes for developing their skills. Solutions such as AI-powered assessment, training and suggestion programmes are becoming increasingly popular, however, these are limited in countries with strict data protection regulations such as France due to the General Data Protection Regulation (GDPR). Elsewhere, these solutions can be tailored to the individual. In chapter 4, the impact of AI is discussed on skills development training imparted to various government officers. These feedbacks are crucial for the improvement of the training programme and the technology-enabled process is helping the organizations to go ahead with quicker solutions and easy implementations. Further, in Chapter 10 the impact of AI-based training in the education sector is detailed to enhance the teaching-learning processes.

Motivation and Social Climate: Towards a Better Understanding of Commitment

AI is revolutionizing the way we manage our employees. Chapter 12 covers the challenges associated with the building of effective teams in the virtual world and the role of technology in strengthening team cohesiveness. By leveraging AI, managers can gain insights into the engagement levels of their teams without knowing who said what. With AI-powered tools, managers can quickly identify employees who are at risk of resigning, as well as gain a better understanding of the underlying social phenomena in the workplace. These tools allow for real-time indicators, helping managers to act quickly and take corrective action when needed. However, the use of AI in HR management is still in its early stages, and questions and criticisms remain. Issues such as data privacy, return on investment and algorithmic governance must be addressed for AI to be effectively and ethically implemented in the workplace.

The Risks and Disruptive Role of Artificial Intelligence

Data is essential for AI to work effectively, and its quality is critical for the accuracy of the results. Amazon's experience is a perfect example of how data quality is essential: the company had to quickly withdraw its first recruitment software since it favoured male resumes. This was simple to understand that the software was built on the datasets of companies having male candidates.

The data associated was almost a decade old. Furthermore, the data sets in the HR field tend to be more limited than in other areas. The number of people employed in large companies is much lower than the number of purchases made by customers, making it difficult to use large data applications. This is unlike predictive maintenance, where expert systems can detect signs of wear in a machine before humans, and just-in-time interventions can be made to overhaul the machinery. However, in human systems, the actions and reactions of individuals are not usually tracked, and can sometimes be unpredictable. Therefore, it is important to take into consideration both the quantity and quality of data, as well as how to use it in a context and time frame that can support analysis and decision-making.

Association of Return on Investment (ROI) and the Dangers of Gimmickry

The debate about whether to invest in AI for HR purposes is a complex one, with HR managers particularly concerned about the budget and returns on investment. The current trend for chatbots and virtual technologies can be attractive, offering a modern image to the company, but often leading to costly investments. Redoing the corporate website can easily cost ten times more than a chatbot, and can soon become outdated due to the frequent advancements in AI. In addition to the financial implications, HR needs to be aware of the potential risks of investing in AI. Gimmicks and a profusion of HR indicators may be presented as desirable, but the relevance and effectiveness of these tools must be thoroughly assessed before being adopted. Start-ups often only offer solutions for a specific area and not the company's entire ecosystem, meaning HR must look for a comprehensive package that fits their needs. Ultimately, HR managers need to evaluate the long-term costs and benefits of implementing AI and consider the risk of jeopardizing employee trust. Before any investment is made, it is essential to carefully weigh the pros and cons of AI to make the best decision for the organization.

Algorithmic Governance

HR managers are increasingly aware of the potential of AI to improve their processes, but at the same time, they fear that it might lead to a loss of the creativity and inventiveness that is so important in the field. They worry that AI will replace the human touch and risk sacrificing the trust that employees have in their HR departments. It is important to note that human behaviour is complex, and it is impossible to capture all of it in data. Automating management and decision-making in HR may not be the best approach, as it ignores the psychological and sociological aspects of the job. The solution is not to replace managerial methods, but to find ways to capitalize on the advances in technology while still keeping the human touch. AI can be used to analyse predictive data and should be seen as a tool to help HR departments become more holistic and innovative. With this in mind, AI can be used to make HR more efficient and effective.

Confidence in HR Reporting with AI Integration

Integrating AI into Human Resources (HR) processes are being seen as a practical move by many reports. A report from Oracle and Future Workplace found that the majority of HR practitioners are open to this change, with 64% of them expressing a willingness to take advice from a robot over their manager. This is a significant shift in attitude when compared to the traditional view of HR and indicates the potential of AI in this field. With the right implementation, AI could revolutionize the way HR departments operate, leading to a more efficient, streamlined process. As AI technology continues to develop, more and more businesses will likely begin to utilize its potential in HR. It has been found that 50% of a majority of workers are currently using some form of AI at work. Further, 32% more significant numbers were reported in 2018. Furthermore, 65% of workers feel optimistic, excited and grateful about having robotic co-workers. It appears that 60% of workers in India, 44% of workers in UAE, and 56% of workers in China are the most enthusiastic about AI, followed by 41% of workers in Singapore, 32% of workers in Brazil, 26% of workers in Australia/New Zealand, 25% of workers in Japan, 22% of workers in the US, 20% of workers in the UK, and 8% of workers in France. Interestingly, according to survey men workers are more likely to have a positive view of AI at work than women workers, with 32% of men optimistic compared to 23% of women.

Chapter 13 discusses how gamification is used in HR practices to transform various functions from the traditional model. Most of the companies who are using gamification for transforming their workplace have AI-based tools for it. The gamification-based practices are equipping the organization for employee engagement and effective HR management. These gamification techniques are largely based on AI. In the past two years, many companies have realized the potential of AI to revolutionize their HR workflows and are beginning to invest in it for their business. This has resulted in a marked shift in the optimism of workers, says Dan Schawbel, research director at Future Workplace. His study shows that AI is changing the dynamics between workers and their managers, and redefining the role of a manager in an AI-driven workplace. Organizations are now realizing the importance of integrating AI into their daily operations, and are adopting it to improve efficiency and productivity. From automating manual HR tasks to analysing data to make informed decisions, AI is becoming the go-to technology for many companies. In addition, AI is also providing much-needed insight into the workforce and workplace, allowing employers to gain a better understanding of their workers. AI-driven technologies such as sentiment analysis are helping organizations identify the emotions and feelings of their workers, allowing them to make decisions based on actual data. The emergence of AI has revolutionized the way companies operate and has enabled them to create a better workplace. As companies continue to invest in AI, they will be able to reap the benefits of improved efficiency, productivity and employee satisfaction.

Talent Acquisition and Management

After the pandemic, organizations have gone through several structural and process changes at the workplace. The hybrid or online mode of working has brought major issues in people management whether it is hiring employees, engaging or retaining them. After the pandemic, more and more people are expected to re-enter employment and companies are expecting intense competition for talent. Technology-equipped recruitment processes are helping HR professionals for smooth functioning and talent acquisition. Chapter 7 of this book throws some light on such issues in which current practices of HR for AI-aided talent acquisition practices are detailed. Another challenge for HR professionals is to train and develop their employees so that they are effectively performed to further add value to the organizations. Chapter 3 emphasizes on the digital upskilling process that organizations are adopting in the present era to manage and engage their employees.

Smart digital forms for candidate resumes

HR departments are increasingly leveraging AI technology to create a more streamlined and personal connection between companies and current and prospective employees. Adriana Bokel Herde, Pega's chief people officer, explains that AI can help automate tedious tasks such as having applicants fill out multiple forms, by recognizing relevant information from their resume and transferring it to digital forms. In addition, AI can be used to analyse candidate work experience and interests to match them with available roles. By using AI, companies can make the candidate experience a priority and assess candidates even before they have interacted with a recruiter. AI technology can also help reduce human bias in the hiring process, enabling companies to create an equitable and personalized experience for their current and prospective employees.

Insights into the employee referrals

AI has the potential to revolutionize the way HR departments operate, by enabling them to delve deeper into employee referrals and extract valuable insights. By analysing performance data of previous referrals, AI can recognize patterns and identify when similar successful candidates are being recommended. In addition, AI can automate many of the repetitive, low-value tasks associated with the onboarding process, freeing HR teams to focus on more strategic activities such as mentoring and gathering feedback. By unlocking the insights from data collected throughout the candidate and employee lifecycle, HR departments can improve employee engagement and retention.

Insights on Data-backed Resources

Michael Cohen, the Chief Product Officer at Achievers, believes that AI has revolutionized the way Human Resources (HR) professionals work. He says that AI provides HR professionals with data-driven resources and information obtained directly from employees. This helps HR professionals to take the right action and provide employees with the experience they desire, leading to increased engagement and lower turnover rates. Cohen further highlighted the importance of AI in the current scenario, saying, 'The pandemic has changed the way we work, and technology has become essential to link workers in all levels of the organization. It is also essential that leaders hear out their employees and take the right action. AI is one of the ways we can connect with all employees and understand their needs'.

AI-backed Chatbots Keep Engagement Conversation Going

Employee engagement is a science that requires careful measurement and analysis of employee sentiment regularly. To facilitate this, AI-based chatbots are being used to enable both employees and HR professionals to continually maintain a dialogue of engagement. These chatbot conversations can be used to gain an understanding of employee concerns, wants and needs. However, it is just as important to take action in response to these discussions as it is to initiate them. With the help of chatbots, organizations can better engage with their employees and ensure their voices are heard.

Summary

In the present time, the pandemic has brought various social and economic changes around the globe, wherein organizations are also not untouched by these changes. There is a new normal working dynamic adopted by maximum organizations coping with the pandemic situations to sustain in the business environment. Chapter 14 of this book discusses the various perspective of HR practices in the IT industry so that an effective way of methodology equipped with modern technology can be adopted for competitive advantages. Technology is playing a major role in this new working dynamic where machine learning and artificial intelligence (AI) are facilitating human functioning at work in an effective manner. At the individual level, the progress and integration of AI into common technologies have a major impact on how individuals are exposed to information, interact, learn, experience life and work and make decisions. Furthermore, at the organizational level, artificial intelligence is being used to assist recruiters in objectively screening and summarizing resumes that match job specifications, as well as managing talents without bias. Here, HR has a major role in embracing AI and it is a significant cultural shift for the employees to adopt and adjust. New employer-employee constructs are predicted to emerge when companies reassess the tasks and competencies that have previously comprised an employee's obligations. To what extent technology is facilitating to physical, emotional and financial well-being of employees is well explained in Chapter 11. These are crucial outcomes of technology-enabled practices and a way towards sustainability.

To utilize AI to its fullest potential, Indian AI development companies must invest in efficient data storage management. This will dramatically alter the HR department's workflow structure. In addition, these companies must invest in a knowledgeable team of employees who are proficient with advanced tools and software.

This book aims to contribute to the understanding and development of sustainable human resource management processes and practices having recent technologies in alignment. It covers the interconnection among three bottom-line sustainable approaches for the growth and development of the organization. In this book, three approaches, i.e., social, economic and environmental are based to link sustainable HRM processes and practices. In this book, it is not only shown that individual-level factors while cultural and organizational factors are equal contributors to sustainable functions of HR with the help of artificial intelligence. This book would help HR practitioners, managers, and policymakers to gain more insight into innovative practices in the field of HR for gaining competitive advantage and making more sense of organizational development. Chapter 15 summarizes the convergence of AI for Sustainable HR practices aiming towards organizational growth. For any company, it is crucial to have both present and futuristic perspectives to be successful and sustain its practices. Technology is one of the facilitators in this venture and organizations have to be adaptive and competitive globally.

Bibliography

[1] Barends, Eric and Denise M. Rousseau. 2018. Evidence-Based Management: How to Use Evidence to Make Better Organizational Decisions. Kogan Page.

[2] LinkedIn. 2018. The Rise of HR Analytics.

[3] KUMAR, BVDS SAI PAVAN, and KOMAL NAGRANI. "Artificial Intelligence in Human Resource Management." JournalNX: 106–118.

[4] Banks, G.C., Woznyj, H.M., Wesslen, R.S., Frear, K.A., Berka, G., Heggestad, E.D. and Gordon, H.L. (2019) 'Strategic Recruitment Across Borders: An Investigation of Multinational Enterprises.' Journal of Management; 45 (2): 476–509. Retrieved from: Aalto Finna Database

[5] Tambe, Prasanna, Peter Cappelli, and Valery Yakubovich. "Artificial intelligence in human resources management: Challenges and a path forward." California Management Review 61.4 (2019): 15–42.

[6] Dalgleish, S. (2005) 'Recruiting Quality.' Quality; 44 (6): 14. Retrieved from: Aalto Finna Database [Accessed on 5 January 2019]. Dennis, M.J. (2018) 'Artificial intelligence and recruitment, admission, progression, and retention.' Enrollment Management Report; 22 (9): 1–3. Retrieved from: Aalto Finna Database

[7] Kaplan, A., and M. Haenlein (2019). "Siri, Siri, in My Hand: Who's the Fairest in the Land? On the Interpretations, Illustrations, and Implications of Artificial Intelligence," Business Horizons 62(1): 15–25

[8] Van Esch, P., J. Stewart Black, and J. Ferolie (2019). "Marketing AI Recruitment: The Next Phase in Job Application and Selection," Computers in Human Behavior 90: 215–222. ation and Selection," Computers in Human Behavior 90: 215–222.

1

Artificial Intelligence and Sustainable Human Resource Management

Neetu Bali Kamra[1], Indranil Mutsuddi[2], Chandranshu Sinha[3] and Ruchi Sinha[4]

[1]Associate Professor, Lloyd Business School, Greater Noida, India
[2]Head of Department and Associate Professor, School of Management Studies, JIS University, Kolkata, India
[3]Department of Psychology, University of Allahabad, India
[4]Professor, Amity Global Business School (AGBS), Amity University, Noida, India

Email: neetu.kamra@lloydcollege.in; indranil.mutsuddi74@gmail.com; chandranshu.sinha@allduniv.ac.in; rsinha1@amity.edu

Abstract

This chapter has presented the best available knowledge about the changing landscape of corporate with the rising impact of artificial intelligence (AI), particularly in the area of human resources. The objective of this chapter is to apply this knowledge in the development of a strategic framework to assist students and professionals pursuing human resources to design effective applications in human resources powered by AI.

The discussion in this chapter begins with a brief summary of the inception of AI in general and some theoretical fundamentals of AI like narrow vs. strong AI. It then presents insights into the way AI actually works, with a brief understanding of machine learning concepts, including supervised and unsupervised learning. This chapter goes on to present the AI tools and techniques in the market today, with special reference to IBM as a key player in the AI industry today. This chapter also talks about how AI is used in human resources through e-recruitment and chatbots, which are virtual HR assistants.

This chapter focuses on one of the most intriguing applications of AI in today's HR practices, which is AI-enabled HR analytics. As HR managers are more and more involved in strategic decision-making, AI applications are constantly providing senior managers with deep-hidden insights into employee engagement and behaviours. The AI-enabled HR analytics applications give real-time action-oriented insights to today's HR managers on issues like productivity, motivation, moods and emotions. This chapter discussed such AI-based HR analytics interventions as text analytics. The rich content of textual data has great business insights, and it has the power to influence people-centric opinions in an organization. Sentiment analysis is one such application of text analytics for business intelligence which has a great scope of application in human resources and is discussed in detail in this chapter. Sentiment analysis involves the process of applying natural language processing (NLP), which has been briefly discussed in the concluding part of the chapter. This chapter concludes with the future scope of AI and HR practices. These inputs would help HR professionals to streamline their theoretical and practical know-how about the way AI is changing the human resources domain.

1.1 Introduction

Artificial intelligence (AI) is gaining momentum in the twenty-first century of the industrial revolution which is characterized by 'cyber physical' spaces. The era of 'cyber physical' spaces is determined by the presence of technology and society in the same space to collaborate with each other for a 'productive' output (Acikgoz, 2019). Artificial intelligence (AI) is one such application of technology that provides society to engage through innovative solutions in their everyday work practices. The advancements through the internet, along with the socio-economic impetus provided by AI, is a resounding socio-technical debate that also addresses 'ethical' implications on the society for which AI has come to the forefront of many corporate debates (Zviran, 2015; Youndt et al., 1996).

Organizations are investing a huge amount of money in AI initiatives in their enterprise systems and processes. With the advent of 'big data' and the use of sensors through the Internet of Things (IoT) for data recording, the environment for AI in organizations is fast expanding. The shift from paper-based to paperless work, using analytics and AI has been a major drift in the way organizations are organizing themselves. The major reason for this shift is due to the advantages offered by AI in the 'transactional' day-to-day activities of employees which involve repetitive tasks.

Human resources is also one such function in organizations which is seeing the advent of AI in creating seamless work processes. The major role of AI in human resources is the elimination of 'labour intensive' roles that are repetitive in nature. Also, the use of analytics in AI for speeding up the processes of 'people' analytics for measuring metrics and improving the human resources functions through data management provides the thrust for organizations to shift to AI. Since the human resources function requires a collaborative view of the employee's activities in the organization, it is imperative to collect data from various sources like performance management, satisfaction survey, etc., and then analyse it for an insightful decision-making process for employee wellness initiatives. The use of advanced data-driven technology has impacted the efficiency of the performance of human resources functions creating an employee-oriented culture (Breaugh, 2008).

So, now that we are aware of the rising needs and opportunities for AI in the human resources function let us explore the exact definition. Artificial intelligence is defined as the leveraging of the intelligence of machines that can mimic the human brain for decision-making effectiveness. Many definitions of AI have surfaced lately, John McCarthy (2004) in his paper defined AI as 'it is the science and engineering of making intelligent machines, especially intelligent computer programs and is related to the similar task of using computers to understand human intelligence. Here, it is referred that AI does not have to confine itself to the biologically observable methods'.

However, the concept of AI originated decades ago in Alan Turing's (1950) seminal work on '**Computing Machinery and Intelligence**'. Turing had defined AI as the 'father of computer science', and had posed the question of whether machines are capable of thinking.

In the history of AI development, turing developed the 'turing test' in which a human interrogator attempt to distinguish between computer responses from human responses. The turing test has been a sediment in AI history as it developed ideas around linguistics which have been a powerful contribution to AI and its applications in industry. Later, Stuart Russell and Peter Norvig published artificial intelligence: A modern approach, which was one of the best novel books on the study of AI (Barber, 1998). This textbook discusses the notion of differences between machines and humans in their abilities to differentiate between rationality and thinking. Alan turing defined AI as systems that are capable of thinking like humans (Mueller & Baum, 2011).

Thus, AI is a field that combines computers and datasets through constructive mathematical modelling to deliver problem-solving solutions (Ambrose & Kulik, 1994). AI also encompasses machine learning and deep learning as its sub-components. Through these systems, AI creates expert systems that use mathematical models on data to create predictions and classifications as the outputs (Galanaki & Parry, 2019; Storey, 2004).

AI is still an emerging technology that needs to be understood, explored and applied. Gartner's hype cycle suggests that product innovations have a typical way of progression which initially begins with over enthusiasm and then disillusionment to finally make a re-understanding of the relevance of the functioning of the innovation in the market.

Lex Fridman in his lecture at MIT in 2019 addressed that a peak of inflated expectations is approaching a trough of disillusionment. However, the challenges AI implementations are facing due to ethical implications need to be ascertained and discussed for effective AI implementation in organizations (Bringsjord & Schimanski, 2008, Gill et al., 2008).

1.2 Theoretical Framework

The AI can be differentiated between weak AI versus strong AI Weak AI which is sometimes referred to as narrow AI or artificial narrow intelligence (ANI) is when an AI is developed that focuses on a 'limited' or specific task of execution. Mostly all the functions and applications of AI that we encounter in our day-to-day activities are applications of weak AI and few examples of weak applications are IBM Watson, Amazon's Alexa, Apple's Siri and various autonomous vehicles.

On the other hand, artificial general intelligence (AGI) and artificial super intelligence (ASI) form the basis of a strong AI system. Artificial general intelligence (AGI) makes machines capable of making themselves capable of decisive decision-making just like humans, where they can understand, explore and solve problems and then retrain to do it again in the future. Artificial super intelligence (ASI) referred to as super intelligence would exceed the intelligence and ability of the human brain which is an extreme performance of a machine (Maguire and Delahunt, 2017). While strong AI so far has been theoretical in reference, limited to laboratories for invention and development but the continuous work on the same is on. ASI can be best understood from the robotics and fiction movies that fascinate all generations.

(a) Deep Learning and Machine Learning

Since machine learning and AI are interchangeably used, it is worth noting the nuances between the two to be able to understand their applications. As was discussed earlier both deep learning and machine learning are components of AI, or as would be stated that deep learning is a subcomponent of machine learning. Figure 1.1 eludes the same.

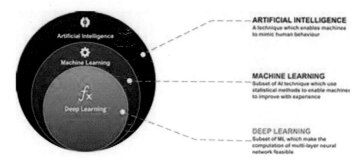

Figure 1.1 Visual representation of how AI, ML, and DL relate to one another.

As seen in Figure 1.1, deep learning is further composed of neural networks.

AI and machine learning are related through the way that AI can be implemented using an algorithm that can learn and process data and then apply this learning to perform specific actions. Through the machine, learning automation is possible, which eliminates manual human intervention. Further, deep learning can be explained as 'scalable machine learning' as defined by Lex Friedman MIT.

(b) Types of Learning

The world is getting 'smarter' every day, especially with the use of digital devices that are powered by computing technology that can process real-time data. To keep up with the expectations, companies are increasingly using machine learning algorithms to automate systems and procedures. There have been so many end-user experiences like face recognition for unlocking smartphones, capturing attendance or detecting credit card fraud (through predictive analytics), that machines can smartly learn and apply solutions to business cases.

The process of learning from data by machines and then executing responses based on the output of the mathematical algorithms is done by two basic approaches: supervised learning and unsupervised learning. The main difference between supervised and unsupervised data is that one uses labelled data to help predict outcomes, while the other does not (Zang & Ye, 2015).

In human resource functions, most of the data which is structured in MS Excel format are labelled, however, data that are unlabelled are texts, images, videos, etc. which can be categorized as unlabelled data. Figures 1.2 and 1.3 are illustrative of the same.

Figure 1.2   Types of learning in machine learning.

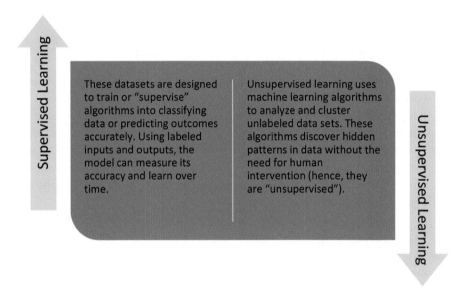

Figure 1.3   Difference between supervised and unsupervised learning.

The data input (labelled/unlabelled) is made to pass through algorithms that produce logical outputs. Figure 1.4 elaborates the process of data analysis for AI that results in logical outputs.

Let us consider an example of employee attrition. Through predictive analytics, in AI the employee who will churn or quit the organization can be predicted. Considering the employee data (labelled data) passes through an algorithm (classification in this case), it would be able to logically predict the outcome of the employee data by providing a binary output which states 1: 'will leave' and 0: 'will continue as the logical output'. Basis this organizations can develop retention programmes to decrease employee turnover and retain employees.

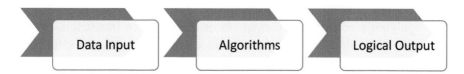

Figure 1.4   Process of data analysis in AI.

1.3 Applications of AI

In today's world, there are numerous examples of AI applications that are real-world applications of artificial intelligence systems. A few commonly used applications of AI are referred to below:

1. Speech recognition: Also referred to as speech recognition or speech-to-text, it is an AI application that can utilize natural language processing (NLP) to convert human speech into text format for processing. Siri is one such example that incorporates speech into text which then processes the required tasks of the users. Its application in human resources in cultural audits and satisfaction surveys can be enacted for recording responses and suggestions.

2. Customer service: Chabot's is replacing human agents along the journey of customer experience. The frequently answered questions (FAQs) provide personalized insights and responses to customer-centric questions used for cross-selling products or handling customer grievances. Such AI applications have changed the way organizations engage their customers across websites and social media platforms. Virtual agents, messaging apps and Facebook Messenger, which can perform tasks of virtual assistants and voice assistants, are examples of messaging bots on e-commerce sites with virtual agents. Its application in human resources through employee self-service for employee policies can provide the employee-centric approach to 24 × 7 employee addresses of queries.

3. Computer vision: This AI technology has enabled computers to derive meaningful insights from digital images and videos. Based on these inputs the machine responds with response actions. This technology is powered by convolutional neural networks (CNN) that can process images and generate likeable outputs. In human resources, this technology can empower the recruitment and selection process, through images and photos, the candidate's profiling and mapping can be conducted successfully.

4.   Recommendation engines: Using past data, AI can be supportive in applying algorithms on datasets to discover hidden trends that can be used to develop strategies for employee retention, promotions, training and development.

1.4 AI Tools and Techniques

To be able to practice and implement artificial intelligence in organizational practices is not easy. Practising data science comes with challenges. Like, for the human resources department, comes with a lot of fragmented data sources from which data needs to be collected, a lack of AI and data science skills in the HR department, and the requirement of powerful AI tools for training and deployment on which the systems can be implemented. It is also challenging to operationalize ML models with unclear accuracy and difficult-to-audit predictions.

However, the market today has saturated with some very powerful data science tools and solutions, which provide accelerated AI-driven innovation with:

- an intelligent data collaboration technique,

- a simplified project development software,

- the ability to run any AI model with a flexible deployment,

- trusted and explainable AI, and

- easy to use GUI (graphical user interface).

Case Illustration: IBM Watson

One such tool that the current chapter discusses is the much-used and known IBM Watson. IBM has been a pioneer in advancing AI-driven enterprise technologies and has paved the way for the future of machine learning systems across multiple industries. IBM has developed the AI Ladder for successful artificial intelligence deployments based on decades of AI research, years of experience working with organizations of all sizes, and learnings from over 30,000 IBM Watson engagements:

1. Collect data: Simplify data collection and accessibility.

2. Organize data: Create a business-ready analytics foundation.

3. Analyse data: Building scalable and trustworthy AI-driven systems.

4. Infuse: Integrate and optimize systems across the entire business framework.

5. Modernize: Bring AI applications and systems to the organization cloud.

IBM Watson provides enterprises with the AI tools they need to transform their business systems and workflows while improving automation and efficiency significantly. One can easily explore the details and information on how IBM can help organizations to complete their AI journey and can explore the various IBM portfolios of managed services and solutions. Users can use Watson to analyse and interpret all of their data, including unstructured text, images, audio and video. By understanding a user's personality, tone and emotion, IBM Watson can provide personalized recommendations. It offers solutions that speed up the development of catboats that can converse (Leg and Hutter, 2007).

1.5 Applications of AI in HR

1.5.1 AI-based recruitment

One of the frequent uses of AI has been prominent in the field of recruitment and selection activities used by organizations.

The purpose of AI-based applications in the recruitment process had been:

- To identify potential job aspirants from multiple job boards at the click of a mouse. AI applications facilitate the prompt conversion of job aspirant resumes into smart cards which further enable quick filtering of candidates suitable for the job profile (Figure 1.5).

- To significantly reduce the lag time for scheduling candidate interviews by automating the process.

- To facilitate prompt integration of the evaluation of the process involving multiple interviews.

- To structure an effective applicant tracking system involving various hiring partners or intermediaries.

- To facilitate effective management of candidate database and ensure prompt retrieval of data for future uses.

- To scan and predict facial expressions of candidates during interviews and identify their moods, emotions and behavioural tendencies during recorded interview sessions as well as during online interviews (Figure 1.6).

Figure 1.5   AI-based candidate calibration (Courtesy: https://demo.turbohire.co/smart-hiring-solution/).

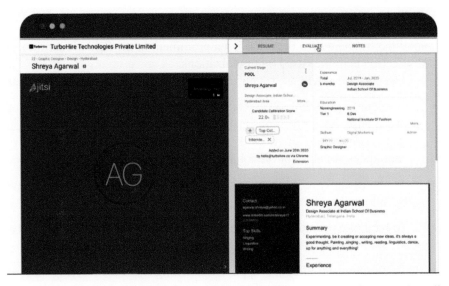

Figure 1.6   AI-based video interviews and online profile assessment (Courtesy: https://demo.turbohire.co/smart-hiring-solution/).

1.5.2 Benefits of using AI-based interview applications

- Accuracy in candidate profiling and screening.

- Candidate interview analysis: predicting candidate's emotions and behavioural reactions based on video analysis and facial recognition.

- Accuracy in terms of candidate fit for job requirements.

- Time-saving solution for HR professionals.

- Effective storage of recruitment data and retrieval as per the needs of the organization and the hiring team.

- Effective reporting of filtered data as per organizational needs.

1.6 AI-enabled Virtual HR Assistant

As organizational operations are becoming more and more complex and HR professionals now engaging themselves in strategic decision-making activities, handling employee queries 24 × 7 is nowadays delegated to AI-based virtual HR assistant applications. These AI-based applications perform the function of meeting the needs of answering employee queries on employment-related issues on a real-time basis. The fully conversational AI-enabled virtual HR agent also can perform simultaneous conversations and chats with multiple employees on a real-time basis. Such AI applications (Figure 1.7) are also powered with applications for facilitating addressing employee concerns or cases by issuing virtual employee tickets using the case management dashboard applications. Employees can access these applications on a real-time basis and raise their concerns by participating in the AI-enabled conversational interface. The virtual HR assistant also acts as the nerve centre for sharing HR information with the employees on a day-to-day basis just like a real-life HR executive in person. An employee by using the conversational interface may ask for his salary slip, key result areas, updates on target achievement, make queries regarding leave status so on.

1.7 AI-based HR Analytics

One of the most intriguing applications of AI in today's HR practices is obviously the application of AI in HR analytics. As HR managers are more and more involved in strategic decision-making, AI applications are constantly facilitating senior managers with deep-hidden insights into employee engagement and behaviours. The AI-enabled HR analytics applications give real-time action-oriented insights to today's HR managers on issues like productivity, motivation, moods and emotions. These inputs are helping HR managers to streamline their strategic manpower planning processes and enhancing the chances of delivering HR solutions to the organization that fosters employee engagement, performance and continuance.

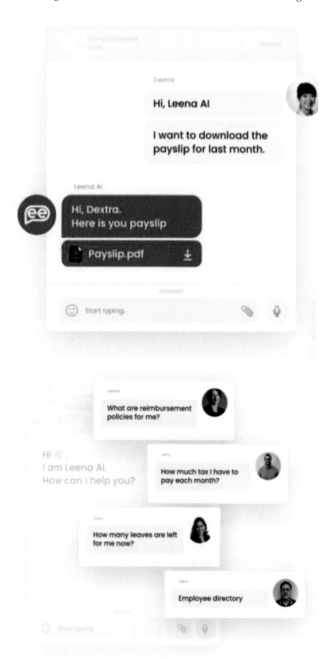

Figure 1.7   AI-based virtual HR assistant (Courtesy:https://leena.ai/ai-in-hr).

Table 1.1 AI-based HR analytics.

AI-based HR analytics	Hallmarks	Benefits to organizations/ HR
Cognitive supporting decision-making	AI-based cognitive solutions are aimed to enable HR decision-makers to integrate HR analytics with big data sources about strategic people management leading to present and unearthing new strategic business insights	Decisions about employee training, performance development, hiring processes, etc would be going to be integrated with the strategic goals of the organization.
Smart HR analytics	AI-based HR analytics applications are meant to deal with big data related to employee performance and predict the future behaviour of people in the organization.	Smart HR analytics (AI-augmented) would facilitate HR managers to collect, analyse and manage employee data to enhance people engagement and developing smarter work teams.

One of the interesting trends in the application of AI in HR practices had been in terms of amalgamating cognitive computing perspectives with the various functional HR domains like training & development, employee orientation and onboarding, employee selection activities, etc. The purpose of AI-based HR analytics would be principally aimed to reinvent and transform the functioning of the existing HR system and practices. Applications of AI-based HR analytics are expected to be in the realm of areas disucussed in Table 1.1 .

1.7.1 How would organizations need to deal in order to implement AI-based HR analytics

The fundamental resources which are essential for organizations to ensure AI-based HR analytics work would be by integrating big data analytics with HR decision-making. In this regard organizations would need to primarily emphasize upon two types of data, namely:

- **HR Record System**: This includes the already existing HR data like employee profiles, employee competency data bank, employee training records, performance data, etc. stored in organizational databases and existing HRMS.

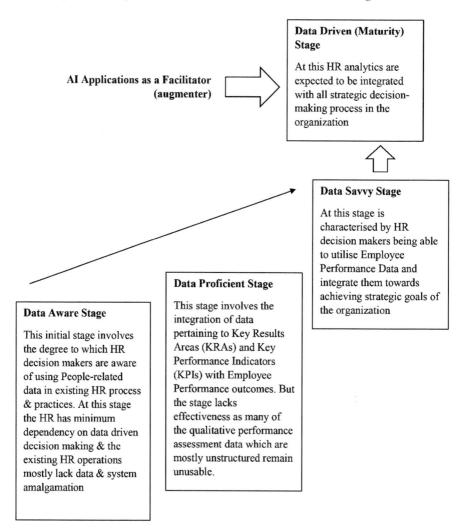

Figure 1.8   Evolution of the HR practices in terms of adopting HR analytics for strategic decision-making.

- **Employee-Made Data:** These data are based on insights, feedback or opinion surveys (e.g. people engagement survey) conducted on employees by the HR team.

To leverage the benefits of AI-based HR analytics and facilitate the evolution of the same at the operational or functional level in the organization, the organizations need to evolve their data dependency about HR-related decision-making. This is illustrated in Figure 1.8.

Figure 1.8 illustrates the four successive stages that are involved in the process of adopting HR analytics and integrating the same with the strategic decision-making process in the organization.

- The first **data awareness stage** involves the preliminary stage where the existing HR system becomes aware of using people-related data in existing HR processes and practices. At this stage, HR has a minimum dependency on data-driven decision-making and the existing HR operations mostly lack data and system amalgamation.

- The second **data proficient stage** involves the integration of data about key results areas (KRAs) and key performance indicators (KPIs) with employee performance outcomes. But the stage lacks effectiveness as many of the qualitative performance assessment data which are mostly unstructured remain unusable.

- The third **data savvy stage** is characterized by HR decision-makers can utilize employee performance data and integrate it towards achieving the strategic goals of the organization.

- The fourth **data-driven (maturity) stage** is characterized by organizations ensuring the integration of HR analytics with all strategic decision-making processes in the organization. This is the stage where HR decision-making is further augmented by the application of '**AI-based HR analytics**'.

1.8 Benefits of using AI-based HR Analytics

The use of AI-based HR analytics could be beneficial for organizations and the overall functioning of the HR in the following ways, namely:

1.9 Emerging Domains of AI-based HR Analytics through Text Analytics

Humans have a language that they use to communicate. Human language is vital for them to express and understand each other. The undercurrent of writing as a medium of propagation and expressing ideas requires an understanding of the conceptual nuances of 'words' and their applications. Technology can act as a facilitator for encouraging people's connectivity through the right use of words and vocabulary with intensive semantic knowledge which a computer program can store, analyse and recommend. This AI-enabled feature in computers like Grammarly Applications offers great insights to study

Table 1.2   Benefits of using AI-based HR analytics.

Benefits of using AI-based HR analytics	Hallmarks
Decreasing biased decisions	The application of AI-based HR analytics significantly decreases the extent of biased managerial decisions particularly in domains of employee performance and behaviour management which are outcome driven. It also brings into place transparency in people management decisions and contributes to employee engagement and satisfaction.
People relationships at the workplace	AI-based HR analytics provide deep and rich insights on the personality and attitude of the employees and help the managers to have an insight and predict their future behaviours. These contribute effectively to strengthening interpersonal relationships and translate the same into effective teamwork.
Assessment centre evaluation	Assessment centre evaluation becomes more pragmatic and data-driven rather than being solely dependent on the rater (evaluator) perception based. This facilitates effective candidate selection during interviews which are further streamlined by AI recruitment applications. On the other hand, data-based assessment reports further help training managers identify employee training needs.
Predictive data analytics	The AI applications can augment and prescribe predictive behavioural and employee performance models impacting future performances.
Enhanced strategic focus	One of the major accomplishments of AI-based HR analytics had been to integrate data-driven employee management perspectives with the strategic goals and aspirations of the organizations. Routine HR activities are taken up by AI applications like the 'virtual HR assistant' enabling HR practitioners investing more time on strategic decision-making in the organization.
Result-driven orientation	AI-based HR analytics strongly facilitate result-driven work culture in organizations by application of predictive models and forecasts leveraging a high performance driven orientation in the organization.

the tone and the content of the words used which could act as an enabler for human resources personnel.

In studies, it is found that 90% of the world's data is unstructured and poorly organized. Daily, unstructured business data is created from emails, support tickets, chats, social media conversations, surveys, articles and documents. However, analysing such large volumes of text for sentiment in a timely and efficient manner is extremely difficult. As human resource specialists, most of the data that they handle and receive is unstructured like reviews, cultural audits, feedback, performance appraisal logs and exit interviews which are mostly in text format. As the power to people-centric opinion in an organization, this rich content of textual data has great insights for business. Here, sentiment analysis comes into a major role to play which provides an automated method for searching for the user's sentiments in any free-form text. Sentiment analysis involves the process of applying natural language processing (NLP). Through this, the users can apply algorithms that can analyse unstructured textual data to explore insights into employee opinions. Using this tool, one can quickly determine whether a piece of writing is positive, negative or neutral. Glassdoor is one such application of deploying employee opinions in textual format which they use to develop dashboards for propagating goodwill of companies among job seekers.

1.10 What is Sentiment Analysis and its Application in HR?

Using natural language processing (NLP) and machine learning techniques, a sentiment analysis system assigns weighted sentiment scores to entities, topics, themes and categories within one or more sentences. In this manner, computerized sentiment analysis function. Machine learning techniques and deep learning algorithms and are employed to train the model to identify parts of speech in a sentence, and then categorize the output as a result of the word classification process.

Applications of sentiment analysis (Figure 1.9) in human resources could be used for measuring the 'VOE' – voice of the employee which is a powerful way to gauge employee wellness and opinions in an organization. As a result of employee churn, human resources professionals face a substantial challenge in retaining employees. Results from different researches show that 20% of workers leave their jobs voluntarily each year, while another 17% are fired or laid off. As a result, to deal with this issue companies are turning to data analytics to understand their employees' voices so that they can monitor and retain them on time. HR directors can use sentiment analysis to analyse employee feedback, surveys, performance reviews,

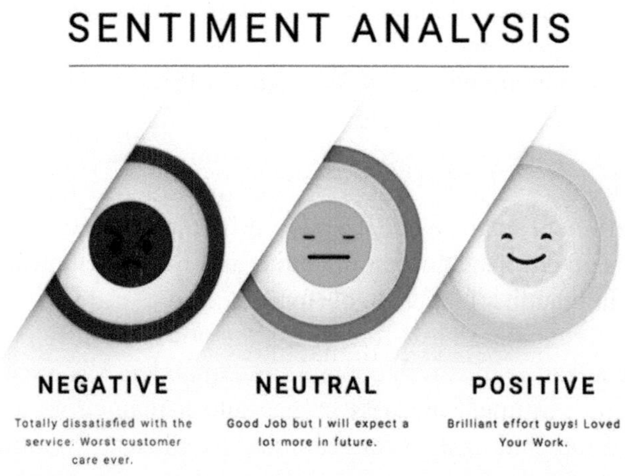

SENTIMENT ANALYSIS

NEGATIVE
Totally dissatisfied with the service. Worst customer care ever.

NEUTRAL
Good Job but I will expect a lot more in future.

POSITIVE
Brilliant effort guys! Loved Your Work.

Figure 1.9   AI-based textual analysis using NLP (Courtesy: https://www.datasciencecentral. com/sentiment-analysis-types-vtools-and-use-cases/).

Data Collection | Preparing The Text | Algorithms and Modellling | Output

Figure 1.10   Steps in sentiment analysis.

and appraisal logs to determine an employee's improvement points and improve morale.

1.10.1 The steps of sentiment analysis

Sentiment analysis is a complex process that consists of four different steps to analyse sentiment data. The steps to sentiment analysis are illustrated in Figure 1.10.

1.   **Data collection**: The first step of sentiment analysis consists of collecting the data which is unstructured and available in blogs, posts, reviews and opinions to extract and classify such data for analysis.

2.   **Preparing the text**: It consists of cleaning the data for anomalies and other deficiencies so that data analysis can begin. The non-textual contents that are irrelevant to the analysis are identified and eliminated during the process.

3. **Algorithm and modelling**: Thereafter, the processed data is analysed through built AI-enabled tools with 'classification' mathematical models that help to extract and classify the data into 'classified' output positive, negative, good, bad, etc.

4. **Output:** The main objective of sentiment analysis is to explore and mine data of text format for hidden insights to understand the underlying sentiments in the data. When the analysis is finished, the results are displayed on graphs like pie charts, bar charts and line graphs.

1.11 Conclusion: Future of HR and AI

The future of artificial intelligence enabled processes in human resources function would intensify in times to come. The reason for this is that human-centric data which is 'big' data needs to be analysed consistently with time to be able to feel the 'pulse' of the employee continuously. With organizations shifting to a 'work from home' format, the challenge for human resources to be connected to its employees would be even more gruesome. Such AI-enabled tools with data analytics practices can provide impetus to new ways of working in the future. We live in a data-driven world that is dominated by data germinating almost every second in every field, which leaves us to decide how to turn it around to our advantage, especially for human resources professionals who require to be 'connected' with the employees all the time for knowing their 'VOE', voice of employee. AI enables human resources with the power of connectivity with employees through data-enabled platforms which make all processes 'people-centric'.

References

[1] Acikgoz, Y. (2019). "Employee recruitment and job search: Towards a multi-level integration". Human resource management review, 29, 1–13.
[2] Ambrose, M., & Kulik, C. (1993). Old friends, new faces: motivation research in the 1990's. Journal of management. 25(3), 231–292.
[3] Andersson, N. (2003). Applicant and recruiter reactions to new technology in selection: A critical review and agenda for future research. International Journal of Selection and Assessment, 11(2–3), 121–136.
[4] Barber, A. E. (1998). Recruiting Employees. Foundation for organizational science.

[5] Baron, I.S., Mustafa., & Agustina, H. (2018). The challenges of recruitment and selection systems in Indonesia. Journal of management and marketing review. 3(4), 185–192.

[6] Breaugh, A.J. (2008). Employee recruitment: Current knowledge and important areas for future research. Human Resource Management Review, 18, 103–118.

[7] Breaugh, A.J., & Starke, M (2000). Research on Employee recruitment: So many studies, so many remaining questions. Journal of management. 26(3), 405–434.

[8] Bringsjord, S. & Schimanski, B. (2003). What is Artificial Intelligence? Psychometric AI as an answer. IJCAI'03 Proceedings of the 18th international joint conference on Artificial intelligence, 887–893.

[9] Broadhurst, K., & Harrington, A. (2016). A thematic literature review: The importance of providing spiritual care for end-of-life patients who have experienced transcendence phenomena. American journal of Hospice & palliative medicine. 33(9), 881–893 Worldwide Hospitality and Tourism Themes, 2(1), 86–93.

[10] Elearn. (2009). Recruitment and selection (Rev. ed., Management extra). Amsterdam; Boston: Elsevier. Erixon, F. (2018).

[11] Galanaki, E., Lazazzara, A., & Parry, E. (2019). A cross-national analysis of e-HRM configurations: integrating the information technology and HRM perspectives. Organizing for digital innovation. 27, 261–276.

[12] Gill, P., Stewart K., Treasure, E., & Chadwick, B. (2008). Methods of data collection in Qualitative research: interviews and focus groups. British dental journal, 204(6), 291–295 Information extraction from CV.

[13] Legg, S. & Hutter, M. (2007). A Collection of Definitions of Intelligence. Advances in Artificial General Intelligence: Concepts, Architecture and Algorithms, IOS press, Issue 157, 17–24.

[14] Leong, C. (2018). Technology & Recruiting 101: how it works and where it's going. Strategic HR Review, 17(1), 50–52.

[15] Maguire, M., & Delahunt, B (2017). Doing a thematic analysis: A practical, step-by-step guide for learning and teaching scholars. All Ireland Journal of Teaching and Learning in Higher education. Vol.3.

[16] Mueller, J.R & Baum, B. (2011). The definitive guide to hiring right, Journal of applied Business & Economics, 12(3), 140–153.

[17] Storey, D.J. (2004). Exploring the link, among small firms, between management training and firm performance: a comparison between the UK and other OECD countries. The international Journal of Human Resource Management, 15(1)

[18] Youndt, M.A., Snell, S.A., Dean, J.W., & Lepak, D.P (1996). Human resource management, Manufacturing Strategy, and firm performance. Academy of management. 39(4), 836–866.

[19] Zang, S., & Ye, M. (2015). Human Resource Management in the Era of Big Data. Journal of Human Resource and Sustainability Studies, 3(01), 41.

[20] Zviran, M. (2015). Relationship between organizational and information systems objectives: some empirical evidence. Journal of management information systems. 7(1), 65–84.

2

The New Era of HRM in the World 2.0

Chinmayee Abbey[1], Anamika Pandey[2] and Chait Rendu[3]

[1]Research Scholar, School of Business, Galgotias University, India
[2]Professor, School of Business, Galgotias University, India
[3]Assistant Professor of Travel, Rosen College of Hospitality Management, University of Boulevard, Orlando, Florida

Email: chinmayee.20gsob3010018@galgotiasuniversity.edu.in;
anamika.pandey@galgotiasuniversity.edu.in; chait.rendu@ucf.edu

Abstract

In any organization, human resources contribute in a big way to building a competitive advantage across industries. It has been a challenging situation for human resource management (HRM) in the wake of the COVID-19 pandemic. The study seeks to provide a comprehensive evaluation of the role of HR in the post-COVID era that we are living in today, often called 'World 2.0'. The pandemic has led to a lot of undue stress for individuals as well as organizations. While everyone has found their own way to cope with these pressures, some individuals have gone through serious stress and burnout. The present study examines the new factors of World 2.0 and the impact they have both externally and internally on individuals and organizations. As a result of the pandemic, managers have been confronted with the ripple effects, as employees re-evaluate their careers and leave their jobs in record numbers. Additionally, the study provides insight into the phenomenon of 'The Great Resignation' and analyses the factors that could predict it. This chapter aims to explore the possibilities presented today by the pandemic and the reasons for 'The Great Resignation'. Additionally, it explains how HR can navigate this new era with an innovative approach to creating an inclusive work environment.

A systematic review of the literature is being conducted in this study. The data is gathered by using a variety of secondary sources, including past research and journal articles and electronic databases such as PubMed, Web of Science and Scopus using the keywords human management, COVID-19, New World 2.0, The Great Resignation, etc.

As part of a new HR strategy, organizations must collaborate with employees to build lives rather than simply work lives and to succeed in the age of World 2.0. This study examines HRM initiatives concerning job changes, working routines, workplaces and remote working conditions. The study explores numerous factors of World 2.0, which primarily focuses on employee well-being and resilience, change management, and the pandemic's overall impact on individuals and organizations. This study has analysed in detail the impact caused by the pandemic on individuals and organizations, investigating the phenomenon of 'The Great Resignation', and the new era of HR in World 2.0.

2.1 Introduction

Human resource management is the backbone of any organization that eventually contributes significantly towards building a competitive advantage across industries. This study aims to take a comprehensive look at the role of HR in the post-COVID era that we are living in today, referred to as World 2.0. Individuals, organizations, society, and the world overall have undergone an unsolicited transformation where no one remains untouched by the impact of the pandemic. While most of our lives got disrupted, the best part about being human is that we learn to adapt, and so we all adapted ways to operate in this new world, the new normal and the new life!'.

The organizations too had to adopt new, innovative business strategies to cope with the insurmountable task of maintaining business continuity. HR has played an imperative role in this transition. Two years roughly into the pandemic already and the latest we hear on the pandemic as I write this, and I quote Rochelle Paula Walensky, an American physician-scientist who is the Director of the Centre for Disease Control and Prevention, said, '*We may be done with the virus, but the virus is not done with us. We cannot get comfortable or give into a false sense of security that the worst of the pandemic is behind us*'.

All this has led to a lot of undue stress—individuals have gone through fear, the loss of a loved one, grief and the things that people took for granted once have now taken priority over others, for instance, health, quality time with the family, well-being and work–life balance. The situation has been unprecedented, and so desperate times call for desperate measures. While everyone has found their own way to cope with these pressures and challenges, some individuals have gone through serious stress and burnout. *These are some of the reasons that have led to 'The Great Resignation' that seems to be here to stay, for now.* Many people have been able to step back far enough from the normalized rat race to think about their lives honestly. People can now acknowledge the meaninglessness of their career pursuits.

A recent Microsoft survey found that 41% of employees are considering leaving their current employers. Due to the pandemic, across industries, attrition is rising and companies are struggling to understand a multi-pronged approach to this new challenge.

HR, now more than ever, has the most critical role to play and they need to re-engineer the way organizations see human capital—not just as employees, but as partners. It is time for a change in basic assumptions to inculcate an integrated approach to building organizations in partnership with employees, building lives, instead of just work lives.

2.2 Factors of World 2.0

The pandemic has disrupted industries, and the role of HR has become more critical than ever in this new normal. HR as a function has come a long way from being a support function to a line function to being a warrior in World 2.0 and now emerging as a business transformer. The definition of work and workplace has changed, and we are still learning to get accustomed to this new change in thinking in the HR landscape. While individuals have struggled to adjust to newer work lives and the blurred lines between work-life and home life, organizations have had to face a different set of challenges altogether.

The present study aims at taking a close look and analysing the HR function as the business transformer in the post-COVID era that we are living in today, referred to as World 2.0. The pandemic has unsolicitedly transformed individuals, organizations, society and the world as a whole. This study examines the effects of the pandemic on employees and organizations as well as the challenges they face.

A few factors and themes that define the organizations in World 2.0 are as follows.

2.2.1 Employee well-being and resilience

Human Resource Management Research and Practice in Asia: Past, Present and Future – The recent pandemic, COVID-19, arrived in late 2019 and has shaken the whole world to its core. Every day, organizations had to reinvent their organizational structures and processes and adopt alternative hybrid work models. There was a shift from on-site to online consulting for employees, and people struggled to adapt their homes to the new way of working (see Zhang & Varma, 2020).

Nevertheless, not all jobs lend themselves well to the work from home model, and many require employees to continue to attend their workplace. Hospital employees, municipal and city services such as public transport and police are deemed 'essential workers', so they must continue working despite being at risk of getting infected. Despite the unprecedented nature of this event, only about 20% of organizations were prepared for it, and they need to improve. This is according to Caligiuri, De Cieri, Minbaeva, Verbeke, and Zimmermann (2020). According to these authors, COVID-19 has been a people-centred crisis, so both HR functions and employees will need more resilience. As a source of organization support during challenging times, Employee Assistance Programs (EAPs) can assist employees. These programmes improve employee well-being and resilience. Thus, there is an enormous need for HR strategies that support their employees to reduce stress, formally and informally.

2.2.2 Change management-responding to the crisis

Building employee well-being and resilience is always critical for businesses, but the pandemic has highlighted its significance more than ever before. These factors are crucial both before and during a severe crisis like COVID-19. Consequently, while improving employee well-being and resilience is absolutely imperative in all industries, numerous HRM-related difficulties are likely to be linked to particular crises that have special effects on businesses and communities as well as people in particular ways (Milburn, Schuler, & Watson, 1983a, 1983b). Many businesses responded to the COVID-19 outbreak by imposing mandatory work from home requirements, forcing employees to do so. As a result, it was also necessary to change HRM practices and policies, including:

- Employee Assistance Programs with an increasing focus on health and well-being
- Business continuity with hybrid work models
- Employee evaluation, appraisal and training
- Decentralizing operations and moving employees out of the headquarters
- New compensation policies

- Layoffs or furloughs

- Empowering managers and leaders to work toward transition and integration

These changes required immediate strategic decisions, adjustment to the uncertain reality, and preparation for the immediate uncertain future to ensure business continuity.

For instance, we adjust and react promptly to lessen societal effects like high unemployment. As a result, the effects of HRM on society, companies and people can be profound (Hutchins & Wang, 2008; Milburn et al., 1983b). The role of HRM and the function of the HR department in managing crises has received very limited research to date (e.g., Farndale, Horak, Philips, & Beamond, 2019; Lee, Phan, & Tan, 2003).

2.2.3 People connect

As a result of the lockdown that was announced with immediate effect, the whole country went into shock without knowing how to move forward. A lot of organizations and industries started facing issues, around people-disconnect, as there was a lot of insecurity and uncertainty. People left for their respective hometowns and villages. There were technical issues related to competency and infrastructure. For instance, working from home was not an option for many people. There were several people who did not have sophisticated systems or headsets, video cameras, high-speed internet connectivity or the skills to manage them all. Agility played a key role here, and people needed to be trained. Many people were also juggling their own work with helping their families cope and keeping their children on a course of study online. There are also social and psychological concerns on the challenges front. People were subjected to stress on a whole new level during extreme adversity like what we faced. Some of the main causes of stress were social distance, uncertainty, threats to life, isolation and disconnect from people.

2.2.4 Infrastructure

To ensure business continuity through this difficult transition, companies needed to transform their tools, technological platforms and infrastructure at a fast pace. They must make sure that staff members are prepared to deal with remote working arrangements. Some businesses now provide employees with a budget to set up a home office where they can do uninterrupted work. A high-speed internet connection, a battery backup, necessary tools, and equipment or even office supplies like desks and ergonomic seats, were all covered by this amount. Businesses have moved forward and opened co-working spaces around the city that could serve as hubs for employees.

2.2.5 Collaboration

One of the serious issues businesses have when allowing workers to work from home is collaboration. Providing effective collaboration required a multi-pronged approach such as ensuring employees were on time for meetings and calls. Spontaneous collaboration has played a crucial role in how people innovate and produce creative solutions, and this has played an important role in crafting a good HR strategy for remote work. A strong collaborative architecture composed of meeting tools, messaging apps and data-sharing software had to be developed by businesses. The feeling of loneliness was significantly diminished by encouraging informal contacts and video calls. Despite operational challenges, leadership played a key role in fostering a culture of collaboration. The managers had to be the messengers of the HR Department not just to convey messages but also to execute these changes with agility and coordinate with teams to maintain the level of trust within teams. The organizations inculcated a collaboration model as shown in the figure below.

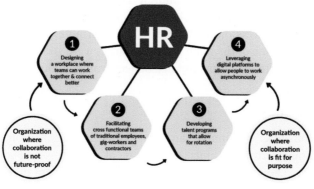

2.3 The Pandemic's Overall Impact on Individuals and Organizations

Some of the top issues for people working in HR and those for employees were:

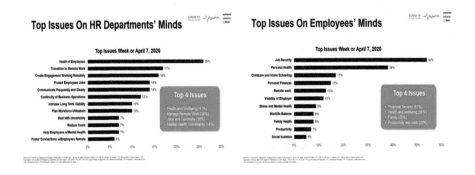

2.3.1 External factors: new work culture and environment (organizations and society)

Organizationally, the uncertainties surrounding events like COVID-19 call for us to build flexibility, integrate tools and technologies, eliminate redundancies and create processes and systems that can adapt to changes rapidly. Unexpected incidents and crisis management will necessitate infrastructure investments and resource allocation. Employers are responsible for aiding in their employees' psychological and skill-based preparation for potential changes. While organizations grapple with the changing role of HR, they must continue to improve and build their HR capabilities in the event of a crisis. As was the case in the early 1990s and 2020s, massive disruptions like COVID-19 might cause large portions of the population to become unexpectedly unemployed. Governments, non-governmental organizations, welfare organizations and private citizens intervened in almost every instance to help those impacted by the sudden change in employment status. Many industries were severely impacted, resulting in corporate disasters and catastrophes for businesses. For instance, because people will not want to travel or stay in hotels, the hospitality and travel industries are likely to be paralyzed for a while. The trend of globalization that we have seen over the past few decades will undoubtedly be reversed as a result of this. Organizations will limit international travel, which could result in 'a change from the great integration to the great fragmentation' in the actual world (Walker, 2020, internet source, n.p.). In other words, nations might become increasingly isolated from one another, which would have significant effects on business and human resource management.

Working from home offers both benefits and drawbacks. We can list the following benefits of working from home:

• fostering a sense of belonging among employees,

• boosting the employee's satisfaction for factors like finding a work-life balance,

• decreasing stress and promoting safety,

• shortening commutes,

• enhancing organizational work flexibility and

• isolating them from the pandemic's social effects and improving the work environment.

Working from home has some disadvantages and obstacles, such as

• social isolation,

• the need for new management techniques,

• conflict between personal and professional life,

• the cost of putting up home office facilities and

• the requirement for time management skills.

2.3.2 Internal factors: definition of career and rethinking priorities, acquiring new experiences (individuals)

Individuals are now focusing on re-calibrating their priorities and are now willing to re-design their careers around the kind of life they desire after riding this tremendous roller coaster. Rethinking and revamping their careers, as well as being open to new experiences, are all part of this. Internal factors that individuals face as World 2.0 leaders include:

• **Morale**
  Keeping and boosting morale among their leadership teams and staff has proven to be the biggest issue. Employees have suffered from acute burnout as a result of an incredibly stressful period. Increased uncertainty, health difficulties and this pandemic have all posed a threat to everyone. All the stress, combined with the expectation to perform or even maintain their jobs, can be exhausting and have an impact on

employee morale. To keep employees engaged and cheerful, a few techniques that have worked to increase morale include taking a break away from work when needed and reinforcing priorities.

- **Workspace Concerns**
  The pandemic has altered the workplace's very definition. Leaders are pondering over issues such as when to return to work and how to do so. Workplaces will need to be reinvented with a new HR strategy that prioritises health and safety. Even while the situation has improved and been brought under control in a few nations, an increasing number of employees are eager to hunt for new professions with restructured priorities, such as working from home. To create a holistic well-being culture, businesses will need to carefully design hybrid workforce models that benefit all stakeholders.

- **Growth**
  Driving and maintaining growth is difficult when there is so much fear, anxiety and stress. Leaders must fully comprehend the state of their market, as well as the changes in consumer demands, wants and behaviours because of the level of transformation their companies have gone through to progress towards growth. As a result, leaders must continue to innovate and evolve to satisfy the changing demands of customers and the environment. Increasing business volumes necessitates the creation of new demand, re-engagement with consumers and the rebuilding of opportunity pipelines. To develop a growth-centric culture, leaders will have to push this shift to adapt to new customer behaviour and reality.

- **Uncertainty**
  Uncertainty regarding the pandemic's duration, the economy's trajectory, and the uncertain impact on the markets has been a persistent source of worry. As pre-COVID financial models have become less relevant, forecasting has become significantly less predictable.

Leaders must rely on the facts available at the time to make decisions immediately. Leaders must also consider the opinions of people they trust, such as tax or financial advisers, as well as research from reliable and objective sources.

The idea is to think about and analyse a variety of viewpoints, make a judgement and then make the best decision possible. Leaders will need to cultivate an agile culture that allows them to quickly pivot to the path that information, data, and instincts indicate and to change that path as often as necessary. To deal with this terrible uncertainty, the best thing to do is to continue forward.

2.4 'The Great Resignation' and Possible Reasons

The idea of 'The Great Resignation' was developed by Professor Anthony Klotz of Texas A&M University and predicts a large number of workers quitting their jobs once the COVID pandemic is finished and society returns to 'normal'.

As workers reassess their professions and quit their employment in unprecedented numbers, people all around the world are currently coping with the pandemic's aftereffects. To investigate what has been driving this recent shift, Ian Cook and his team conducted a thorough examination of more than nine million employee data at 4,000 global organizations. Their findings highlighted two trends:

- mid-career workers are most likely to resign, and

- the technology and healthcare sectors have the greatest resignation rates.

Four million Americans left their jobs in July 2021, according to the US Bureau of Labour Statistics.

There are several theories about what the causes of this phenomenon are, with some of them being enhanced unemployment benefits, fear of COVID-19, remote work and general job dissatisfaction. Another possibility is suggested by a recent Gallup poll. Three-quarters of workers—the highest number ever—are disengaged from their employment, and many—particularly women—feel worn out.

It is also believed that one of the causes of 'The Great Resignation' is that people are now re-calibrating their priorities and seeking a holistic life with a healthy work-life balance.

The strongest predictor of employee resignations, according to a different study by a team from MIT (who dug through enormous quantities of data to discover the underlying causes of 'The Great Resignation'), was a toxic culture. As per this research, the following five predictors seem to be the causes of this phenomenon:

- **Toxic culture**
  According to the report's authors, 'a toxic corporate culture is 10 times more influential than compensation in predicting turnover and is by far the biggest predictor of industry-adjusted attrition'. The term 'toxic culture' describes several things, such as a failure to advance diversity, equity and inclusion; a feeling of disdain among employees; and unethical behaviour.

- **Reorganization and job insecurity**
  Employees become disengaged as a result of this feeling, and their fear of losing their jobs leads them to begin looking for new employment. Previous studies have discovered that a key predictor of attrition is how negatively employees feel about their company's future.

- **High levels of innovation that cause burnout**
  This one is counterintuitive, and it has been observed that the more enthusiastically people spoke about innovation at their workplace, the more probable it was that they would leave. The likely cause of this is that, while innovation motivates people, it can also result in burnout because it is difficult for those who participate in it.

- **Failure to recognize performance**
  Employees are more likely to quit jobs and organizations that do not distinguish between high and low achievers when it comes to praise and prizes. When one produces outstanding work, it is more important to feel appreciated and seen than to receive payment.

- **The COVID-19 reaction was poor**
  According to the study, employees who spoke negatively about their employer's handling of the pandemic or who referenced COVID-19 more frequently in their reviews were more likely to leave.

2.5 Conclusion: New Era of HR in the World 2.0

As discussed above, this work aimed to describe the World 2.0 that we live in today and the new emerging themes of human resources claiming to be a business transformer.

Despite the constantly evolving environment, HR plays a key role in defining not just the future of HR but the future of businesses and society as a whole. This work has analysed in detail the factors of World 2.0, the impact on individuals and organizations caused by the pandemic, investigating the phenomenon of '**The Great Resignation**', and the new era of HR in World 2.0. Employees will have to become resilient and open to sudden and unexpected changes and build a career around the lifestyle they want to live rather than run a rat race.

The definition of 'career' should be redesigned with priorities, well-being and work-life balance at the forefront. The pandemic has disrupted lives and the way business is done. A few qualities that people need to develop are agility, resilience and learnability.

Organizations will need to be flexible, add redundancies, and develop systems and processes that can deal with unplanned changes as a result of the uncertainty brought on by unforeseen events. A crisis management plan needs to be implemented, infrastructure needs to be built, and technology needs to be invested. The only way to move forward is to prepare for change and move forward towards better, despite the change.

HR, now more than ever, has a critical role to play, and they need to re-engineer the way organizations view human capital—not just as employees, but as partners. The new HR strategy must include an integrated approach to establish organizations in collaboration with employees for them to construct lives rather than simply work lives and thrive in a World 2.0 environment.

Some of the future HR trends and top priorities for HR leaders in this new era of HR in World 2.0 are:

- Structure talent management around skills and building critical skills and competencies for the organization.

- Facilitate effective organizational design and change management based on trust, teamwork and empathy.

- Encourage employee health and well-being, thereby increasing resilience and preparing a future leadership bench.

- Design and integrate HR strategy with the business to evolve into the new era of HR.

- Drive the change by taking collective accountability to focus on diversity, equity and inclusion.

References

[1] Adam, J. P. (2021). Management of human resources of a pharmacy department during the COVID-19 pandemic: take-aways from the first wave. Research in Social and Administrative Pharmacy, 17(1), 1990–1996.

[2] Bersin, J. (2020). MIT Sloan Management Review and CultureX. Top Issues on HR department's minds, .

[3] Caligiuri, P. D. (2020). International HRM insights for navigating the COVID-19 pandemic: Implications for future research and practice. Journal of international business studies, 51(5), 697–713.

[4] Chugh, A. (2021). What is 'The Great Resignation'? An expert explains,. World Economic Forum.

[5] Cooke, F. L. (2020). Human resource management research and practice in Asia: Past, present and future. . Human Resource Management Review, 30(4), 100778.

[6] Farndale, E. H. (2019). Facing complexity, crisis, and risk: Opportunities and challenges in international human resource management. . Thunderbird International Business Review, 61(3), 465–470.

[7] Gartner for HR Top 5 Priorities for HR Leaders. (2022). Gartner HR Priorities Survey.

[8] Hutchins, H. M. (2008). Organizational crisis management and human resource development: A review of the literature and implications to HRD research and practice. Advances in Developing Human Resources, 10(3), 310–330.

[9] Ian Cook, H. B. (2021). Who Is Driving the Great Resignation,. Harvard Business Review,.

[10] Joe Galvin, V. (2020). 4 Major Pandemic Challenges Facing Leaders and How to Solve Them. Inc.com.

[11] Josh Bersin. (2020). Top Issues on HR department's minds. MIT Sloan Management Review and CultureX.

[12] Lee, S. H. (2003). Impact of the Asian economic crisis on training intentions and outcomes. Human Resource Management Review, 13(3), 467–486.

[13] Mala, W. A. (2020). How COVID-19 Changes the HRM Practices (Adapting One HR Strategy May Not Fit to All). SSRN 3736719.

[14] Meenakshi Kaushik, N. G. (2020). The Impact of Pandemic COVID -19 in Workplace. European Journal of Business and Management.

[15] Milburn, T. W. (1983). Organizational crisis. Part I: Definition and conceptualization. . Human relations, 36(12), 1141–1160.

[16] Milburn, T. W. (1983). Organizational crisis. Part II: Strategies and responses. Human Relations, 36(12), 1161–1179.

[17] Stillman, J. (2022). These Are the Top 5 Reasons People Are Quitting During the Great Resignation. According to a Massive New Analysis.

[18] Verlinden, N. (2021). Top 10 HR Trends for 2021 and Beyond. AIHR.

[19] Walker, A. (2020). Coronavirus: UK economy could be among worst hit of leading nations. OECD. BBC.

[20] Zhang, Y. &. (2020). Organizational preparedness with COVID-19: strategic planning and human creativity. . The European Business Review, 22–33.

[21] Zhongming, Z. L. (2021). The Great Resignation: American Workers Suffering a Crisis of Meaning.

3

Emerging HR Practices—Digital Upskilling: A Strategic Way of Talent Management and Engagement

S. Gomathi[1], A. Rajeswari[2] and Seifedine Kadry[3]

[1]Professor, VIT Business School, Vellore Institute of Technology, Vellore, Tamil Nadu, India
[2]Research Scholar, VIT Business School, Vellore Institute of Technology, Vellore, Tamil Nadu, India
[3]Professor, Noroff University College, Kristiansand, Norway

Email: sgomatthi@vit.ac.in; rajeswari.arunachalam2020@vitstudent.ac.in; skadry@gmail.com

Abstract

Digital upskilling is creating a positive shift and new implications in the field of human resource management. The introduction of digitization in HR practices like automation, artificial intelligence and big data analytics changes the dimensions of work at a greater pace. Therefore, companies are realizing the importance of digital upskilling for their workforce to stay competitive and more productive than before. As a result, it is unavoidable for organizations to effectively plan, manage, engage and retain digital talent. There is a knowledge gap among the employees in developing technological skills to perform their jobs and tasks. Rather than concentrating on hiring and training new employees with expected skills, which is an expensive and hectic process, it is better that the organization identify this knowledge gap and teach additional skills to their existing employees to enrich their performance. This strategy of teaching additional skills to the existing employees is termed 'upskilling'. Upskilling involves continuous learning of skills to adapt to changing environments and avoid becoming obsolete. Digital upskilling refers to teaching technology-oriented skills to employees to meet the demands of the technologies and digitalization involved in their businesses. This paper attempts to review the digital upskilling of the employees in the organization which is a key strategic approach to effectively managing and engaging talent. This paper emphasizes the importance and benefits of digital upskilling in the workplace. The contribution of this paper relies on pointing out some of the effective and successful approaches to developing digital upskilling strategies in organizations.

3.1 Introduction

Technology in the workplace helps organizations be more effective, efficient and well organized. It is one of the key determinants for gaining a competitive advantage. Every business organization has been technology-driven in its production and service processes. Technology plays an integral and beneficial role in all aspects of business processes. In recent scenarios, work is being reformed by artificial intelligence, technology and other innovative applications, with possible and considerable effects. Employers and employees alike must possess the requisite digital and soft skills in order to meet the new demands and upcoming opportunities that are expected to arise. The contemporary environment is hastening the demand for digital transformation while also generating significant and extensive personnel and skills challenges. The correct combination of talented and flexible individuals, linked with the right culture and the right mindset, may help companies with their empowerment and long-term sustainability. Digital skills will increase the economic growth of the country and societal wellbeing.

3.2 Theoretical Review

Gekara et al. (2019) have identified that by enhancing the digital skills of the workforce, the organization could increase their productivity and also contribute to a high level of the global economy. The study also suggests that organizations could upskill the employees' digital skills by incorporating a multifaceted approach with the support of government and corporate stakeholders. In the year 2016, Adam states that in consideration of the evolution and increasing dependency on digitalization in our work and personal lives, digital intelligence is a much-expected new competency that employees need to develop and train. Mithas (2017) has coined 'digital intelligence' as 'the ability to understand and utilize the power of IT to our advantage'. Boughzala et al. (2020) have identified that the framework of digital intelligence comprises three levels of analysis, namely the individual level, organizational level and societal level, that facilitate the outline of digital learning and intelligence.

3.2.1 Digital upskilling versus hiring new skills

According to reports, roughly half of the work and tasks in the world have the technical capacity to be digitized using currently available technologies. While some skills are likely to become redundant faster than the world has probably thought and some new skills will rise in demand. In this case, there are two possible options for the management: either to hire new talent or upskill the existing workforce. Among these two, hiring new talents with the required technical skills is expensive, whereas digital upskilling of the existing workforce is quite cost-effective. Therefore, the management has to take the right decision on digital upskilling for the existing talent, which would be an effective managerial outcome.

When firms consider bringing new technical capabilities to their staff, hiring fresh people is usually the first idea. Individuals, from their perspective, expect their organization to provide digital upskilling programmes and to prepare them for new job role demands. Hence, the question arises as to which is more economical and viable for the organization—hiring new talent or upskilling.

Research conducted in the year 2018 by the Society of Human Resources Management says that companies aim to hire skills from outside the organization which is nearly equivalent to the amount spent on six to nine months of an employee's compensation. "This carries its own set of costs, as well as increased hours and cultural implications." Furthermore, there is a high demand for talent with digitally competent skills and abilities, which seems to be difficult to locate.

In such a scenario, it is evident from the above-mentioned statement that upskilling the existing workforce makes sense and is also the most economically efficient option in the long run, as it contributes to talent retention and talent engagement, thus improving organizational productivity.

Krishnakumar (2018), founder and CEO of Simplilearn, states that 'the skill gap has made professionals and enterprises highly vulnerable, and digital upskilling is the only way out, and companies are acting very fast to ensure their employees are technically skilled across newer and more advanced technologies'. He added that companies are partnering with training companies to deliver online training on digital skills for their employees.

It's also worth noting that not every employee is interested in digital upskilling and reskilling training programmes. Therefore, it is the organization's part to identify for which group of employees it should invest time and money in digital upskilling programmes.

Sundar Subramanian (2018), President of Mphasis, says that employers must establish a good balance between hiring and upskilling. In the long run,

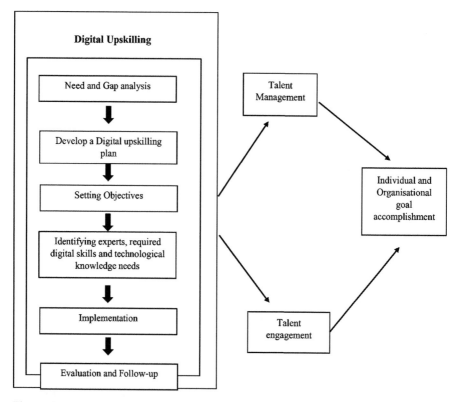

Figure 3.1 Conceptual framework of digital upskilling for talent management and talent engagement.

multiskilling employees at various levels may be an alternative. He continued that hiring new talent and training individuals is easy since they pick up new abilities rapidly. On the other hand, experienced professionals and employees have subject knowledge and a good awareness of their clients' needs. Customers frequently have a lot of unspoken criteria in terms of service and process delivery and meeting service-level agreements and deliverables, which new hires may not be aware of. They're also more outcome-oriented.

The conceptual framework of digital upskilling mentioned in Figure 3.1 describes how digital upskilling of the workforce is initiated with an effective need and gap analysis where the organization identifies whether there is actually a need for upskilling the employees and, if so, what are the areas, skills, and competencies of the employees that are to be improved and what are the potential knowledge and skill gaps that are to be addressed through upskilling. The next step is drawing up a plan that establishes the course of actions involved in providing digital skills training to the employees, followed by defining clear and specific goals and objectives for upskilling. After setting up the objectives, the organization should identify the required skills and technological knowledge and methods. Whether the organization chooses artificial intelligence tools, big data analytics or MOOC methods to upskill their employees, all are highly impactful and are demanded by the organization for talent knowledge development and business sustainability. This also includes finding the right experts to impart digital upskilling training, where the organization can choose in-house experts or they can choose to outsource the experts. Then the organization should execute the plans and evaluate the upskilling process and continuously monitor the activities and outcomes to ensure whether the objective of upskilling the employees and enhancing the digital intelligence of the workforce has been met or not. In case of discrepancies, the organization should identify the gaps and should make necessary revisions in the previous phases, whichever is subject to improvisation.

The beginning of digital upskilling of employees leads to effectively engaging the talent on their tasks, work, team and organization as a whole, as well as effective workforce management, which in turn impacts the organization's performance in terms of achievement of individual and organizational goals and objectives.

3.3 Research Methodology

The study is conceptual, and several scholarly contributions, concepts and ideas have been reviewed and analysed for the study. Secondary data is used to conduct this study where journals, books, articles and websites have been referred to for the conceptualization of this article.

3.4 Managerial Reviews on Digital Upskilling

Top executives of various corporate have shared their viewpoints on digital upskilling.

Vinay Pradhan (2018), Country Manager of Skillsoft (India), says that 'Effective upskilling requires a balance of technical and soft skills for organizations to nurture the talent they need for open jobs'.

Another executive, Kumar (2018), shares that online courses were once thought to be inferior to traditional learning methods. However, in today's environment of shifting business strategies and technological advancements, digital upskilling has taken centre stage. The demand for online training has risen dramatically as businesses expect their employees to be more up-to-date on the latest abilities. Online learning has taken over normal training with ease due to its flexibility, integrated manner of communication, engagement and ability to apply skills on the job.

Ruchi Bhalla (2018), Vice President (Human Resources) of Pitney Bowes Inc. insists that India is one of the greatest job providers in the global technology business. At the same time, the implementation of technology in the Indian IT sector is not rapid enough. He also says that there are a plethora of job specialties for which India lacks the essential educational infrastructure, and online learning courses fill that void. People gain greatly from specialized technology like blockchain, and their lives and career pathways are altered as a result. To stay up with the market, the IT ecosystem as a whole needs to advocate for a more holistic view of upskilling the workforce.

Dr. Rahmyn Kress (2018), Chief Digital Officer and founder of Henkel-X, opines that the organization can strengthen and expand its global business by embracing digital transformation. According to him, this can be done if everyone in the organization shares the same perspective and expertise.

Ravi Kaklasaria (2019), Co-Founder & CEO of Spring People, said that their organization's artificial intelligence study route, machine learning with Python language, and Programme in Data Science were in high demand among the stakeholders, and it was surprising to learn that 95% of these inquiries resulted in enrolling in a matter of days. He also reports that the majority of the learners have shown considerable benefits following the upskilling or reskilling programme. These benefits can include recognition from their employer, a rise in income, a promotion or an incentive.

Sarita Digumarti (2017), Co-Founder & COO, of Jigsaw Academy, shared that since April 2017, around 4,000 fresh talents have registered and about 5,000 individuals have signed up for the emerging technological and technical courses in total. She added that as companies shift towards a more data-driven strategy, professionals, experts, and new graduates are investing in digital upskilling courses to improve salaries and stay ahead of the curve. According to her, the salaries of the users increased from 20 per cent to 100 per cent depending on the competencies and functionalities they had.

According to the research conducted by Gartner in 2017, a worldwide research and consultancy group, it is predicted that artificial intelligence will generate more employment than it will remove. By 2020, 2.3 million new jobs will have been generated to replace the 1.8 million ones that will be eliminated. This disparity is expected to widen with each passing year, resulting in a skill divide. As a result, staying current with current trends and digital abilities is critical. Every new technology introduces some sort of disruption. Automation, on the other hand, allows people to focus on their strengths, including creativity, invention and emotional intelligence while managing activities that humans are not equipped to handle. These technologies will be implemented by businesses to improve productivity and long-term planning. As a result, ensuring that employees are not only focused on the task at hand, but also receiving training in management, services, career advancement, mentorship and other areas would enable the business to develop strategic competency in the digital transition process.

3.5 Demand for Digital Skills

Technology-driven business improves productivity, increases efficiency and stimulates creativity and innovation in the workplace. As a result, there is a huge demand for gaining expertise in hybrid technical skills like cyber security, mobile app development, UI and UX, big data analytics, cloud computing, Internet of Things, automation, robotics, process automation, AI machine learning, natural language processing, augmented reality, virtual reality, pervasive computing, etc.

Digital upskilling in areas like big data analytics, cloud and distributed computing, data mining, data sciences, platform engineering, DevOps and testing automation is also in the pipeline of improvement.

3.6 MOOCs (Massive Open Online Courses) and Digital Upskilling

Access to digital technology in the organization has accelerated its business performance and also emphasizes learning in the workplace through MOOCs. MOOCs are an effective means of upskilling the workforce. MOOCs provide the organization with a quick and cost-effective way to improve its workforce's digital abilities. A MOOC is a professional learning and development tool used in many human resources functions like recruitment, training and development and performance enhancement.

Employers and employees are increasingly using MOOCs, indicating a shift towards recognizing the need for more inexpensive, up-to-date and flexible professional and digital skills development. MOOCs, according to Dezube (2019), are 'ongoing, flexible content to sharpen skill development'. Therefore, the adoption of MOOCs for upskilling must be embraced by HR managers for digital upskilling and employee talent management at the workplace.

3.7 Implementing Digital Upskilling in the Workplace

The learning content needs to be designed and updated by subject matter experts, and industry and corporate leaders, and it also needs to be aligned with applied learning projects and real-time case studies, with hands-on practice. The delivery must combine self-paced online content as well as instructor-led live virtual classrooms. Furthermore, the progress of upskilling initiatives can be ensured with pre and post-course assessments and certifications.

3.7.1 Benefits of digital upskilling

3.7.1.1 Higher levels of productivity

Digital upskilling may bring high levels of productivity. It also costs the business the least amount of money to replace talent. Therefore, by upskilling the digital skillset of the employees, the company could be more dynamic, flexible, entrepreneurial and well-rounded and may have an equipped workforce that can adapt quickly to change.

3.7.1.2 Talent retention

Employees do not desire to work in an organization that does not care for employees' personal growth and development. Employees wish to work in an organization that encourages them in the active learning and development process. Digital upskilling will prevent their skills from being obsolete and also help employees to move forward on the career ladder. Thus, digital upskilling helps in talent retention.

3.7.1.3 Workforce engagement

Since the company is providing learning and upskilling opportunities to the employees, it psychologically makes employees committed to the organization and thus fosters employee engagement.

3.7.1.4 Increased customer satisfaction

Through digital upskilling, the employees can gain insights and updates on relevant industry trends, which leads to improved service quality that may lead to increased customer satisfaction and better customer experience..

3.7.1.5 Company reputation

If the organization engages itself in promoting active learning and development for its employees, it substantially creates a win-win environment and constructs synergistic organizational development. This, in turn, results in an improved company's reputation in the industry.

3.8 Corporate Practices in Digital Upskilling

Companies like Microsoft, Amazon, PwC, Henkel, Salesforce.com Inc., and Google have invested in and launched programmes to upskill their workers. These companies are dedicated to the continuous upskilling of employees with advanced technological skills and knowledge.

3.8.1 Amazon's digital upskilling

Ryan Roslansky (2021) mentions that Amazon has a diversified workforce with different backgrounds, education levels and varied skill sets. To cope with this diversified education level and varied skillset, Amazon is committed to investing $700 million in the digital upskilling of its workforce. The digital upskilling programme includes computer-based or e-learning and certifications, curriculum redevelopment and other technical programmes. The objective of the programme is to provide the workforce with required job skills and to close the gap between acquired and required job skills.

3.8.2 Salesforce.Inc digital upskilling

In the newsletter released in the year 2019 by Salesforce.com Inc, a California-based cloud-based software corporation, it was mentioned that the corporation has made a free investment in upskilling half a million US workers. Salesforce's Trailhead training platform is available to employees in any field who need to learn new skills.

3.8.3 Google digital upskilling

In 2017, Google started a digital upskilling programme. Through a broad partner network of schools, libraries and non-profits, it has trained over 3 million US workers in digital skills. Workers have received important job-related technical skills as a result of this programme, which will help them compete in the job market. For computer workers, students, military personnel, educators and families, Google offers certification courses and programmes, as well as basic skill workshops.

3.8.4 Microsoft digital upskilling

By the end of the year 2020, Brad Smith (2020), President & Vice Chairman of Microsoft, states that Microsoft will have provided digital upskilling programmes to 25 million US workers affected by the COVID-19 Pandemic.

Their digital upskilling programme integrates existing and new materials from LinkedIn, GitHub, and other sources to equip people with the digital skills they need to succeed in the workplace or progress up the professional ladder from their current job.

3.8.5 Henkel digital upskilling

Henkel's press release in 2019 mentioned that Henkel has initiated a global, companywide digital upskilling programme. Their primary approach is an in-depth analysis of the existing skill set of the workforce. It conducts online self-assessments to evaluate employees' digital skills. The self-assessment is carried out under two main criteria. First is 'Digital Base Fit', which tests general knowledge of the workforce, and second is 'Digital Expert Fit', which tests the advanced job-specific expertise of the workforce. These tests were meant to identify the knowledge level of employees for digital skills. This phase evaluates the types of training that should be provided based on the gaps identified. Based on the results obtained, Henkel develops customized training programmes and recommendations, that match the 'ideal future skill set up' as per the training needs analysis. The training programme on digital upskilling covers aspects like analytics, e-commerce and sourcing the future workforce.

For upskilling programmes, Henkel has partnered with Cornerstone which is a pioneer in cloud-based workforce management software, to create a new learning platform to help employees navigate their digital learning experience. The use of this platform provides true personalized content to its employees that encourages continuous improvisation in upskilling of the workforce and ensures learning on demand through this intuitive platform.

3.8.6 PwC—digital upskilling

Mike Fenlon and Sarah McEneaney (2018) of PricewaterhouseCoopers (PwC), a multi-professional service-based business firm, state that their company has developed a holistic workforce upskilling approach to empower all employees' 'digital fitness'. It aims to empower the entire workforce with a wide range of knowledge across all the domains deemed essential for today's business people, such as big data and business intelligence analytics, blockchain, artificial intelligence systems, design thinking and robotization. PwC's primary business competency is the digital upskilling strategy. PwC is developing digital fitness through tech-enabled learning, which includes immersive skill-building, podcasting, gamification, multiple media content and quiz assessments delivered via mobile and digital platforms, bypassing the limitations of traditional classroom learning. They have also created a digital fitness application that gives all of its employees a tailored assessment of their digital skills and directs them to the tools and resources they need to fill in the gaps and develop. This programme creates a personalized learning route for the entire workforce and helps in workforce planning and digital upskilling plans.

3.9 Impact of COVID-19 on Digital Upskilling

The reliance on technology in the post-pandemic period has been proven by remote work. As a result, today's businesses are more willing to spend on future-proofing their employees' skill sets and adapting to the quick speed of technological development. As a result of the pandemic, hybrid workplace architecture has emerged, resulting in a greater reliance on digital services and remote working. The current situation, according to industry experts, has increased the need for upskilling and reskilling in trending areas of technology like big data, digital HR, cyber forensics and security, workforce analytics, cloud technology, AI and machine learning, DevOps, data mining with ETL and the Internet of things. Experts also believe that digital upskilling has to be upgraded to future-proof the careers of employees. Consequently, digital upskilling efforts have regained prominence owing to the economic uncertainty brought on by the pandemic, especially in the job market.

3.10 Conclusion

Digital upskilling is an ongoing process. Digitalization of businesses involves the integration of technology into all areas of business activities. By integrating technology into the business processes, the organization could keep them updated in today's ever-changing digital era. Therefore, organizations and employees should understand the significance of digital upskilling and should implement it for the continuous commitment and growth of the organization. It should be noted that there is a huge demand for digital upskilling in today's quickly expanding digital environment. And while it's not just the individuals in the IT function in the organization who have to be digital-ready, it is more crucial for all the leaders of the organization to possess all those skills and competencies that are required to mobilize and drive the digital agenda. There is a tremendous opportunity for digital transformation in developing countries, and that is possible only if the workforce can be upskilled to live up to the challenge, which is a strategic way of talent management and competitive advantage for the business. Hence, organizations need to increase their investments in employee training and digital upskilling at all levels of the organization. Therefore, organizations need to address the employees' skillset gaps through digital upskilling or reskilling, to meet digital transformations and technological initiatives that match expected business outcomes.

3.11 Discussion

Digital upskilling allows for continuous growth and professional development of talents. At the organizational level, practising digital skill enhancement philosophy improves organizational efficiency and develops strategic intent to withstand sustainability competition. It can also be noted that digital upskilling or reskilling prepares employees for their successive growth and development. Digital upskilling also ensures employee engagement by increasing the level of engagement of low-engaged and disengaged employees and focuses on successful talent management. On the other hand, imparting digital skills will substantially reduce the employees' frustration that arises due to fear of the unknown and obsoleteness. Therefore, effective implementation of digital upskilling practises and programmes is vital for the organization to yield the best results and outcomes at all levels of the organization.

References

[1] Amrita Nair Ghaswalla, Ravi Kaklasaria (2019, April 16), "Workforce needs to enter the digital age: Experts", The Hindu: Business Line. Retreived from Workforce need to enter digital age: Experts - The Hindu BusinessLine

[2] Bersin, J. (2017, June 11), "How do you define digital learning?", Chief Learning Officer, Vol 16, No 5. Retrieved from: https://www.chieflearningofficer.com

[3] Brad Smith (2020, June 30), "Microsoft to help 25 million people worldwide acquire new digital skills needed for the COVID-19 economy", Microsoft News Center. Retrieved from https://news.microsoft.com/2020

[4] CIPD. (2021), "Digital learning in a post-COVID-19 economy: a literature review" London: Chartered Institute of Personnel and Development.

[5] Hanna Phillips (2019, March 28), "How to prepare a Company for the future", Henkel: Press release. Retrieved from www.henkel.com/press

[6] Krishnakumar (2018, July 1) Upskilling workforce for Digital Age, Dataquest: Business Trends. Retrieved from PressReader.com

[7] Mike Fenlon, Sarah McEneaney (2018, October 15), "Employment and jobs: How teach digital skills at PwC", Harvard Business review & Aspen institute. Retrieved from https://www.aspeninstitute.org/

[8] Dr.Rahmyn Kress (2018, July 9) "Digital Transformation-No one can do it alone", Henkel: Spotlight Magazine. Retreived from Digital transformation – no one can do it alone" (henkel.com)

[9] RobVan Der Meulen, Christy Pettey (2017, December 13), "Gartner says by 2020, Artificial Intelligence will create more jobs than it eliminates", Gartner: Newsroom Press releases. Retrieved from AI Will Create More Jobs Than It Eliminates | Gartner

[10] Ruchi Bhalla (2018, July 1) Upskilling workforce for Digital Age, Dataquest: Business Trends. Retrieved fromPressReader.com - Digital Newspaper

[11] Ryan Roslansky (2021, June 08), "Hiring and Recruitment: You need a Skills-based approach to hiring and developing talent", Harvard Business Review. Retrieved from https://hbr.org/2021

[12] Salesforce.Inc (2019, May 16), "Company signs White House Pledge to America's Workers", Salesforce: News and Insights. Retrieved from https://www.salesforce.com/news/press-releases/2019

[13] Sarita Digumarti (2017, May 23), "IT Professionals can increase salaries through upskilling", India Today: Press Trust of India. Retrieved from IT professionals can increase salaries through upskilling - PTI feed News (indiatoday.in)

[14] Soma Tah (2018, August 1), "Upskilling workforce for the Digital Age", Dataquest: DQ India online. Retrieved from Upskilling Workforce For The Digital Age (dqindia.com)

[15] Sundar Subramanian (2018, July 1) Upskilling workforce for Digital Age, Dataquest: Business Trends. Retrieved from PressReader.com

[16] Vinay Pradhan (2018, July 1) Upskilling workforce for Digital Age, Dataquest: Business Trends. Retrieved from PressReader.com

4

Impact of Artificial Intelligence on Skill Development Training in India

Biswabhushan Behera[1], Mamta Gaur[1] and Mohammad Asif[2]

[1]School of Business, Galgotias University, India
[2]College of Administrative and Financial Sciences, Saudi Electronic University, KSA

Email: bbb222@rediffmail.co; mamtagaur@galgotiasuniversity.edu.in; asif.alif35@gmail.co

Abstract

Skill development has gained focus in the corporate sector as skills are among the top three external forces that impact the business next to technology and market factors. Corporates are waking up to the criticality of skill and the adverse impact of skill gaps as skills can have a direct impact on the company's ROI. With an effective system of skill development, human resources can be developed which can translate into increased productivity and ultimately the development of the nation.

Artificial intelligence has created a radical disruption in the world of work. It can address many issues about skill development training like innovative training and learning practices. It can amplify technology, make data-driven analysis for faster decisions and help in working smarter and faster, and achieve better outcomes.

The earlier traditional jobs are now efficiently and cost-effectively done through AI-powered systems/robotic process automation/humanoids. Industries need new skill sets to handle such AI-powered machines/systems and match with AI as conventional skills are no longer sufficient or relevant; hence the need for skill development for re-positioning/upgrading/ upskilling.

This research paper endeavours in understanding (i) the relationship between artificial intelligence and skill development and (ii) how artificial intelligence is impacting skill development training in India.

The research paper has made exploratory and descriptive research and made an in-depth analysis based on available secondary data collected from the web, books/journals/magazines, news media and government portals.

The researchers finally concluded that to match the disruption due to the technological advancement of AI, the skill development system needs to be prepared and equipped to respond and match the required emerging skills. How human interacts with AI-powered machines keeps on changing which recommend the need for skill development to be inbuilt and navigate these interactions to grow so that workers/trainees do not remain excluded/exploited.

4.1 Introduction

The concept of artificial intelligence was introduced from 1940 to 1956 as it rolled for the first time with the turing test by Alan Turing in 1950 but the term 'artificial intelligence' (AI) was coined in 1956 at a conference held at Dartmouth College. The period 1956–1974 marked the golden years. In 1959, machine learning was used to beat human players in Samuel's checkers programme. In 1961, arithmetic was performed through voice command using IBM's Shoebox. In 1966, the first mobile robot, Shakey was launched and Joseph Weizenbaum created ELIZA an artificial conversational 'therapist' Chatbot. There was an AI winter from 1974 to 1980 and then the AI boom was again witnessed during 1980–1987 with the introduction of expert machines like the R1/XCON for assisting sales personnel. There was again an AI winter from 1987–1994. Thereafter, the modern age of AI started in 1994 when the world was surprised by twin robotic cars VaMP and Vita-2 travelling around 1000 KM on the Paris highway. In 1997, IBM's intelligent machine, deep blue, defeated the human champion in chess. In 2000, Kismet, a social machine capable of expressing emotion, was introduced. In 2004, Honda Ashimo, a personal robot was released. In 2011, the Watson Computer system of IBM competed against Brad Rutter and Ken Jennings on the quiz show 'Jeopardy' and defeated the champions. Subsequently, in 2016, Virtual Agents like Apple's Siri, Google's Now and IPSoft's Amelia were also introduced. In 2017–2018, Google introduced AutoML which uses AI to generate AI to train high-quality models as per the business need.

Artificial intelligence is commonly understood as human intelligence exhibited by smart machines. Systems powered by AI can approximate, automate, imitate and eventually improve human thinking. Now, machines and systems are getting smarter as AI helps the computer systems, robots and humanoids process data to perform intelligent tasks of humans, that is, thinking and perceiving, visualizing and acting, understanding language, reasoning and decision making, etc. Many of our daily services have already been leveraged by AI to improve the user's experience. E-commerce sites like Amazon etc use machine learning to recommend products based on the search made by the user. Apple's Siri, Microsoft's Alexa, etc., use AI in their speech-to-text conversation and optimization. Even our email and SMS services also use AI to filter spam.

In today's world, our learning does not stop with our school or university, we need to keep updating and reskilling to match with the ever-evolving and ever-innovating world of work. There is a paradoxical situation, as a huge gap between the demands versus supply of skill is evident. The skills possessed by the existing and potential workforce through traditional education and training do not match the demand of the industry. This skill gap has further widened with the advent of Industry 4.0 and artificial intelligence (AI).

Many jobs that were traditionally done by humans are now done more cost-effectively and efficiently by AI-powered systems/robotic process automation/humanoids. Industries now require new skill sets to handle such AI-powered machines/systems to match with AI as the conventional skills of existing and potential workforce are not enough or relevant. The workforce and the industry need to re-position or upgrade/upskill to be in the race. Hence, the importance of skill development training has gained momentum.

The objective of the present study is to determine:

(i) The relationship between artificial intelligence and skill development trainings.

(ii) The impact of artificial intelligence on the skill development trainings in India.

4.2 Literature Review

McKee and Gauch (2021) in their research paper 'Implications of Industry 4.0 on Skills Development' concluded that there are huge possibilities for educational transformation due to emerging and converging technologies. However, as the world moves towards this educational transformation, it is imperative that the world also transforms into a more useful, productive, secure place and better place for all.

Pelau et al. (2021) in their research article 'The Impact of Artificial Intelligence on Consumers' Identity and Human Skills' concluded that the development of AI can be beneficial to humans and humanity only if they learn to use such robots and intelligent machines properly for the benefit of humans.

Paek and Kim (2021) in their research paper 'Analysis of Worldwide Research Trends on the Impact of Artificial Intelligence in Education' concluded that nowadays artificial intelligence is omnipresent, impacting human civilization and is also becoming instrumental in the revolutionary change in the education sector. AI forces us to change our perspective of education starting from its purpose, content and teaching methods.

Hui (2020) in his research paper 'The Impact of Artificial Intelligence on Vocational Education and Counter Measures' indicated that vocational education requires upgrading learning contents and methods to adapt to the changes in the job market and change in level and quality of the talent demand due to the advent of artificial intelligence.

Panigrahi and Joshi (2020) in their research article 'Use of Artificial Intelligence in Education' opined that focused efforts are required by all the stakeholders of the Education sector to comprehend, admit and utilize AI-based products which benefit them and which can be used to create customized, pertinent, appealing, understandable and controllable solutions for every learner.

Goksel and Bozkurt (2019) in their research article 'Artificial Intelligence in Education: Current Insights and Future Perspectives' brought out that AI undoubtedly helps in easing human lives and advancement of human progress. However, it is very important to develop a serious stance before integrating AI into educational processes. An ethical policy needs to be developed and the ethical boundaries of the usage of human-generated data by AI need to be first defined. Then, it needs to be ensured, by testing and retesting, that the AI-featured educational processes do not produce any automated processes and machine learning.

Ray (2019) in his article 'Digital Skills, Transmedia and Artificial Intelligence' brought out that AI should solve human problems and if it does not it would rather be a nuisance and another problem for the world to tackle with.

Tao et al. (2019) in their paper 'Digital Skills, Transmedia and Artificial Intelligence' brought out that caution is required and precautions need to be taken to ensure that robots and artificial intelligence do not dominate situations without human supervision, especially in matters of education.

Poola (2017) in his article 'How Artificial Intelligence is Impacting Real Life Every day" brought out that the implementation of AI has resulted in the saving of time, which ultimately enhanced business results and facilitated day-to-day human activities. Moreover, the use of AI-based computerized methods and automated systems has also eased human effort. It is evident that AI has immensely impacted people's lives with the automation process of almost all their manual activities and enables them in moving ahead.

Patil (2016) in his article 'Study of Teaching in Artificial Intelligence Track' concluded that for actually implementing the Study of teaching it is essential that the students have high consciousness and Lecturers have the required expertise to analyse and stimulate students, the benefit in research of teaching.

4.3 Research Methodology

The study is exploratory research based on the secondary data sourced mainly from articles and reports available on the web or published in books, journals, magazines and Government portals. The research design is a descriptive and in-depth analysis of the research study have been adopted. Available secondary data have been extensively used for the study.

4.4 Analysis and Findings

4.4.1 Importance of skill development training in India

The human factor has a great impact on the national and regional economies. Organizations devoid of a skilled workforce struggle to innovate, deliver value to stakeholders, grow and create more job opportunities. Under such situations, many companies migrate to other locations in search of workers with the required skills so that they remain competitive. The economic competitiveness of the region can be severely impacted by the decline of the skills of the workforce. Regions with mainly low-skilled and low-wage jobs can witness a drop in GDP, reduced tax revenues and become dependent on public services. The human factor is the most critical consideration in making location investment decisions by companies. Skill development has gained focus in the corporate sector as skills are among the top three external forces that impact the business next to technology and market factors. Corporates are waking up to the criticality of skill and understanding the adverse impact of skill gaps as skills can have a direct impact on a company's ROI. Around 70% of leading companies report that they continuously invest to improve their workforce skills. With an effective system of skill development, human resources can be developed which can translate into increased productivity and ultimately the development of the nation.

4.4.2 AI in skill development training

AI should be for all and everyone should be able to take advantage of the technological revolution in terms of innovation and knowledge. AI can address many of the issues in skill development training and helps in innovative training and learning practices. It can amplify technology, make data-driven analysis for faster decisions and help in working smarter, and faster and achieve better outcomes. In skill and development approaches, AI can filter complicated processes of data via machines. For example, it can filter trainee's preferences to provide a personalized skill development option directly. With help of machine learning or AI, trainees can maximize their learning process by arranging their preferences based on their skill and experience. Content can be personalized to suit the trainee's requirement, focus on their weaker areas, recommend suitable content based on past behaviour and generate content using various algorithms. To utilize AI to the fullest it is required to harness the huge amount of data with help of machine learning, data analysis and AI programmes. The output from such data enables the skill development trainers to gain insight into the trainees' journey and help them to create training programmes that enable adaptive learning and drive value.

AI can analyse big data in real-time and provide solutions in terms of smart content and other specified training parameters that help in meeting trainees' requirements of targeted practice and feedback. It also facilitates trainers to understand the performance of trainees better and formulate personalized training plans which are more effective.

4.4.3 Impact of AI on skill development training programmes

Automation of data-driven enterprise tasks started with the introduction of enterprise resource planning (ERP) systems and has now evolved into robotic process automation (RPA). Today, most customer services are performed by machines (bots), not men. Bank of America in a report stated that by 2025, AI would result in an annual industrial expansion of around $14–33 trillion.

The relation between AI and skill development training involves (i) AI for skill development and (ii) skill development for AI.

4.4.3.1 AI for skill development

Skill development training largely involves human-to-human interaction. The integration of AI in development required human-like qualities, for example, repetitiveness, resourcefulness and thoughtfulness are still a long way to go. Yet, there are many areas where the strength of AI helps in filling the 'gaps'. AI is augmenting the training industry including skill development training in the following ways.

4.4.3.1.1 Smart training contents

AI is helping in creating smart digital training content, like smart training guides, customizable training digital interfaces, online assistants or chatbots, etc. The content in burdening troubleshooting guides can be condensed into easily digestible study guides with step-by-step troubleshooting summaries, flashcards, intelligent simulations, etc., which the trainees can easily understand.

4.4.3.2 Smart training systems

AI can also tutor a trainee based on the challenges they are facing. It involves mastery learning which facilitates in the training room with individualized training and instructions. For example, air force technicians are trained with 'SHERLOCK', a smart system, to diagnose electrical system faults in aircraft. Army officials before proceeding on international assignments are trained with Avatar-based training modules. Such smart platforms adapt to a wide variety of learning styles and are of great help to both the trainer and trainee.

4.4.3.3 Virtual environment and facilitators

The smart 'touchless' or 'gesture recognition' technologies empower virtual facilitators with the ability to respond to verbal as well as nonverbal cues and perform like humans. Currently, AI-augmented reality, computer animation and 3-D gaming are used for training purposes in smart training environments and platforms. In the future, the human trainer may soon be replaced with humanoids/robots to a great extent.

4.4.3.4 Content analytics

With help of AI, the content trained to trainees can be analysed for the best effect and can be optimized to cater to the needs of the trainees. The trainers and content providers create, and manage their E-learning content and also gain important insights into the trainee's progress and understanding through the use of analytics.

4.4.4 Skill development for AI

AI is being taught in many Universities for the last three decades and it generally requires some basic knowledge of computer science and mathematics. Recently, academic interest in data science, AI and machine learning has gained momentum. Still, it is difficult to introduce AI as a new computing curriculum without enough trained trainers in the field. The trainers need to adapt to the new applications, be digitally aware and also be trained to prepare for digital skills. AI applications are now omnipresent. As such, we just need to add the usage of the applications to the individual skills required by a trainer.

Due to technological advancements, many jobs will be lost due to robotization, and at the same time, new jobs would emerge too. Many of such new jobs would be directly or indirectly linked with the technical aspects of AI. The learning environment would radically change and would include AI. Intelligent training systems and tools that allow personalized learning/training experiences would also require a good understanding of these AI tools. AI definitely would help trainers but at the same time, the trainers would be penalized if they are not able to access or make proper use of these AI tools. Skill development in AI would be the prerequisite to make the right use of the AI tools.

4.5 Skills for the Current AI Age

The nature of jobs and skills has always been impacted by innovation in technology and disruptions. Hence, it is a continuous endeavour of industry and the workforce to adapt to such disruption. This disruption has been all the more accelerated by the advancement of AI.

As predicted by NASSCOM, by the year 2022, 46% of the Indian workforce would be engaged in completely new jobs which are non-existent today or jobs with emerging skill sets. It is also estimated that a considerable demand for AI, machine learning specialists and data analytics professionals would persist over the next 10 years.

In the IT sector, instead of traditional software developer roles, there would be demand for new roles like computer vision engineers, cloud architects, language processing specialists, robotic process automation engineers and 3D modelling engineers, etc. With AI, such a transition would also impact other sectors like education, health, agriculture, finance, etc., requiring many new skill sets. Hence, in each sector, the required new skill sets need to be identified and proper skill development training programmes are required to be designed to make the workforce ready for the new technologies of the AI age.

4.6 AI Impact on the Future of Skill Development Training Programmes

Skill development training programmes are greatly influenced and transformed by AI in the following ways:

1. **Personalization:** The skill development training programmes can be personalized according to the needs of each trainee. Trainees can achieve their learning goals faster as AI provides prior information based on their personal preferences. The AI learning system analyses the past performance and objectives of each trainee and encourages their engagement.

2. **Automation:** The entire learning process can be automated.

3. **ROI:** Faster learning and greater engagement can bring better learning results, which can further translate into a positive ROI on the company's investment in skill development.

4. **Integration**: The skill development training can be integrated into the routine workflow as the AI-powered learning systems can provide personalized programmes, materials and schedules for each trainee.

5. **Reinforcement:** The AI-powered skill development programmes can improve reinforcement as training processes can be automated to save time.

6. **Success rate:** The completion rate improves as the trainees are more engaged in completing their personalized training modules.

7. **Access**: The AI products make training programmes more accessible to a wide group of trainees, including people with various disabilities, as AI delivers programmes and solutions that create alternate texts for pictures and images. For example, the Automatic Captions Video App from Google is a great help to deaf people.

8. **Effectiveness**: The training effectiveness can be measured more effectively as the AI system helps in collecting and analysing data quickly to get insights on learning effectiveness.

9. **Smart Trainers**: AI-based digital tutors can replace human trainers.

10. **Anytime Training**: The AI-based training enables 24/7 training options for trainees.

4.7 Conclusion

To match the disruption due to the technological advancement of AI, the skill development system needs to be prepared and equipped to respond and match the required emerging skills. As can be witnessed from the trends, many jobs are becoming obsolete due to automation. This calls for continuous upskilling, reskilling and lifelong learning. Like how humans interact with and intersect with AI-powered machines keeps on changing, the need for skill development to understand and navigate these interactions also grows so that workers/trainees do not remain excluded/exploited. This necessitates the demand for investment in infrastructure, development of trainers, review of curriculum/content, etc. to meet the emerging challenges. The AI disruption may also pose a threat of financial and human capital shortages, forcing the industry to reconsider its traditional working methods.

Despite all these challenges, the AI era is very exciting with the change in perspective, methods for connecting and discovering, tools it offers and solutions it provides. This excitement is available only to those individuals and organizations who adapt themselves to the changing times. Many training institutions have adapted fast and are now offering distance learning on virtual and online platforms, thus generating possibilities for more flexible training programmes and methodologies.

Governments, industry and skill development institutions need to collaborate and work towards the creation of required infrastructure and the development of appropriate human capital for ensuring the ethical design and value-based utilization of AI for generating quality skilling opportunities and impacting the progress, growth and development of the nation.

References

[1] Arora, R., & Chhadwani, M. (2019, Jan - Mar). Analysing the impact of Skill India as a tool for reshaping Indian economy. International Journal of Research and Analytical Reviews, 6(1), 392–396.

[2] Damioli, G., Roy, V. V., & Vertesy, D. (2021). The impact of artificial intelligence on labor productivity. Eurasian Business Review, 11, 1–25. doi:https://doi.org/10.1007/s40821-020-00172-8

[3] Göksel, N., & Bozkurt, A. (2019). Artificial Intelligence in Education: Current Insights and Future Perspectives. In S. Sisman-Ugur, & G. Kurubacak, Handbook of Research on Learning in the Age of Transhumanism (pp. 224–236). IGI Global. doi:10.4018/978-1-5225-8431-5.ch014

[4] Hui, F. (2020). The Impact of Artificial Intelligence on Vocational Education and Countermeasures. Journal of Physics: Conference Series. 1693. Inner Mongolia, China: IOP Publishing. doi:10.1088/1742-6596/1693/1/012124

[5] Kanchan, S., & Varshney, S. (2015). Skill Development initiatives and strategies. Asian Journal of Management Research, 5(4), 666–672.

[6] McKee, S., & Gauch, D. (2020). Implications of Industry 4.0 on Skills Development. In B. Panth, & R. Maclean, Anticipating and Preparing for Emerging Skills and Jobs, Education in the Asia-Pacific Region: Issues, Concerns and Prospects (Vol. 55, pp. 279 - 288). Singapore: Springer. doi:https://doi.org/10.1007/978-981-15-7018-6_34

[7] Panigrahi, A., & Joshi, V. (2020). Use of Artificial Intelligence in Education. SSRN Electronic Journal, 55, 64–67. doi:10.2139/ssrn.3666702

[8] Pelau, C., Ene, I., & Pop, M. I. (2021, February). The Impact of Artificial Intelligence on Consumers' Identity and Human Skills. Amfiteatru Economic, 23(56), 33–45. doi:10.24818/EA/2021/56/33

[9] Ray, G. (2019). Transmedia and Artificial Intelligence. STEM Journal, 20(4), 163–177. doi:10.16875/VWeP.2019.20.4.163

[10] Tao, H. B., Parez, V. R., & Guerra, Y. M. (2019). Artificial Intelligence and Education : Challenges and disadvantages for the teacher. Arctic Medical Research, 72(12), 30–51.

[11] Verma, J. P. (2016). Need and challenges: Skill development in India. International Journal of Multidiscriplinary Education adn Research, 1(10), 35–38.

5

An Empirical Investigation on the Effect of Applying Artificial Intelligence Tools in Human Resource Analytics

Bhaswati Jana[1], Surya Kant Pal[2], Jayanta Chakraborti[3], Manish Mohan Baral[4], Subhodeep Mukherjee[4] and Hari Shankar Shyam[5]

[1]GD Goenka University, India
[2]Department of Mathematics, School of Basic Sciences and Research, Sharda University, India
[3]Symbiosis Skills and Professional University, India
[4]Department of Operations, GITAM Institute of Management, India
[5]School of Business Studies, Sharda University, India

Email: bhaswati.chk09@gmail.com; suryakantpal6676@gmail.com; jaychak072@gmail.com; manishmohanbaral.31@gmail.com; subhodeepmukherjee92@gmail.com; harishankar.shyam@sharda.ac.in

Abstract

The new millennium has seen an increase in the demand for talented manpower, which has become scarce. To acquire, manage and retain talented manpower, HR personnel have been using applications like human resource analytics (HRA). The HRA applications performed functions like descriptive analytics, diagnostic analytics, predictive analytics and prescriptive analytics. However, these applications are based on basic statistical functions like correlation, regression and time series analysis. The application of artificial intelligence and machine learning (AIML) tools like the logistic regression classifier, decision tree classifier, random forest classifier and support vector machines classifier has served to increase the effectiveness, accuracy and predictive power of HRA applications. Our research work was carried out to understand the implications of applying AI to HRA for managing talent acquisition, talent management, and talent retention and creating an effective predictive decision-making (PDM) application. The cross-sectional research was carried out in eight cities with HR managers and HR professionals as the respondents. The major findings of this research are that AI plays a significant role in increasing the effectiveness of HRA applications. In the current study, the integrated HRA-AI application will help both academics and professionals make accurate, unbiased and powerful predictions using the integrated HRA-AI.

5.1 Introduction

The twenty-first century is marked by rapid advancement in technology and the adoption of technological processes like artificial intelligence and machine learning (AIML), Internet of Things (IoT), big data analytics, and robotic process automation (RPA). Most of the functions are now less dependent on the human interface and more dependent on cognitive computing (Davenport, Harris & Shapiro, 2010). Industrial robots are now being used in manufacturing, drones are being used to deliver products, chatbots are being used in customer relationship management (CRM), algorithmic trading is being used on stock markets, and a flight-risk model is being used to predict when an employee is likely to leave the company (McIver, Lengnick-Hall, and Lengnick-Hall, 2018).

Like in other domain areas, human resource management, henceforth referred to as HRM, has also seen a major transformation in work processes. Manpower planning has now been re-designated as 'Talent-Gap Analysis', recruitment and selection are now called 'talent acquisition', and the other HR functions like manpower deployment, training and development, performance appraisal, and succession planning come under 'talent management'. The focus has now shifted from attrition management to 'talent retention'. The emphasis is now on 'talent' as relented manpower is now in high demand because of the complicated technological processes, and also in short supply as several companies are vying for the same talent pool (Marler, & Boudreau, 2017).

To run the processes seamlessly, the human resource department has started using human resource analytics (HRA) in a big way. HRA is defined as 'the use of statistical techniques, research design, and algorithms to evaluate employee data and translate results into evocative reports' (Levenson, 2005). HRA is also defined as 'the application of statistical tools to analyse data pertaining to employee functions in an organization to draw insights and inferences on how to deploy and maximize the productivity of human resources and resolve HR-related challenges' (Chakraborti, Tripathi, and Khan, 2017). HRA 1.0 was characterized by tools for descriptive analytics, diagnostic analytics, predictive analytics and prescriptive analytics whereas, HRA 5.0 is equipped with tools for artificial intelligence and machine learning, cognitive computing, and automation processes like robotic process automation (Perkin & Abraham, 2021).

In today's competitive scenario, the top management not only wants answers to what is happening and what has happened but also what can happen and how mishaps can be prevented from happening. That is where HRA is now depending on artificial intelligence and machine learning (AIML) tools like Gaussian Naive Bayes, logistic regression classifier, decision tree classifier, random forest classifier, and support vector machines (SVM) classifier. These tools help to build AIML-based models that are trained on a specific set of data to draw inferences for predictive decision-making (Fallucchi et al., 2020).

Although there is extensive research work carried out on the application of HRA for predictive decision-making, the application of AIML in the area of HRA is relatively new. However, there is extensive use of AI now in different industries like information technology, banking, financial services and insurance (BFSI), and manufacturing. There is a dearth of quality research work carried out on the application of AI in HRA to manage talent acquisition (TA), talent management (TM), and talent retention (TR) (Qamar & Samad, 2021). We propose to conduct exploratory research to address the following research questions:

RQ1: Does the effectiveness of predictive decision-making regarding TA, TM and TA increase by the application of HRA?
RQ2: Does the effectiveness of predictive decision-making regarding TA, TM and TA increase by the application of AIML?
RQ3: Does AIML have a significant impact on the HRA application?

Our research paper is structured into seven sections. Section 1 gives the introduction. Section 2 gives the literature review and hypothesis formulation. Section 3 explains the research methodology. Section 4 gives the data analysis and findings. Section 5 gives the discussion. Section 6 gives the theoretical and practical implications. Section 7 gives the conclusion, limitations and directions for further studies.

5.2 Literature Review and Hypothesis Formulation

5.2.1 Use of HR analytics and artificial intelligence for talent acquisition

One of the key functions of the HR department is recruitment and selection. The activity is also called staffing. The HR staff does the need-gap analysis, writes the job description and job specification, advertises the job in news-papers or online, receives applications, shortlists them, calls the candidates for interviews, conducts the interviews, negotiates salaries, checks the candidates' backgrounds, and sends out the offer letter (Tursunbayeva, Di Lauro, and Pagliari, 2018).

The whole process is time-consuming and complicated and needs huge investment in terms of time, money and manpower. To save on crucial resources like time, money and manpower, organizations have now changed the system of talent acquisition. There are social media promotional campaigns that do employer branding and motivate potential employees to register on job boards (Agarwal, Arya & Bhasin, 2021). The HR analytics software screens the resumes of applicants and shortlists the resumes. The interview is scheduled using recruitment bots. The questions for the interview are selected by AIML-based software (Bock, 2015).

The responses are recorded and analysed using the HRA software. The recruitment bot updates the candidate on whether they are selected or rejected and issues the offer letter. With the use of HRA and AIML, the process is automated to reduce the quantum of human intervention and thus reduce the investment required in time, money and manpower. This is now being actively used in top organizations like IBM, Google, Microsoft, Oracle and Accenture where the talent acquisition (TA) processes are being facilitated and enhanced using HRA and AIML (Pessach, et al., 2020). Thus, we hypothesize that:

> H1a: The process of talent acquisition (TA) is getting enhanced by the application of HR analytics (HRA)
>
> H1b: The process of talent acquisition (TA) is getting enhanced by the application of artificial intelligence (AI)

5.2.2 Use of HR analytics and artificial intelligence for talent management

The functions of manpower deployment, performance appraisal, training and development, and succession planning are now grouped under talent management (Fitz-Enz, 2010). It is critical not only to hire the most talented people but also to understand their capabilities and assign them to the right tasks. The shift is also now towards real-time performance appraisals where the employee gets instant feedback on the tasks performed. Coca-Cola and General Electric use the nine-box grid where employees are classified as 'Potential Gem', 'High Potential', 'Star', 'Inconsistent Player', 'Core Player',

'High Performer', 'Risk', 'Average Performer' and 'Solid Performer' (Mabe et al., 2021). The classification is done based on HR analytics and AIML-based tools like the logistic regression classifier, decision tree classifier and random forest classifier (Pessach, 2020). The bias in performance appraisal is greatly reduced by the use of analytical and AI tools. Tableau, Power BI, and Google Data Studio dashboards are used to map performance, training needs, training effectiveness, and succession planning (White, 2021). These tools help to make the talent management process faster, error-free, fair, transparent and devoid of any bias. Thus, we hypothesize that:

H2a: The process of talent management (TM) is enhanced by the application of HR analytics (HRA)

H2b: The process of talent management (TM) is enhanced by the application of artificial intelligence (AI).

5.2.3 Use of HR analytics and artificial intelligence for talent retention

One of the core issues in modern organizations is the low engagement rate and high attrition rates (Branham, 2012). With talented employees being in short supply and in high demand, they tend to stay in organizations for a shorter tenure. This entails a higher cost for the organization as they have to spend on fresh recruitment, training and relocation expenses. Also, many projects get stalled or disrupted when key personnel leave midway (Falletta & Combs, 2020).

To solve this problem, HR people have created software based on HRA and AI to predict when and why an employee is likely to leave. Hewlett Packard (HP) has created a software called 'Flight Risk Score' that can predict which employees are at high risk of leaving. At the same time, AI and HRA are helping organizations shift their focus from attrition management to retention management (Siegel, 2013). Thus, we hypothesize that:

H3a: The process of talent retention (TR) is enhanced by the application of HR analytics (HRA)

H3b: The process of talent retention (TR) is enhanced by the application of artificial intelligence (AI)

5.2.4 HR analytics and artificial intelligence

The process of HR analytics (HRA) comprises steps like data collection, data extraction, transformation and loading, data warehousing, data mining and data visualization (Chakraborti, Tripathi & Khan, 2017). The various HRA models used are descriptive analytics, diagnostic analytics, predictive analytics and prescriptive analytics. Under descriptive analytics, data is collected about what is happening and reported. Under diagnostic analytics, the data is analysed to understand the cause and effect. Under predictive analytics, forecasts are made about what is going to happen. Prescriptive analytics talks about what measures should be taken to prevent mishaps from happening (Fitz-Enz, 2010).

HR analytics has traditionally depended on statistical tools like correlation, regression and time series modelling to do the analysis and draw inferences. For example, AI has brought in tools like ARIMA (autoregressive integrated moving average), fuzzy logic, and cognitive analytics that help to reduce statistical bias and errors and make the analytical process much sharper, incisive, and error-free (Pessach, 2020). Thus, we hypothesize that:

> H4: The application of AI helps to make the HRA process much more accurate and incisive

5.2.5 HR analytics, artificial intelligence and predictive decision-making

In a modern organization, the HR manager is expected to make decisions based not only on what has happened or is happening but also on what is about to happen (Mohammed, 2019). To take futuristic decisions, the manager needs to rely on predictive models like correlation, regression and time series. Artificial Intelligence has added to the effectiveness of predictive analytics by introducing tools like Gaussian Naive Bayes, logistic regression classifier, decision tree classifier, random forest classifier, and support vector machines (SVM) classifier (Pessach, 2020). Both HRA and AI have significantly contributed to the building of robust predictive decision-making models. Thus, we hypothesize that:

> H5: HRA enhances the process of predictive decision-making with forecasting tools
>
> H6: AI enhances the process of predictive decision-making with forecasting tools

The proposed conceptual model is given in Figure 5.1:

5.3 Research Methodology

The conceptual model and the hypotheses were validated by conducting a cross-sectional study in seven major cities in India. The cities were Delhi

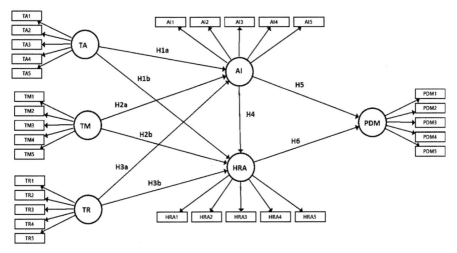

Figure 5.1   Proposed conceptual model.

NCR, Chandigarh, Mumbai, Pune, Chennai, Bengaluru, Hyderabad and Kolkata. The data was collected through a structured questionnaire from managers and owners of information technology companies. The items in the questionnaire were scaled with a 5-point Likert scale with 1 indicating 'Strongly Disagree' and 5 indicating 'Strongly Agree'. The sampling method used is simple random sampling. The questionnaire was administered to 375 respondents residing in eight cities in India. We received valid responses from 358 respondents which indicate a response rate of 95.46%.

The minimum required sample size was calculated with Daniel Soper's "A-Priori Sample Size Calculator for Structural Equation Models" (Soper, 2022). The recommended minimum sample size was found to be 161 for the effect size of 0.3, the statistical power of 0.8, six constructs, thirty-six and a probability level of 0.05 (Cohen, 1988). Our sample size of 358 is much above this recommended level and hence acceptable for the research. The data was analysed following the partial least square-structural equation modelling (PLS-SEM) guidelines given by Hair et al., 2019. Smart PLS v3.3 software was used to analyse the data.

The demographic details of the respondents are given in Table 5.1.

5.4 Data Analysis and Findings

The conceptual model was analysed using PLS-SEM (partial least squares-structural equation modelling) method (Dijkstra and Henseler, 2015). The PLS-SEM approach was taken because this provided the scope to do predictive analytics (Hair, Risher, Sarstedt & Ringle, 2019). The data

Table 5.1   Demographic details of the respondents.

Demographic variable	Category	Number of respondents	%
Gender	Male	199	55.6
	Female	159	44.4
Age	20–30	72	20.1
	30–40	123	34.4
	40–50	96	26.8
	Above 50	67	18.7
Designation	HR Manager	122	34.1
	HR Head	95	26.5
	VP (HR)	84	23.5
	CHRO (Chief HR Officer)	57	15.9

was analysed in two stages. In the first stage, the measurement model was assessed. In the second stage, the structural model was assessed. Mediation analysis has also been carried out to find the mediating effects. The data was analysed using Smart PLS 3.0 software.

5.4.1 Measurement model assessment

To do the measurement model analysis, we have followed the steps given by Hair et al. (2019). The first step is to measure the indicator loadings. All the indicator loadings are above the threshold value of 0.708. This indicates that all the constructs explain 50% of the indicator's variance, thus establishing indicator reliability (Hair et al., 2019).

The second step is to measure the internal consistency and reliability of the constructs. This is measured by assessing Cronbach's α, composite reliability and rho_A (Jöreskog, 1971). The values of Cronbach-α, composite reliability and rho_A should be between 0.70 and 0.95 (Hair et al. 2019). In our case, all the values are above 0.70 and below 0.95, which indicates satisfactory internal consistency and reliability of the constructs.

The next step is to measure the convergent validity of the model, which is assessed with the average variance extracted (AVE). The AVE values of our constructs are above the threshold value of 0.5, which indicates that the construct explains more than 50% of the variance of its items (Hair et al. 2019).

The assessment of the measurement model is given in Table 5.2.

The final step in the assessment of the measurement model is to measure the discriminant validity. This is done in two ways. It can be assessed with the Fornell-Larcker criterion (Fornell, and Larcker, 1981), or by calculating the heterotrait monotrait (HTMT) Ratio, as given by Henseler et al. (2015). To

Table 5.2 Indicators and constructs validity and reliability.

Constructs	Items	Factor loadings	Cronbach's alpha	rho_A	Composite reliability	Average variance extracted
Talent acquisition (TA)	TA1	0.774	0.888	0.889	0.918	0.691
	TA2	0.835				
	TA3	0.841				
	TA4	0.877				
	TA5	0.828				
Talent management (TM)	TM1	0.817	0.870	0.871	0.906	0.659
	TM2	0.799				
	TM3	0.763				
	TM4	0.835				
	TM5	0.843				
Talent retention (TR)	TR1	0.816	0.869	0.869	0.905	0.657
	TR2	0.797				
	TR3	0.775				
	TR4	0.838				
	TR5	0.826				
Human resource analytics (HRA)	HRA1	0.869	0.888	0.889	0.918	0.691
	HRA2	0.829				
	HRA3	0.823				
	HRA4	0.808				
	HRA5	0.826				
Artificial intelligence (AI)	AI1	0.775	0.876	0.879	0.910	0.669
	AI2	0.847				
	AI3	0.816				
	AI4	0.819				
	AI5	0.833				
Predictive decision-making (PDM)	PDM1	0.754	0.768	0.782	0.842	0.516
	PDM2	0.677				
	PDM3	0.725				
	PDM4	0.695				
	PDM5	0.738				

Table 5.3   Discriminant validity: Fornell-Larcker criterion.

	AI	HRA	PDM	TA	TM	TR
AI	0.818					
HRA	0.578	0.831				
PDM	0.737	0.745	0.737			
TA	0.58	0.608	0.62	0.832		
TM	0.617	0.633	0.79	0.604	0.812	
TR	0.562	0.627	0.718	0.562	0.587	0.811

NB: TA = talent acquisition, TM = talent management, TR = talent retention,
HRA = HR analytics, AI = artificial intelligence, PDM = predictive decision-making.

Table 5.4   Discriminant validity – heterotrait monotrait (HTMT) ratio.

	AI	HRA	PDM	TA	TM	TR
AI						
HRA	0.698					
PDM	0.664	0.774				
TA	0.661	0.684	0.752			
TM	0.598	0.823	0.697	0.686		
TR	0.542	0.612	0.616	0.64	0.675	

NB: TA = talent acquisition, TM = talent management, TR = talent retention,
HRA = HR analytics, AI = artificial intelligence, PDM = predictive decision-making.

satisfy the Fornell-Larcker criteria, the AVE of each construct should be more than the squared inter-construct correlation of that same construct. For our research model, the values are given in Table 5.3. The readings show that conditions given by Fornell-Larcker (1981) for establishing discriminant validity are fulfilled.

To check for discriminant validity, we have also assessed with the heterotrait monotrait (HTMT) ratio (Henseler et al., 2015). The HTMT values should be ideally below the threshold value of 0.90 (Hair et al., 2019). The HTMT values of our model are given in Table 5.4. All the readings are below the threshold value of 0.90, which satisfies the condition for discriminant validity.

5.4.2 Structural model assessment

After a satisfactory assessment of the measurement model, we now move to the assessment of the structural model. In the first step of this assessment, we measured the collinearity with VIF (variance inflation factor). The VIF values are expected to be below the threshold value of 3 (Hair et al., 2019) to

Table 5.5 Path coefficient.

Hypothesis	Path	Path coefficient (β)	T statistics (|O/STDEV|)	p-values	95% confidence intervals	Significance (p < 0.05)
H1a	TA → HRA	0.252	4.096	0.000	[0.115, 0.323]	Yes
H1b	TA → AI	0.220	4.515	0.000	[0.114, 0.361]	Yes
H2a	TM → HRA	0.333	4.765	0.000	[0.150, 0.356]	Yes
H2b	TM → AI	0.252	5.340	0.000	[0.210, 0.452]	Yes
H3a	TR → HRA	0.225	5.257	0.000	[0.173, 0.380]	Yes
H3b	TR → AI	0.277	3.583	0.000	[0.103, 0.350]	Yes
H4	AI → HRA	0.139	2.721	0.007	[0.036, 0.238]	Yes
H5	AI → PDM	0.460	11.174	0.000	[0.378, 0.540]	Yes
H6	HRA → PDM	0.479	12.167	0.000	[0.403, 0.557]	Yes

establish that collinearity does not exist. For our model, all values of VIF are below the threshold value of 3, indicating that there are no collinearity issues.

After checking the collinearity issue, we have assessed the validity of the proposed hypotheses. The path coefficients, t-values, p-values and confidence intervals are shown in Table 5.5.

The path analysis shows that all the hypotheses from H1a to H6 are supported at a 0.05 level of significance. This means that the constructs TA, TM and TR have a significant impact on both HRA and AI. AI has a significant impact on HRA. Both AI and HRA have a significant impact on PDM.

In the next step, the predictive power of the model is assessed by measuring the R^2 value of the endogenous constructs (Shmueli and Koppius, 2011). The endogenous constructs construct artificial intelligence (AI) has reported an R^2 value of 0.478, HR analytics has reported an R^2 value of 0.547 and predictive decision-making (PDM) has reported an R^2 value of 0.696. We can say that the predictive power of the model is high as the R^2 values of the dependent latent variables HRA and PDM are above 0.50 (Hair et al., 2019).

The next step is to assess the effect of the constructs by measuring the f^2 values (Cohen, 1988). The f^2 value of HRA on PDM is 0.503 and AI on PDM is 0.464, which are quite high. However, the effect of AI on HRA is 0.022, which is relatively low. The effect of TA on AI is 0.069, the effect of TM on AI is 0.116, and TR on AI is 0.057, which is moderate. The effect of TA on HRA is 0.057, the effect of TM on HRA is 0.068 and TR on HRA is 0.094, which is moderate.

The predictive relevance of the model is calculated through the blind-folding method by calculating Q^2 (Hair et al., 2019). Artificial intelligence has a Q^2 value of 0.313, HRA has a Q^2 value of 0.372 and PDM has a Q^2 value of 0.341. As all the endogenous variables have shown values above 0, we can say that our research model has predictive relevance (Hair et al., 2019).

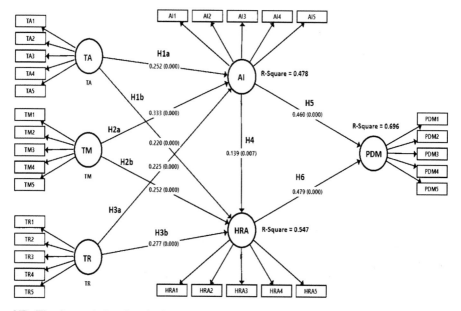

NB: The figures in brackets indicate *p*-values. The figures outside brackets indicate the path coefficient (β).

Figure 5.2   Validated research model.

The goodness-of-fit of the conceptual model is measured with SRMR (standardized root mean square residual) value (Hair et al., 2019). The SRMR value of the research model is 0.066 which is below the threshold value of 0.08 and represents a good fit (Hu and Bentler, 1998).

The validated structural model is given in Figure 5.2.

5.4.3 Mediation analysis

We conducted a mediation analysis to examine whether the constructs AI and HRA were acting as mediators between TA, TM and TR on one side and PDM on the other. Our analysis shows that AI acts as a mediator between TA and PDM ($\beta = 0.116$, $p < 0.001$), TM and PDM ($\beta = 0.153$, $p < 0.001$), TR and PDM ($\beta = 0.104$, $p < 0.001$). HRA acts as a mediator between TA and PDM ($\beta = 0.105$, $p < 0.001$), TM and PDM ($\beta = 0.121$, $p < 0.001$), and TR and PDM ($\beta - 0.133$, $p < 0.001$). HRA acts as a mediator between AI and PDM ($\beta = 0.067$, $p < 0.01$). The results of the mediation analysis are given in Table 5.6.

Table 5.6 Mediation analysis.

	Original sample (O)	T statistics ($|O/STDEV|$)	*p*-Values	Result
TA → AI → PDM	0.116	4.324	0.000	Supported
TA → HRA → PDM	0.105	4.135	0.000	Supported
TM → AI → PDM	0.153	4.334	0.000	Supported
TM → HRA → PDM	0.121	4.034	0.000	Supported
TR → AI → PDM	0.104	3.360	0.001	Supported
TR → HRA → PDM	0.133	4.462	0.000	Supported
AI → HRA → PDM	0.067	2.629	0.009	Supported

5.5 Discussion

The new millennium has seen intense competition to acquire talent, manage talent and retain talent. Talented employees have multiple options and will switch jobs if not treated in a fair and justified manner. Hence, there is immense pressure on the HR department to adopt technology in the various processes like recruitment and selection, deployment, performance appraisal, training and development, rewards and compensation, succession planning and employee retention.

HRA 1.0 was characterized by the use of statistical tools like correlation, regression and time series analysis for predictive analytics. HRA 5.0 is characterized by the use of artificial intelligence and machine learning (AIML) tools like Gaussian Naive Bayes, logistic regression classifier, decision tree classifier, random forest classifier, and support vector machines (SVM) Classifier. These AIML tools have helped to remove the bias and increase the accuracy of the predictive decision-making process.

The cross-sectional study was carried out among 358 respondents in eight cities in India. The respondents are mainly HR professionals working in different companies. A structured questionnaire using a 5-point Likert scale was administered to collect the data. The data was analysed using partial least square – structural equation modelling (PLS-SEM) method.

Our analysis showed that hypothesis H1a was supported ($\beta = 0.250$, $p < 0.001$) which implies that the talent acquisition process can be enhanced using the HRA technology. The hypothesis H1b was also supported ($\beta = 0.220$, $p < 0.001$) which implies that the talent acquisition process can be enhanced using artificial intelligence. We also infer that HRA ($\beta = 0.252$, $p < 0.001$) has a stronger impact on PDA than AI ($\beta = 0.220$, $p < 0.001$). We are now seeing the use of job boards for getting resumes, the use of software like Oracle PeopleSoft and IBM Kenexa to screen the resumes and shortlist the ones which fit the required specifications and the use of recruitment bots to schedule and conduct interviews. These tools and technologies are leading to a superior and error-free process of talent acquisition. Our findings are in sync with the findings of experts and published in extant literature (Pessach, et al., 2020; Mohammed, 2019).

Our analysis showed that hypothesis H2a was supported ($\beta = 0.333, p < 0.001$) which implies that the talent management process can be enhanced using the HRA technology. The hypothesis H2b was also supported ($\beta = 0.252, p < 0.001$) which implies that the talent management process can also be enhanced using artificial intelligence. We also infer that HRA ($\beta = 0.333, p < 0.001$) has a stronger impact on PDM than AI ($\beta = 0.252, p < 0.001$). Talent management is a critical process which involves functions like how to deploy manpower and make the best out of them by giving them proper guidance and training. It is also important to conduct performance appraisal fairly and transparently and give rewards where it is due. These functions are also vulnerable and prone to human bias and that is where the tools of HRA help to reduce the bias and increase the accuracy. AI serves to further enhance the predictive power of HRA by incorporating automated tools. The findings are similar to those reported by experts in extant literature (Chalutz Ben-Gal, 2019; Levenson, 2011).

Our analysis showed that hypothesis H3a was supported ($\beta = 0.225, p < 0.001$) which implies that the talent retention process can be enhanced using the HRA technology. The hypothesis H3b was also supported ($\beta = 0.277, p < 0.001$) which implies that talent retention process can also be enhanced using artificial intelligence. We also infer that AI ($\beta = 0.277, p < 0.001$) has a stronger impact on PDM than HRA ($\beta = 0.225, p < 0.001$). In most organization, attrition management has been replaced by retention management. Instead of reacting to resignation letters given by employees, the HR personnel are using software like 'Flight Risk Score' to gauge when an employee is likely to leave and take pre-emptive actions to resolve the issue before it goes out of control. This is facilitated by the use of both AI and HRA. The findings are in sync with the inferences given by experts in extant literature (Fallucchi et al., 2020).

Our analysis showed that hypothesis H4 was supported ($\beta = 0.139, p < 0.01$) which implies that HRA functions are getting enhanced by the application of AI technology. HR analytics was traditionally run with statistical tools like correlation, regression and time series modelling. AI has brought in tools like ARIMA (autoregressive integrated moving average), fuzzy logic and cognitive analytics that helps to reduce statistical bias and errors and make the analytical process much sharper, incisive and error-free. This is similar to the findings of experts that have been published in extant literature (Berhil, Benlahmar & Labani, 2020; Lengnick-Hall, Neely & Stone, 2018).

Our analysis showed that hypothesis H5 was supported ($\beta = 0.460, p < 0.01$) which implies that PDM functions are getting enhanced by the application of AI. Hypothesis H6 was also supported ($\beta = 0.479, p < 0.01$) which implies that PDM functions are getting enhanced by the application of HRA. Our analysis also shows that HRA ($\beta = 0.479, p < 0.01$) has a stronger impact on PDA than AI ($\beta = 0.460, p < 0.01$). Predictive decision-making was previously dependent on models built with statistical tools like correlation, regression and time series analysis. Now, it has become more incisive with the application of AI tools like autoregression, cognitive computing and fuzzy logic. The tools like logistic regression classifier, decision tree classifier, random forest classifier and support vector machines (SVM) classifier serve to further increase the predictive power of HRA. This is in sync with the findings by experts which have been published in extant literature (Mohammed, 2019; Falletta, 2014).

5.6 Theoretical and Practical Implication

With talent becoming scarce and the competition to acquire talent intensifying, organizations have been looking at effective strategies for talent acquisition, talent management and talent retention. HRA has been a tool that has been extensively used with models like descriptive analytics, diagnostic analytics, predictive analytics and prescriptive analytics. With modern computing taking a quantum leap and the introduction of tools like chatbots, cognitive computing and fuzzy logic, the accuracy and the predictive power of HRA have rapidly increased.

Although there are a lot of research works that have been conducted on studying the application of HRA and the various tools associated with it, the studies done on AI are relatively new and scarce in number. Our research work will help research scholars and theoretical analysts to understand the implications of applying AI tools in HRA. Their future research can include the study of AI tools to further understand the practical applications of how to increase the effectiveness of HRA.

Our research work also has far-reaching practical implications. With most organizations now adopting HRA, the challenge is now to stay ahead of the competition and get a competitive advantage. In this regard, AI tools like logistic regression classifier, decision tree classifier, random forest classifier and support vector machines classifier can help organizations to automate the

HRA functions and reduce the dependence on human intervention. This will help in increasing the effectiveness and incisiveness of the HRA functions and reducing the human errors and bias.

5.7 Conclusion, Limitation and Future Research

A cross-sectional research was carried out in eight cities in India to understand the process of enhancing the functions of HRA by using AI. Our research found that AI and HRA did have a significant impact on TA, TM and TR. AI and HRA also played a significant role in the development of PDM Models which were useful, effective and had high predictive power. HRA had a stronger impact on TA and TM, while AI had a stronger impact on TR. AI had a significant impact on both HRA and PDM, while HRA had a significant impact on PDM. The effect of HRA on PDM was stronger than the effect of AI on PDM. Both AI and HR played a mediating role between TA, TM and TR on one side and PDM on the other.

The research work has significant theoretical and practical implications as it will help both the scholars and practitioners to apply the integrated HRA-AI Model to get accurate, unbiased and powerful predictive inferences. The limitation of this research is that it was carried out only in eight cities with limited sample size. Future researchers can increase the scope by increasing the sample size and conducting the research in more Indian and International cities. The research study was quantitative and had limitations in the responses received. Future researchers can conduct an open-ended qualitative study to get more incisive inferences. This study was cross-sectional. Future researchers can do a longitudinal study to understand the long-term impact.

References

[1] Agarwal, T., Arya, S., & Bhasin, K. (2021). The Evolution of Internal Employer Branding and Employee Engagement: The Temporal Role of Internal Social Media Usage. Journal of Information & Knowledge Management, 20(01), 2150012.
[2] Bassi, L. (2011). Raging debates in HR analytics. People and Strategy, 34(2), 14.
[3] Ben-Gal, H. C. (2019). An ROI-based review of HR analytics: practical implementation tools. Personnel Review.
[4] Berhil, S., Benlahmar, H., &Labani, N. (2020). A review paper on artificial intelligence at the service of human resources management.

Indonesian Journal of Electrical Engineering and Computer Science, 18(1), 32–40.

[5] Bock, L. (2015). Work rules!: Insights from inside Google that will transform how you live and lead. Twelve.

[6] Branham, L. (2012). The 7 hidden reasons employees leave: How to recognize the subtle signs and act before it's too late. Amacom Books.

[7] Chakraborti, J, Tripathi R & Khan S. (2017). HR@Analytics. Global Vision Publishing House.

[8] Chatterjee, S., Rana, N. P., Dwivedi, Y. K., &Baabdullah, A. M. (2021). Understanding AI adoption in manufacturing and production firms using an integrated TAM-TOE model. Technological Forecasting and Social Change, 170, 120880.

[9] Cohen, J. (1988). Statistical Power Analysis for the Behavioral Sciences (2nd Edition). Hillsdale, NJ: Lawrence Earlbaum Associates.

[10] Davenport, T. H., Harris, J., & Shapiro, J. (2010). Competing on Talent Analytics. Harvard Business Review, 88(10), 52–58.

[11] Dijkstra, T.K. and Henseler, J. (2015), "Consistent partial least squares path modeling", MIS Quarterly, Vol. 39 No. 2, pp. 297–316.

[12] Falletta, S. (2014). In search of HR intelligence: evidence-based HR analytics practices in high performing companies. People and Strategy, 36(4), 28.

[13] Falletta, S. V., & Combs, W. L. (2020). The HR analytics cycle: a seven-step process for building evidence-based and ethical HR analytics capabilities. Journal of Work-Applied Management.

[14] Fallucchi, F., Coladangelo, M., Giuliano, R., & William De Luca, E. (2020). Predicting employee attrition using machine learning techniques. Computers, 9(4), 86.

[15] Fornell, C.G. and Larcker, D.F. (1981), "Evaluating structural equation models with unobservable variables and measurement error", Journal of Marketing Research, Vol. 18 No. 1, pp. 39–50.

[16] Fitz-Enz, J. (2010). The new HR analytics. American Management Association.

[17] Garvin, D. A. (2013). How Google sold its engineers on management. Harvard Business Review, 91(12), 74–82.

[18] Hair, J. F., Risher, J. J., Sarstedt, M., &Ringle, C. M. (2019). When to use and how to report the results of PLS-SEM. European business review.

[19] Henseler, J., Ringle, C. M., &Sarstedt, M. (2015). A new criterion for assessing discriminant validity in variance-based structural equation modeling. Journal of the academy of marketing science, 43(1), 115–135.

[20] Hu, L. T., &Bentler, P. M. (1999). Cutoff criteria for fit indexes in covariance structure analysis: Conventional criteria versus new alternatives. Structural equation modeling: a multidisciplinary journal, 6(1), 1–55.

[21] Jöreskog, K.G. (1971), "Simultaneous factor analysis in several populations", Psychometrika, Vol. 36 No. 4, pp. 409–426.

[22] Lengnick-Hall, M. L., Neely, A. R., & Stone, C. B. (2018). Human resource management in the digital age: Big data, HR analytics and artificial intelligence. In Management and technological challenges in the digital age (pp. 1–30). CRC Press.

[23] Levenson, A. (2005). Harnessing the power of HR analytics. Strategic HR Review.

[24] Mabe, D., Esmael, G., Burg, M., Soares, P., &Halawi, L. (2021). Optimization of Organizational Design. Journal of Computer Information Systems, 1–13.

[25] Marler, J. H., & Boudreau, J. W. (2017). An evidence-based review of HR Analytics. The International Journal of Human Resource Management, 28(1), 3–26.

[26] McIver, D., Lengnick-Hall, M. L., &Lengnick-Hall, C. A. (2018). A strategic approach to workforce analytics: Integrating science and agility. Business Horizons, 61(3), 397–407.

[27] Mishra, S. N., Lama, D. R., & Pal, Y. (2016). Human Resource Predictive Analytics (HRPA) for HR management in organizations. International Journal of Scientific & Technology Research, 5(5), 33–35.

[28] Perkin, N., & Abraham, P. (2021). Building the agile business through digital transformation. Kogan Page Publishers.

[29] Qamar, Y., & Samad, T. A. (2021). Human resource analytics: a review and bibliometric analysis. Personnel Review. https://doi.org/10.1108/pr-04-2020-0247/full/html

[30] Ringle, Christian M., Wende, Sven, & Becker, Jan-Michael. (2015). SmartPLS 3. Boenningstedt: SmartPLS. Retrieved from https://www.smartpls.com

[31] Shmueli, G. and Koppius, O.R. (2011), "Predictive analytics in information systems research", MIS Quarterly, Vol. 35 No. 3, pp. 553–572.

[32] Siegel, E. (2013). Predictive analytics: The power to predict who will click, buy, lie, or die. John Wiley & Sons.

[33] Sikaroudi E., Mohammad A., Ghousi R., Sikaroudi A. A data mining approach to employee turnover prediction (case study: Arak automotive parts manufacturing) J. Ind. Syst. Eng. 2015;8:106–121.

[34] Tursunbayeva A., Di Lauro S., Pagliari C. People analytics: a scoping review of conceptual boundaries and value propositions. Int. J. Inf. Manag. 2018;43:224–247

[35] Soper, D.S. (2022). A-priori Sample Size Calculator for Structural Equation Models [Software]. Available from https://www.danielsoper.com/statcalc

[36] Valle M.A., Varas S., Ruz G.A. Job performance prediction in a call center using a naive Bayes classifier (2012). Expert Systems with Applications 39:9939–9945

[37] White, D. (2021). Business Predictive Analytics: Tools and Technologies. In Data Analytics in Marketing, Entrepreneurship, and Innovation (pp. 31–51). CRC Press.

6

Artificial Intelligence in Reinventing Strategic Human Resources

Ankur Kumar[1], Harish Chandra Singh Negi[2] and Olena Nikylina[3]

[1]School of Computer Science and Engineering, Galgotias University, India
[2]School of Business, Galgotias University, India
[3]Department of Management, The University of Life and Environmental Sciences, Ukraine

Email: ankur2022sd@gmail.com;
harish.chandra_phd20@galgotiasuniversity.edu.in; Nikulina7@hotmail.com

Abstract

AI is an important branch of science. Technology is revolutionizing a massive number of industries at a very alarming rate. It enables hiring managers to produce multiple solutions, which include basic recruiting tools, and intermediate applications, as well as advanced AI solutions that help predict more accurately a candidate's success in the future about a company. At a very explicit rate, artificial intelligence is revolutionizing the human resource industry. The technologies that are based on artificial intelligence are and will be a leading factor in the building of smart systems in the future. This will eventually lead to human resources being more dependent on advanced technologies. AI makes the overall process of human resource management relatively easier and thus provides a great deal of efficiency in the HRM processes. Also, there are many AI-based advanced technologies present in the current scenario which help to predict and find out whether, for example, a given candidate is best suited for a particular organization by judging by various parameters. This reduces the chance of error in the selection of a candidate and thus helps in improving the overall parameters of an organization. The intelligence displayed by machines, in addition to that displayed by humans and other animals, is referred to as artificial intelligence. Also, basic AI programmes can help recruiters in sourcing and screening candidates using applications like chatbots and other automated scraping tools. Employees are a very important part of an organization, as their skills and performance play a very keen role in the development of an organization and staying profitable. AI is a technical tool that generates results after combining technology and human intelligence with ease.

6.1 Introduction

In the current scenario, AI is termed as the intelligence displayed by machines; also, the natural intelligence displayed by human beings as well as animals. AI provides the computer with the ability to think and react in specific situations as humans do. It also provides the ability to think logically and easily carry out complex mathematical operations and produce the output in a relatively short amount of time. Here, we will discuss how artificial intelligence will help in the strategic reinvention of human resources. AI has been applied at the management and enterprise-level to help managers or people at the enterprise-level speed up their repetitive and tedious jobs [1]. An AI is fit to work as a human brain and provide fruitful output from a given set of inputs. HR professionals need to prepare a strategic plan using AI and human intelligence to carry out HRM practises like performance management, hiring, talent management, competency mapping, etc. It provides analytical and database support to enterprise-level employees and managers, allowing them to devote their time to more valuable tasks that require a greater amount of attention. HRM refers to the series of human resource policies concerning management activities carried out by the enterprise. HRM includes a set of activities like recruitment and selection of employees; creation of corporate human resource strategies, training and development, performance management, etc. Although in the current scenario, HRM needs to be integrated with artificial intelligence applications to achieve higher economic benefits. With the help of the self-regulation process, artificial intelligence enables organizations to save a large amount of time as well as the efforts made by employees. Thus, it is changing the working pattern in the workplace from the traditional practices of human resources. Using AI-based applications, numerous applications and even the most complex problems are solved in a relatively short period of time. It is broadly classified into three types of systems, that is, analytical, human-inspired and humanized artificial intelligence. Analytical AI is made up of cognitive intelligence and the representation of the modern world using past experiences. Inspired AI has cognitive elements and human understanding. Humanized artificial intelligence dictates characteristics of all types, including cognitive, emotional and social intelligence, self-consciousness and awareness in interaction with others. To reinvent strategic human resources, intermediate AI applications are used in the hiring process in an organization, such as selection tests, gamification, etc. Candidates must spend some time playing games based on their neuro-science abilities as part of the hiring strategy. These games are fully capable of judging a candidate's memory ability, risk-taking ability, and attention power. All these parameters help a manager in choosing the best candidates for the organization-job fit analytically. However, AI applications may be unable to judge a candidate based on the domain he/she may be working on and to detect whether a candidate is best suited for a specific business requirement in an organization. Organizations can address such issues by using customer-designed advanced artificial intelligence applications with an algorithm that identifies candidates with the best qualities based on specific job performance metrics.

6.2 Artificial Intelligence and HR Practices and Processes

The HR department in today's scenario is moving towards a complete digitalization with AI, including processes like screening, recruitment, selection, etc. Digitalization not only helps in reducing the burden of repetitive, tedious jobs and promotes learning but also enhances the efficiency of each function and process followed by organizations. Asynchronous video interviews (AVIs) are a new type of AI-based interview technique used by several organizations to streamline and speed up the selection process. With the use of this latest technique, it is possible to conduct these interviews anywhere, 24 × 7, improving the overall efficiency of the hiring process. These types of interviews have been opted for by a maximum number of organizations around the world now and are considered the best for the screening and onboarding process. In addition, AI-based talent acquisition and talent development have also been consistently used to improve the processes of acquiring competent workforces and their development. Companies like IBM, Oracle, etc. are using online hiring platforms that employ a predictive analysis technique with a machine learning algorithm. It enables the company's best talent to have a transparent career path, which further facilitates succession planning. Additionally, the AI-based process also facilitates accurate data collection from resumes in a structured format, which allows shortlisting candidates according to job specifications. Employers can avoid unnecessary rehire costs and attrition by utilizing predictive analysis using these AI tools and applications. Companies that are using AI-based tools and applications for the hiring process have been shown to produce better results than traditional recruitment processes with human intervention, which further contributes to a significant reduction in attrition rates in companies, thereby improving employee stability.

6.2.1 AI-based onboarding and induction process

Information related to job profiles can be easily accessed by new joiners using an AI application during the onboarding process carried out by the organization. The implementation of AI allows the Human Resource Department to enable a customized response application to handle frequent queries by new employees, such as questions about the company's rules, regulations and policies, job responsibilities and key result areas, employee welfare and facilities, HR policies, etc. These AI-based applications include the details of the manager in a hierarchy with their contact details. These details may result in a simple and painless onboarding process for new employees.

6.2.2 Implementation of artificial intelligence in training and development programmes

As reported by many companies, AI-based systems help employees enhance their current skill set. These training and developmental programmes examine the present skills of the employees and allocate them to a specific training module accordingly. These types of training and development programmes are self-paced, which enables employees to enhance their skills on their own to meet the present market demands. An AI-based identification of training needs is also done for the existing employees of the organizations while analysing real-time past performance and individual development of employees to further decide the relevant training for them. This process not only enables one to attain a specific skill set at the right time while saving money on training.

6.2.3 AI-enabled performance management system

Many organizations in the current scenario are consistently adopting AI-based tools for automating the evaluation of employees' performance. Performance evaluation functions are very crucial and most of the time, employees feel injustice due to human biases and errors. The AI-based evaluation process removes such errors and is carried out without any emotional or mental biases to extract excellent to bad performance review reports objectively. This system is also used for retaining the right talent at the right time, which is important for organizations' growth and success. The traditional method of carrying out the assessment is found to be outdated in the new normal and underrated in business value. Organissations can improve employee performance and the organization's performance with the help of AI and machine learning techniques.

Many of the HR functions are supported through AI applications where six processes are identified for the major interventions. Semantic search engines for candidate search, artificial neural networks (ANN) for turnover prediction, genetic algorithms for staff roster, resume data acquisition and information extraction, employee self-service integration, and text mining for HR sentiments are the six processes (Strohmeier, 2015). These are highlighted in the broad usage and implementation of artificial intelligence in all fields of HRM, along with chatbots and help centres.

Additionally, data mining techniques are also used to enhance the effectiveness of various HR functions like reward and incentives, learning and development, exit interviews, identification of talents, etc. Intelligent agent techniques are also used for employee development and improvement of the current skill sets of the employees. Furthermore, deep learning-based techniques can measure employee engagement based on personalized learning data and personality assessment. A predictive analysis based on this system provides data about the needs of employees for their growth, salary, stress from jobs and so on. In the current scenario, almost 60% of companies face the problem of employee retention in their organization globally. Artificial intelligence can also help a company address security and privacy concerns. AI may also help in the detection of fraud or compliance of an employee regarding his/her bad record or bad intention towards a company's data network. Although there is some chance of error with this process also, the result of AI is based on past records and is not completely transparent, leading to the possibility of error in analysing the data of a person with 100% accuracy. To achieve accurate results, advancements in AI would be required to produce transparent results and analyse the profile of an individual accurately.

6.3 Role of AI for Sustainable HR Functions and Processes

AI-based systems extend support to various HR functions and processes which is increasing trust and positive attitudes among HR professionals towards the implementation of AI for organizational effectiveness. Although many organizations have adopted artificial intelligence in a variety of areas, some are still in denial and attempting to use data analytics and predictive analytics for decision-making and problem-solving. Moreover, organizations that have adopted AI in HR are still experiencing challenges in its implementation, but the fact that cannot be overlooked is that all efforts are being made so that employees can use predictive analytics for any action plan. As artificial intelligence advances and implementations continue to take place in the organizations, the structure of work will change shortly which is further expected to change many processes and functionalities of HR. In the new normal after the pandemic the HR department must open up for changes and do advancements in the system to be competitive and survive in the business market. With the integration of AI tools and applications, HR departments would be more effective in saving time and increasing the efficiency of various functions like recruitment, screening, help desk, learning and development, competency mapping, compensation management, performance management, etc.

The following are the AI-based HR processes practiced by companies at present for the effective management of their workforce:

- **Personalized employee experience**: IBM has an automated system that replies to new joiners about critical job-related questions to guide them extensively for a comfortable stay in the company. This system guides various areas, such as names, locations, or contact information of the concerned people to whom new members have to connect on their first day, information regarding documents required for joining, etc.

- **Smart recruitment and selection:** AI helps recruitment managers to screen the applications and provides the candidate with quick responses. AI algorithms analyse resumes deeply and further assist in shortlisting qualified, relevant and good candidates. In addition to it, fair and human biased free decisions are taken for hiring and recruiting candidates. Many organizations have also started using Gamified Assessments for screening candidate resumes. The success rate for attracting good candidates has increased by 30% with the use of these methods. SAT, Facebook and GE are among the organizations that are currently utilizing digital technology for screening, personality assessment, interviewing and identifying new talent.

- As a result of the use of AI in HR, traditional recruiter jobs have been reduced by 60% to 65%. It has also resulted in an 80% automation of help desk jobs equally supported by cloud-based chatbots. AI is quite helpful in the automation of the interview process. The interview process is conducted through word or speech pattern exams. Many organizations nowadays use digital interview techniques to conduct interviews, which not only enrich the candidate's experience but also increase the efficiency of the selection process. There are various other tools available on the markets which are used for scheduling meetings and interviews, such as Amy and Clara.

- **Cognitive support in decision-making:** Cognitive engines in AI facilitates the effective implementation of HR policies and assist employees in their day-to-day activities and decision-making processes at work. IBM Watson, for example, is a portal within IBM that promotes natural AI capabilities for the following routine HR activities:

  o **Vacation requests:**
  The Cognitive Engine Support provides information to employees about the chances of approval or disapproval of their leaves or vacation days by the authorities in advance based on who has already applied for leaves from their department during that time period.

  o **Mood determination:**
  Employees get highly stressed and, at times, anxious while handling clients frequently and their calls. A cognitive-based solution equipped with deep learning facilitates measurement of the stress levels of employees, which guides and prepares them to schedule another meeting after break.

  o **Hiring procedure:**
  Cognitive Procedures provide organizations with insight into data sources as well as assist in the development of a candidate profile by giving them access to multiple data sources.

- **Automation of low-value-added tasks:** AI assists in the automation of redundant and low-value-added tasks, resulting in effective time savings and allowing the HR team to focus more on strategic work, laying the groundwork for future success for the organization. AI provides precise solutions to problems and aids in increasing the efficiency of human resources in an organization. Thus, AI in HR is beneficial in terms of reducing workload and saving time.

- **Human-bias elimination**: For a variety of processes in human resources, artificial intelligence eliminates bias in decision-making. For example, religions, castes, language, gender, and so on, are some of the factors that are widely considered in recruiting and selecting candidates in organizations. Such hiring bias patterns can be identified and eliminated with AI algorithms, allowing HR professionals to make effective selection decisions based on data.

- **Smart people analytics:** To gain insight into future stakeholder behaviour, companies gather and analyse stakeholder data. HR Teams need to catch up a lot when it comes to analysing these people's data. As a result, AI will play a larger role in a company's HR department after determining what to track, examine and analyse.

- **Litigation strategy:** Legal litigation faced by companies or employees can be well handled using AI tools to access legal databases and finding out the best approach to deal with it. The system provides cost-effective solutions, assisting with contract drafting, due diligence, legal analytics, etc. to the organizations.

- **Equitable pay and rewards:** Performing data analytics can prove to be a very useful tool for assessing pay equity and incentive equity. Additionally, the legislation in this scenario is rapidly changing at the central and state levels. The latest technological advancements and the use of disruptive technology can be very useful in monitoring employee compensation discrepancies, and in designing pay systems based on performance.

- **Chatbots:** Chatbots help employees access certain important pieces of information from anywhere at any time. Intelligent and easy interactions are made possible by the new generation chatbots. Many companies like IBM, ServiceNow, Xor, Maya, Ideal, Paradox, etc., are using chatbots to answer common employee queries and reply using text. A survey result shows that employees are more comfortable with chatbots as compared to any other form of contact related to transactional queries, company policies, etc. One needs to make sure that they do comply with data security laws, policies, disability, as well as other state laws while making use of chatbots.

- **Enriching learning and employee development:** The Global Learning and development industry is worth over $200 billion, and most professionals believe that half of it is wasted. It is necessary to make learning interesting for it to be interactive and useful. These 'Netflix-like' algorithms are making their way into the learning platform, attempting to make learning more interesting so that employees can get the most out of everything they learn. The market considering L&D is young but massive. There are ample opportunities for growth considering the learning and development market. Research has shown that due to a busy work-life schedule, an average employee has even less than 25 minutes a week to learn as well as develop their skills. If this learning can be made interesting so that employees can get 100% out of it and contribute significantly to an individual's performance improvement.

- Technological advancements have enabled industries to handle behind-the-scenes roles in the current scenario. The various advancements in artificial intelligence have equipped organizations to manage bulk data, provide real-time feedback and provide futuristic solutions for industry growth and success. For effective functioning, the industry recommends certain tools like Microsoft 365, Engazify, Obie & Niles, Wade & Wendy, and many more. It aids employees in increasing workplace efficiency.

- **Management and leadership:** AI can help with leadership development to improve organizational management. According to a study, clients reported that after three months of using AI-based coaching tools and systems, their leadership qualities and team building improved by 25% which included requesting for feedback, reading comments and intuiting sentiments from them.

- **Well-being and employee engagement:** Artificial intelligence is also used to identify the behaviour that is causing poor performance. Artificial intelligence also aids in the identification of risky behaviours and experiences. A recently introduced survey tool assists in the identification of stress and bad behaviours and alerts HR or Line Managers if any such incidence occurs.

The role of artificial intelligence can be categorized majorly in three areas of HRM viz. maximizing engagement, automating workflow and finding talents which are depicted in Figure 6.1. Figure 6.2 shows the companies' trends and areas for the implementation of AI for organization sustainability and success.

6.4 Advantages and Disadvantages of Adopting AI-based System in HR

- The field of AI allows rapid analysis of data, pattern recognition and trend prediction through algorithms and machine learning tools. These algorithms are fast and not intuitive like humans, and they can analyse millions of pieces of data in fractions of seconds.

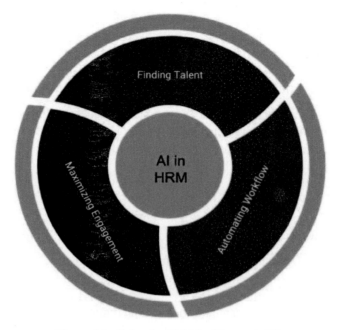

Figure 6.1   Role of artificial intelligence in HR.

How Companies Around the World Are Using Artificial Intelligence

IT activities are the most popular.

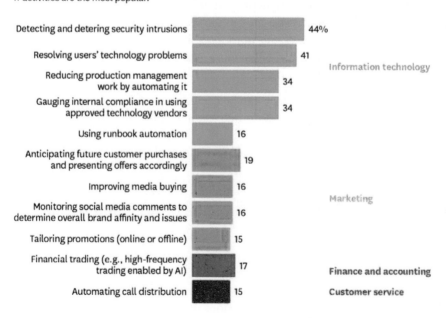

Figure 6.2   Use of AI by various organizations.

- The chance of errors is almost negligible using AI-based tools and techniques. It also reduces manpower involvement and increases the efficiency of work.

- There are numerous risks associated with machine learning applications and algorithms. The most significant disadvantage of artificial intelligence is that it requires training for data handling and management. Algorithms based on AI can also learn from previous experiences.

- The overall success of organizations is determined by a variety of factors, including the accuracy and completeness of its automated system, as well as the ease of using the system. Organizations can use 'narrow-AI', which would provide more specific solutions for problems.

- Artificial intelligence facilitates predicting employee retention rates and the major reasons for their leaving organizations. Based on these predictions, organizations can come up with better employee engagement mechanisms and tools.

- A system based on artificial intelligence can eliminate redundancy of daily tasks so that routine work in the organization can be carried out efficiently and each department operates efficiently.

- AI-based tools and techniques are increasingly used in HRM in hiring, performance management, employee engagement, talent management and predicting future actions, which will become a necessity if a company wants to stand out in today's market.

- However, artificial intelligence is one of the best analytical tools for suggestions and improvement but it still is incapable of making independent decisions. There is also a high risk of data exposure and accidental use of this system.

- The system can also institutionalize bias. Assume a company has never hired a woman, and African engineers are also in short supply. The Artificial Intelligence System would conclude that women and African engineers are very less likely to move into management in an organization. This type of typical bias is likely to be removed from algorithms through advancements in artificial intelligence.

- Every company's management and people decision - making are frequently based on culture. Furthermore, there is a significant time investment required to implement these systems in the real world and optimize them for exceptional performance. The present technological tools are not context-oriented and then lack applicability.

- It can be difficult for HR departments to acquire and retain competent and talented candidates to handle new-age AI-based systems, given the huge challenges facing companies today. Furthermore, technology restricts HR from taking decisions during normal day-to-day operating hours since artificial intelligence (AI) has taken away the authority of HR as well as the role that HR plays in making decisions for an organization.

6.5 Conclusion

In today's competitive environment, artificial intelligence is indeed a great tool for business organizations. AI-based techniques and solutions enable organizations to automate many of their departments, such as HR, Finance, Operations, IT Departments and so on. The implementation of artificial intelligence in the HR department has been extremely beneficial for reducing workload by automating repetitive and redundant tasks, allowing managers and HR professionals to focus more on strategic tasks, resulting in increased efficiency. AI is not only useful in reducing the workload of HR professionals but it is also used for monitoring the stress level and mental health of employees, improving their personalized experience at work, and staying ahead of the competition.

AI is also contributing to enhancing the efficiency of many functions and operations in the HR area. For example, an automated AI-based screening process of resumes and interviews is increasing the effectiveness of the recruitment process. In addition to that, it analyses the cognitive ability of candidates in order to ensure organization-person-job fit. The overall process of acquiring talent supported by AI is cost-effective as well as time-saving. This predictive and analytic-based system done through AI algorithm is helping the organization to design effective employee engagement mechanisms and reduce the attrition rate. Human intelligence in HRM is replacing the entire traditional system of recruitment where human interactions are involved, which further helps in establishing transparency in the recruitment system. Such processes, adopted by various business firms globally, ensure sustainable recruitment practices by maintaining transparency, removing biases with technology and promoting trust and compliance.

The advancement of technology is transforming business processes and functions rapidly, requiring smarter features in AI for better predictability and decision-making accuracy. Various machine learning-based applications are being widely adopted by business firms. Applications such as chatbots, gamification and robot automation are used to provide 24 × 7 support to employees in need of any assistance from the company. These automated systems are programmed with advanced algorithms enabling processes or employees to the best possible solutions for effective functioning. People fear that such automation will result in unemployment, so they are resistant to adopting such systems. The fact is that these technologies would not reduce employment opportunities, but they would require a well-trained and capable workforce to handle them.

6.6 Discussion

Artificial intelligence is a collection of algorithms and machine learning tools capable of rapidly ingesting data, analysing patterns, identifying patterns and generating insights from it. These sets of algorithms are not "intuitive" like humans, but rather can analyse huge amounts of data in a fraction of second and correlate them among patterns.

To select the most appropriate candidate for the designated profile, the acceptance criteria and candidate profiles must be matched. This type of data processing is becoming highly valued in the current scenario among business firms to identify passive candidates and not involve them in any recruitment process to save cost and time. AI-based screenings equip organization to avoid passive candidates very well beforehand. Furthermore, AI is also essential in the recruitment process for sourcing the right candidates for interviews and shortening the recruitment time cycle. As a result, the talent acquisition team is able to engage proactive candidates, predict their ability to perform specific roles, and speed up the recruitment process.

Artificial Intelligence, in conjunction with machine learning Algorithms, has automated almost the entire process of candidate recruitment in an artificial intelligence technology requires a White Box Implementation to ensure complete transparency with employees, which also leads to the establishment of trust and compliance within an organization. For effective HR management, Artificial Intelligence has also been taken to monitor and record the behaviour of an employee in the workplace. At the workplace, artificial intelligence is also being used to monitor the mental health of employees. So, Artificial Intelligence in the current scenario is used to monitor the overall well-being of an employee in an organization. It also helps in improving mental health by enabling HR to extend additional support if necessary.

Many HR functions are equipped with artificial intelligence technology and are working efficiently. However, there are still many areas of HR where intervention is needed and the predictive feature can better enable organizations for effective decision-making. Assessment centres, personality tests, learning transfer, budgeting and procurement of intellectual capital are just some of the areas where AI-based approaches can be used to help organizations achieve better results.

References

[1] Artificial Intelligence And How It is Reinventing The HR – Practices In Making The Organisations More Visible And Competitive [EPRA International Journal of Multidisciplinary Research (IJMR)], ISSN (Online): 2455–3662.

[2] The Growing Role Of Artificial Intelligence in Human Resources. [EPRA International Journal of Multidisciplinary Research (IJMR)], ISSN (Online): 2455-3662.

[3] Artificial Intelligence in HR. [(E-ISSN 2348-1269, P- ISSN 2349-5138)], 2018 IJRAR December 2018, Volume 5, Issue 4.

[4] Bhagyalakshmi, R., & Maria, E. F. (2020). Artificial Intelligence In Human Resource Management, [Studies in Indian Place Names, 40(40), 1453–1458].

[5] Artificial-Intelligence-in-Human-Resource-Practices-With-Challenges-and-Futu re-Directions, [January 2022, DOI:10.4018/978-1-7998-8497-2.ch015].

[6] Hmoud, B., & Laszlo, V. (2019). Will Artificial Intelligence Take Over Human Resources Recruitment and Selection? Network Intelligence Studies, 7(13), 21–30

[7] Archer, N. & Yuan, Y. F. (2000) Managing business-to-business relationships throughout the e-commerce procurement life cycle. Internet Research-Electronic Networking Applications and Policy, 10, 385–395.

[8] Biswas, S. (2018). Employee Experience, Jobs and Skills: How AI will Impact HR. Retrieved from https://www.hrtechnologist.com/articles/digital-transformation/employee-experience-jobsand-skills-how-ai-will-impact-hr/

[9] Kapoor, B. (2010). Business Intelligence and Its Use for Human Resource Management. The Journal of Human Resource and Adult Learning, 6(2), 21–30.

[10] Murgai, A. (2018). Transforming Digital Marketing with Artificial Intelligence. Retrieved from https://www.ijltemas.in/DigitalLibrary/Vol.7Issue 4/259–262.pdf.

[11] Emilia Bratu (2018). A short history of AI, Future Horizons, September 20th, 2018.

7

The New HR Inclination for Artificial Intelligence Aiding Talent Acquisition

Alka Agnihotri[1], Kavita Mathad[2] and Seifedine Kadry[3]

[1]School of Business, Galgotias University, India
[2]GIBS Business School, Bangaluru, India
[3]Noroff University College, Norway

Email: alka.agnihotri@galgotiasuniversity.edu.in; drkavitamathad@gmail.com; skadry@gmail.com

Abstract

In the present scenario, HR functions face the challenge of a lack of future-ready skills. This in turn results in a shortage of talent and also impacts the business adversely. Basically, there is pressure on chief human resource officers (CHROs) to upgrade and transform to a more dependable and quicker AI-supported acquisition of talent for a better consumer experience through a multifunctional and multidisciplinary approach. Thus, large companies are inclined to promote work through technologies such as artificial intelligence (AI), digital assistance, machine learning, etc. The top Indian companies have installed AI-driven talent acquisition systems internally and/or externally through outsourcing. Many top companies in India, like TCS and Oracle, are using AI in an exemplary manner. At Oracle, AI, ML and digital assistants are being used in HR functions like talent acquisition, best applicant identification, personalized candidate experience, smarter offers, anytime feedback, goal setting, performance evaluations, intelligent career planning and planning of learning activities for the employees. The paper aimed to examine how the use of AI tools and products has aided in HR functions such as talent acquisition and learning by outperforming humans in large corporations. The paper also tries to analyse the contribution of AI and ML tools and products to more effective talent acquisition.

A comparative study was conducted using secondary and primary source data to identify the major global HR AI platforms that have been torch bearers and how major companies, especially Oracle in India, are using AI in HR functions, mainly in talent acquisition. Analysis of pre and post-AI scenarios is done to explore the impact on responsible management of removing bias, delays, data-based, open and verifiable, etc. The major findings of the study are that the application of artificial intelligence, machine learning, and digital assistance in talent acquisition has not only improved the operational and financial aspects of work but has also promoted responsible management. It is not only cost and time-saving but also creates a cordial and positive work environment through removing bias from the data collection processes and thus making the decision-making and application more accurate. The data from websites of the companies and vendors of AI-driven acquisition platforms was examined in detail to bring out the clear connection between AI and its use in talent acquisition.

7.1 Introduction

The use of AI in HRM is of recent origin. In India, many top companies like Oracle, TCS, Infosys and Wipro are using AI ML and digital assistance in many HR functions, especially for talent acquisition functions. Oracle is using AI in a much more elaborated way for HR functions. Thus, it is interesting to look at their work in detail. Looking at the Oracle story started in 1977 when software development laboratories was founded by engineers Larry Elision, Bob Miner and Ed Oates. In 1982, the company changed its name to Oracle Corporation. Since its inception, Oracle has aimed at challenging work domains. Oracle's mission is to promote an inclusive environment in which all employees, suppliers, customers and partners can thrive, leading to responsible management. It also involves harnessing and maximizing the gains that may accrue from the diversity of perspectives and backgrounds of all stakeholders. Discovering insights into data and exploring endless opportunities is another focus of Oracle. Introducing AI in HR goes in line with the mission and philosophy of Oracle as shared on the Oracle website (AI in Human Resources: The Time is Now (oracle.com)). Through this, Oracle aims to acquire a sustainable global competitive advantage. At Oracle, AI is being used in almost all important HR functions like talent acquisition, performance evaluations, intelligent career planning, learning, etc. AI is remodelling the HR roles in Oracle (John, F. 2014). The same report informs us that workers are more optimistic, excited, and grateful about having robot co-workers (who may handle riskier work portions and simplify work) (WGS,

2019). The company looks at AI as being capable of aligning with responsible management. Oracle's initiatives about AI, white-box approach, machine learning and digital assistance have resulted in responsible management.

For understanding, defining the important concepts related to AI is as follows:

- **Artificial intelligence (AI):** AI involves using machines to perform tasks that are suited to human intelligence. Oracle is leading the way in leveraging AI and providing candidates, employees, managers and HR organizations with a variety of role-specific benefits. In addition to that, AI also helps in designing and recommending accurate and efficient learning and development programmes.

- **The white-box approach:** A key component of Oracle's AI strategy is the white-box approach. This approach requires the transparent, logical functioning of AI with proven relevance. The white-box approach can instil trust and faith in users because they can understand the workings, relevance and rationality of AI processes. Due to the white-box approach, AI has become much more acceptable.

- **Digital assistant:** The digital assistant platform of Oracle uses AI and can understand user intent and is enabled to customise according to it and provide a satisfactory relevant service or response to the users. It keeps a record of usage and preferences and uses them in making recommendations. Thus, it can satisfy the users by meeting their needs and expectations. Also, it can answer queries related to HR, supply chain, finance, customer-related issues, etc. Machine systems also enable the system to learn and respond accordingly. Many HR functions are now being conducted with the help of these technological developments, such as talent acquisition, compensation management, learning and development at Oracle, all done using AI. It helps in the identification of the ideal candidate by matching the qualifications with the job openings. A global study by Talentfly has revealed that every bad hire may cost on average $14,900. This cost is significant and can be reduced by using AI-driven talent acquisition. Based on the interaction, AI may provide a customised experience for all applicants and may make job recommendations.

Talent management and acquisition processes have become smarter with AI as it can analyse the market data and can optimize job offers and close them with the preferred ones. It is also able to leverage HR information to forecast the acceptance or rejection of candidates. Furthermore, AI also helps in verification of achieved goals by comparing them to the targeted goals set at regular intervals, and the data can be used for performance evaluation and management. In addition, digital assistants have simplified the feedback system, making it more transparent, user-friendly and accessible at any time. The digital assistant helps employees complete the evaluation process by informing them about the status of completion and any required follow-up. The most significant contribution of AI is the contribution to the career planning of employees. It can connect the employees with mentors who are capable of guiding and also suggesting vacant positions matching the qualifications and even suggesting courses of training relevant to the positions.

Similarly, a lot can be improvised when AI and related technologies are applied in the training and learning domains of employees. Tailored, customised training and learning plans may be developed for internal and external customers based on the areas of their interest, career plans and job expectations. In Oracle, the learning nudges provided under digital assistance help not only in content search but also in giving status updates about the timelines of the courses enrolled. To enhance the productivity of the employees, managers can recommend a particular training course useful for a particular project at hand at present or shortly using the digital assistant. Thus, AI is being used in Oracle's workforce upskilling and reskilling.

7.2 Role of AI for Talent Management in the Present Era

AI has become popular as it helps in talent management in several ways (LinkedIn, 2018). There are many software and applications that may be used by companies in talent management and acquisition. It has also helped in enhancing employee experience and reducing attrition. Incorrect or non-accurate hiring is a cost to the company. Right hiring is a top priority for companies who want to seek a competitive advantage. In a study in the US, researchers found that three out of four employers reported hiring the wrong person for a position, due to which a loss of an average of $14,900 per bad hire was incurred by their company.

AI is being used as an aid to talent acquisition. Bad talent acquisition is a costly affair for companies for several reasons, like advertising, replacement and training costs, staff time, adverse impact on team performance, productivity and quality of work, project disruptions and loss of customers. The way out of this is by recruiting and hiring a good fit for the vacant positions in an organization. This requires accurate and relevant data collection from all relevant sources and timely solutions for the issues arising therefrom. The

HR department is always under pressure to be more analytical (Cappelli, P. 2017). This may not be well achieved if only human manual work is involved. Software on talent acquisition and learning may help. Also, the latest developments like AI and ML digital assistance are being utilized for data collection, analysis and decision-making. Thus, recruitment and talent acquisition have become data-driven processes. Thus, IT companies are becoming more and more AI-driven companies. Another reason for this is the IT company's first encounters with such inventions, innovations and creations in the fields of AI and ML. Thus, IT industries are more AI-driven. Is AI more visible in IT companies? Expert opinion is that the IT sector is more in touch and gets first-hand information about such developments. Also, all developments, innovations, improvements and creations about AI, ML, and digital assistance take place in their R&D or related companies. They are the breeding grounds for AI and other applications.

7.3 Talent Acquisition and AI

The process of filling the talent, skills and/or competency gaps is known as talent acquisition. The latest trend in talent acquisition is that it is now a data-driven fiat utilizing AI, ML and digital assistance in informed decision-making for hiring the right talent. This is a new field of talent acquisition analytics where big data is utilized for data-driven skill gap analysis and informed timely decision-making.

AI is proving to be a very versatile field of technology. It is finding utility in developing automated cars, humanoid robots, financial, legal, healthcare, advertising recruiting, learning and training tools, etc. AI is predicted to change work as an enabler in the area of talent acquisition.

In the Global Recruiting Trends 2018 released by LinkedIn, big data is now in use by *50% of hiring professionals* as part of their strategy, which has helped them with talent acquisition and has also positively impacted employee retention by 56%. *In different companies, AI is sparing the employees of repetitive processes and they help in sorting resumes, application tracking, etc.*

Many companies like Oracle, Infosys, cognizant, etc., are using chatbots AI assistants to efficiently handle talent acquisition by guiding the recruitment and hiring process through application sorting, talent and opportunity matching and also answering questions through natural language processing. HR is thus relieved of the daunting process of filtering a huge number of candidates, skill matching and scheduling an interview. Bots automate work and free up time.

7.4 Talent Acquisition Platforms

The HR function of talent acquisition has transformed due to several companies developing AI platforms for talent acquisition in South Asia (Kshetri N, 2020) and the USA. New York is a breeding ground for many AI applications that are now being used worldwide. A summary of some of the popular apps is produced below.

Gloat, a New York-based AI platform connects with job seekers via chat. It matches the job opportunities with the skills and preferences of the users. All the information regarding the users is kept anonymous until they choose to reveal their information to the selected companies.

Companies like Accenture, Deloitte, Wayfair, Macy's, Adidas and Quicken Loans use an AI platform called Restless Bandit, which is based in San Francisco, California. It is a very powerful bot recruiter which algorithmically connects with qualified candidates. It is a very powerful platform as it can work on 120 million job descriptions, 50 thousand hours of data analysis, and about 30 million resumes of applicants, and discover from them the most suitable and relevant candidates.

Companies that employ workers on an hourly basis like Thred Up use AI recruitment platform TextRecruit, which interacts with the candidates and employees through text and live chat. TextRecruit (a San Jose, California-based company) is very beneficial here and provides speed and accuracy to the whole communication process.

Wade and Wendy, a New York-based TA platform, have become very popular. Both are personal AI assistants that are of huge help in the recruitment process. Wade collaborates with job seekers and helps in matching and seeking personalized opportunities for jobs.

On the other hand, Wendy provides assistance in several other useful ways, like smoothening of the tedious tasks like email, which it automates and also provides with feedback.

AI-driven systems and processes increase our outreach tenfold and our engagement by 24 hours a day, seven days a week. On average, it saves 30 hours for every 100 candidates handled. XOR is an AI assistant tool which is very popular in the retail, healthcare and hospitality industry. It uses chatbots to help the candidates in the application process, not only scheduling interviews but also asking questions and gathering information about their experience and skills. For quality talent identification, the Leoforce company has developed an AI platform named ARYA. Similar to ARYA is Entelo Company's Envoy platform, which is being successfully used by companies like Credit Karma, Sony, Hallmark and SpotX to find top potential employees. Hiretual is another very popular AI-driven talent search and matching

Steps in the TA
Platforms on TA

AI platform for TA

Impact of AI

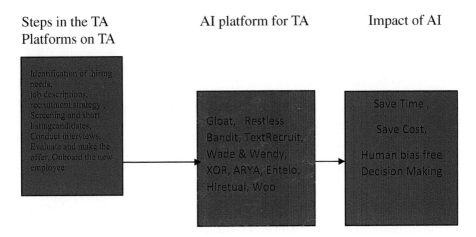

Figure 7.1 Model of AI-driven talent acquisition process and impact

platform which the tech giants like Intel, Verizon, IBM and eBay, etc. are using for talent acquisition. Hiretual sources talent through AI technology, aggregating more than 700 million professional profiles across the web and 30 public platforms and analysing information about experience, skills, market value and availability.

Cosmetics giant L'Oreal has saved itself from recruitment costs and time (an average of 40 minutes per candidate review, which over six months translates to about 45 working days) by using another AI recruitment platform, MyaSystems. Companies like Microsoft, Lyft, Uber, Wix.com, and WeWork all partner with Woo to find new team members.

7.5 Steps in Recruitment

The seven-step recruitment process (Figure 7.1) involves the following steps:

1. Determine the hiring requirements. The available AI platforms for this purpose are GLOAT, Restless Bandit, TextRecruit, and Wade & Wendy.

2. Prepare job descriptions. The available AI platforms for this purpose are GLOAT and Restless Bandit.

3. Create a recruitment strategy. The available AI platforms for this purpose are GLOAT, Restless Bandit, Wade & Wendy.

4. Screen and shortlist candidates. The available AI platforms for this purpose are GLOAT, Restless Bandit, Wade & Wendy.

5.   Conduct interviews. The available AI platforms for this purpose are XOR, etc.

6.   Evaluate and make the offer. The available AI platforms for this purpose are XOR and ARYA.

7.   Onboarding the new employee The available AI platforms for this purpose are Entelo, Hiretual and Woo.

7.6 AI Advantages

Although there are incidences when AI does not work well, as in the case of Amazon, where AI could not be stopped from discriminating against women in the recruitment process (Meyer, David. 2018), its benefits still outweigh the disadvantages. AI is based on talent acquisition analytics and this gives a lot of benefits (as reported by TalentLyft)

The analytics can be used to improve recruitment and candidate experience (Junque de Fortuny, E., Martens, D., & Provost, F. 2013). AI-driven talent acquisition analytics can predict the rate of successful performance by applicants in future jobs. Second, people analytics is used by companies to develop a profile of a successful employee, which may serve as a benchmark for standard performance for employees and their appraisal. It is also used to quickly identify the right kind of candidates for jobs (predictive HR analytics). Elimination of bias is another very important benefit of AI. Third, manual HR tasks, which consume a lot of time, have been automated and AI-driven. It includes updating the important key performance indicators by analysis of market trends, costs in hiring, psychographic and demographic differences and trends. There is all-in-one recruitment software now available which can analyse the data, suggest actions and thus save cost.

7.7 AI in Talent Acquisition in India

The Indian companies have realized that the new era of recruiting and hiring through software like TurboHire claim to save 70 % on recruitment cost. Another very popular AI platform MeritTrac established in 2000, is India's leading pure-play Testing & Assessment provider. We are now a part of UNext Learning Private Limited, a wholly owned subsidary of Manipal Education and Medical Group. MeritTrac offers assessment services and examination management services to corporate organizations, educational institutes and government agencies. MeritTrac Platforms has Talent Assessment Tests named Pariksha which has a battery of online tests with a different purpose. The online assessment platform under it is named SmartTest and it comprises 10,000 assessments of skills relating to cognition behaviour and performance. For assessment of coding skills CodeTrac coding platform is popularly being used. Similarly, SpeechTrac is used as an automated spoken English assessment platform.

7.8 The Rising AI Market

AI has come to stay. This can be predicted from the popularity attained by these AI platforms in recent times because they have given advantages to these companies. Fortune Business Insights reported in 2018 that the AI market was expected to grow by 33% annually (2019–2026) and reach $203 billion. primarily businesses based on 5G technology, connected devices, cloud-based services and applications, machine learning and so on. There are unlimited areas for AI applications. From stocks to IT, health education, security and so on, to space research and other R&D areas, AI has become a fixture due to the benefits and cutting-edge advantages it provides to users. Amazon's uses the AI machine learning system Rekognition to know what the customer demands and then supply the same. This has given Amazon an edge over competitors.

Data analytics is at the core of Google. In 2014, after acquiring DeepMind Technologies, it further deepened its base in AI and ML. It has the potential to build business models using data analytics and AI. It is predicted to end jobs for specialists, e.g., consultants, accountants, etc., involved in creating new businesses for large companies. Companies like Verint use AI in communicating with their customers using intelligent virtual assistants (IVA), which leverage machine learning to understand the communications better and save on providing services to their customers, enabling a few companies to save as much as $1 million in customer service emails. Twilio, a cloud-based communication company could make its turnaround only through AI and ML improvements. IBM could succeed in its market development and market penetration only by building on its AI capabilities, through which they are helping its more than 20, 000 clients across 20 industries to make better decisions. Companies like Stitch Fix (SFIX) are using AI to learn the preferences, styles and personalities of busy people and offer them products accordingly. Amazon created personal shopper by Prime Wardrobe to provide customer profiles and personality-based curated products. many companies are tapping the potential of AI and ML to know and analyse their clients' and customers' preferences and priorities.

7.9 Conclusion

The assessment and the evaluation of both talent management use AI platforms for the cognitive, communicative and behavioural assessments of employees or prospective candidates for the job. The AI platforms are capable of doing background checks and also skills and qualification analyses of potential candidates (Gosh, Prartha, 2020). Several AI platforms are being used now for this function. As a result, the hiring or talent acquisition has not only been made lean but also spares the HR managers for more important discussion and decision-making functions. It has also made the acquisition function efficient, less costly, more timely, better hiring decisions and long-lasting hiring relations.

7.10 Findings and Recommendations

The research has brought to light many useful findings, as under:

1. Most of the AI platforms are US-based. Thus, in India, a lot of scope is there for developing indigenous AI platforms.

2. AI-driven processes are time-saving. This has allowed HR to focus on the right analysis and decision-making about important issues.

3. Due to AI and automation, a lot of activities are eliminated. This actually reduces cost-saving.

4. AI and data-driven HR processes are more effective. It is because more informed decisions are taken and implemented. Also, better candidate matching is possible.

5. AI can collect huge amounts of data and also analyse it efficiently and put it in a simplified manner. Thus, helping analysis of results and decision-making.

It is recommended that first more indigenous AI platforms customised to Indian HR work be developed. Second, HR in companies may adopt AI-driven HR processes so that time and cost are saved and HR processes become more efficient. Third, it will make data analysis and decision-making quick, integrated, collaborative and effective.

References

[1] Acktar, Reese, Dave Winsborough , Uri Ort , Abigail Johnson , Tomas Chamorro Premuzic. 2018. Detecting the Dark Side of Personality Using Social Media. Personality and Individual Differences, 132:90–97.

[2] AI in Human Resources : The Time is Now , https://www.oracle.com/a/ ocom/docs/applications/hcm/oracle-ai-in-hr-wp.pdf 1 Jan 2022

[3] Agnihotri, Alka. (2021) Systemic- Processual shared leadership model with reference to team variables in IT industry in India. Turkish Journal of Computer and Mathematics Education (TURCOMAT). 12. 608–618.

[4] Agnihotri, Alka. (2020). Comparative Study of Team Characteristics under Shared Leadership in Large and Small companies in IT Industry in India. 10.1109/ICRITO48877.2020.9197938

[5] Bloomberg, J. 2018. Don't Trust Artificial Intelligence? Time to Open the AI Black Box. Forbes.

[6] Cappelli, Peter. 2017. "There's No Such Thing as Big Data in HR." Harvard Business Review. June.

[7] Cappelli, Peter and AnnaTavis. 2017. The Performance Management Revolution. Harvard Business Review, November.

[8] Carrillo-Tudela, C., Hobijin, B., Perkowski, P., and Visschers, L. 2015.

[9] Cowgill, Bo (2017) The Labor Market Effects of Hiring through Machine Learning Working Paperowgill, Bo. 2018. "Bias and Productivity in Humans and Algorithms. Theory and Evidence from Résumé Screening." Working paper.

[10] Gosh, Prartha , 2020, Top 20 AI in HR Trends of 2020: The HRT Trend-watch , HR Technologisthttps://www.hrtechnologist.com/articles/ ai-in-hr/20-ai-in-hr-trends/

[11] John,F., Larry Ellison Talks Talent, Teamwork, And 'Insanely Great' Products Larry Ellison in Forbe Feb 2014 ,https://www.forbes.com/sites/ oracle/2014/02/12/larry-ellison-talks-talent-teamwork-and-insanely-great-products/?sh=428a0577332c, accessed on December 16,2021

[12] Junqué de Fortuny, E., Martens, D., & Provost, F. (2013). "Predictive modeling with big data: is bigger really better?" Big Data, 1(4), 215–226.

[13] Kshetri N, (2020) ."Evolving uses of artificial intelligence in human resource management in emerging economies in the global South: some preliminary evidence". Management Research Review, 44 (7), pp. 970 –990.

[14] Lee, M. K., Kusbit, D., Metsky, E., &Dabbish, L. 2015. Working with machines: The impact of algorithmic , data-driven management on human workers. Proceedings of the 33rd Annual ACM SIGCHI Conference: 1603–1612. Begole, B., Kim, J., Inkpen, K & Wood, W (Eds.), New York, NY: ACM Press.

[15] Lind, E. Allan and Kees Van den Bos. 2002. "When Fairness Works: Toward a General Theory of Uncertainty Management." Research in Organizational Behavior 24: 181–223.

[16] LinkedIn. 2018. The Rise of HR Analytics.https://business.linkedin. com/content/dam/me/business/en-us/talent-solutions/cx/2018/pdf/ leaders-perspective.pdf, accessed on December 12, 2021.

[17] Meyer, David. 2018. Amazon Reportedly Killed an AI Recruitment System Because It Couldn't Stop the Tool from Discriminating Against Women. Fortune. October 10th. http://fortune.com/2018/10/10/ amazon-ai-recruitment-bias-women-sexist/

[18] Monthly Labor Review. 2017. Estimating the U.S. Labor Share. Bureau of Labor Statistics, February. https://www.bls.gov/opub/mlr/2017/ article/estimating-the-uslabor-share.htm

[19] Multi-Process Human Resources Outsourcing (MPHRO) Services PEAK Matrix Assessment 2021, Anil Vijayan, Priyanka Mitra, Sharath Hari N, Everest Group, January 19, 2021

[20] Nandini, S., How Can Workers Stay Relevant In A World Dominated By AI? Artificial Intelligence in HR - Insights | Infosyshttps://www.info- sys.com/insights/human-potential/how-can-workers-stay-relevant-in-a- world-dominated-by-ai.html, accessed on January 15, 2022

[21] Pearl, Judea. 2018. The Book of Why: The New Science of Cause and Effect. Basic Books.

[22] Spielkamp, Michael. 2017. Inspecting Algorithms for Bias. MIT Technology Review. June 12. https://www.technologyreview.com/s/ 607955/inspecting-algorithms-forbias/

[23] Srivastava, Sameer and Amir Goldberg. 2017. "Language as a Window into Culture." California Management Review 60(1): 56–69.

[24] Tucker, Catherine. 2017. "Privacy, Algorithms, and Artificial Intelligence." In The Economics of Artificial Intelligence: An Agenda. Edited by Ajay K. Agrawal

[25] Samantha Marsh,2018. Talent Acquisition Analytics: What it is & Why it Matters, TalentLyfthttps://www.talentlyft.com/en/blog/article/233/ talent-acquisition-analytics-what-it-is-why-it-matters. November

[26] Somen Mondal, 2021,The 25 Top Recruiting Software Tools Of 2021 , https://ideal.com/top-recruiting-software/

8

Artificial Intelligence in Recruitment: An Impact Assessment of Organizations

Indira Priyadarsani Pradhan[1], Parul Saxena[2], Chandrani Ganguly[3] and Marija Benei Penava[4]

[1]Institute of Management Studies, Ghaziabad (University Courses Campus), India
[2]Sharda University, India
[3]School of Business, Galgotias University, India
[4]University of Dubrovnik, Department of Economics and Business, Lapadska, Croatia

Email: indirapradhan2004@gmail.com, Parul.saxena@sharda.ac.in; chandrani.ganguly@galgotiasuniversity.edu.in; marija.benic-penava@unidu.hr

Abstract

Artificial intelligence (AI) is considered the most promising and dynamic technology of the present era, revolutionizing the lives of humans and significantly impacting nearly every aspect of business. Many technological advancements have driven firms to improve their value-creation processes. The fundamental goal of this study will look critically at the impact of AI on Human Resource management functions, particularly in the area of recruitment and selection in businesses. The study aims to focus on AI's capabilities and how they affect the selection and recruitment process. The researcher has also used external secondary data (articles and papers) to highlight some of the conclusions of the impact of AI capabilities on the recruitment and selection of employees. Researcher finds that AI has the potential to favourably influence the recruitment and selection process, resulting in benefits such as time and cost savings, accuracy and the removal of bias.

8.1 Introduction

The evolution of artificial intelligence (AI) is a significant technological breakthrough. The term 'AI' refers to computer software that assists humans in performing their daily jobs. There are several business processes where artificial intelligence has been successfully adopted due to its ability to assist and help in strategic planning and decision-making, both of which can be extremely tough and sophisticated activities for business management. If a machine or device can learn and solve a specific problem in the same way that humans do, it can be considered to have artificial intelligence (AI). As a result of its programming, it can think and act like a human being. Or to put it another way, artificial intelligence (AI) can be defined as a set of technologies modelled after human intelligence, but the term AI encompasses a much broader range of concepts. It is necessary to fully demonstrate its significance, benefits and applications. An interview suite survey indicated that 76% of employers were persuaded that AI-based solutions would play a major role in providing HR services going forward. Artificial intelligence (AI) was employed for recruitment in 2021 as a result of the pandemic (Dashveenjit & Kaur). As a result, AI has become an integral part of business management, which has not only altered the way businesses are run but also the nature of work itself. To remain competitive and adapt to rapidly changing conditions, firms must constantly improve their management methods to stay ahead of the curve. A huge amount of data and information is being generated in today's businesses, which necessitates a complete digital transformation of the organization and a shift in the business mode. Human Resources is not exempt from this scenario, and it will either have to join the disruptive technology wave or face disruption. To deal with the competence and knowledge problems posed by AI technologies, businesses will need to implement new comprehensive and sustainable human resource management. An increasing number of large, established corporations, including Fortune 500 firms, are already embracing AI technologies to make better decisions and deliver predictive insights to their employees. Simply said, AI-equipped firms are better able to withstand fierce market rivalry while simultaneously achieving operational excellence.

AI has been demonstrated to have a positive impact on workforce management in business. AI application in HR functional areas was recommended as a way to move HRM to the next level, and the study notably focused on the recruitment process as a place to make use of this technology. The study's goal was to see if artificial intelligence can help with the hiring process at specific organizations. According to the research, AI has a favourable impact on the workplace. In the initial phases of the recruitment process, AI is believed to be quite advantageous; It was suggested that, in the time of salary negotiation in the interview human interaction is advisable. We can achieve bias-free good quality and speed derive process by applying AI in the recruitment process.

8.2 Landscape – Artificial Intelligence in Recruitment and Selection

The current developments in e-recruitment technology can be seen in AI-powered digital tools, for example, machine learning, natural language processing, deep learning and neural networks (Eubanks, 2018). Numerous regular procedures in recruitment and selection can be automated to save time and money (Bafna et al., 2019). An increasing number of companies are realizing the importance of investing in current digital HRM solutions, according to Bondarouk and Brewster (2016). With AI, e-recruitment can achieve considerable process gains by automating tedious selection processes and allowing recruiters to concentrate on their strategic work (Upadhyay and Khandelwal, 2018). Artificial intelligence (AI) is being used to automate routine processes like screening resumes, sending emails, setting reminders, and arranging interviews (Leong, 2018). When it comes to recruiting and hiring, the avoidance of boring chores such as applicant profile checks and screening interview scheduling is an important benefit (Taylor, 2018). As stated by Leong (2018), the application procedure may take several weeks, depending on the number of applicants. As a result, AI-enabled automation can free up recruiters to focus on finding and hiring the finest people. AI, according to Leong (2018), may help companies better understand their talent requirements by automating processes like candidate sourcing, resume scanning and application screening, all of which can help eliminate unconscious human bias in the hiring process. 'Recruitment cost efficiencies' (Dhamija, 2012; Sylva and Mol, 2009), 'reductions in paperwork', 'faster recruitment times' (Kim and O'Connor, 2009), and the 'increased possibility of finding and hiring the right candidate' (Lee, 2007; Parry and Tyson, 2008; Voermans and van Velthoven, 2007) can also be a benefit in the ability to attract passive candidates (McDougall, 2001).

8.3 AI in Screening

Recent advances in e-recruitment technology have shown up in the form of digital tools that make use of artificial intelligence (AI) capabilities like

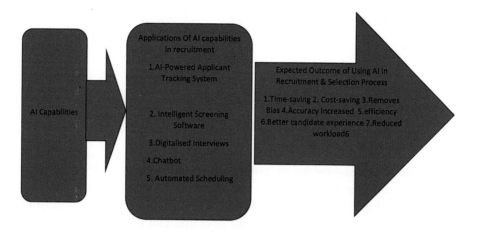

machine learning, natural language processing, deep learning and neural networks. (Eubanks, 2018).

As reported by Forbes in June 2018, the adoption of AI natural language generation (NLG) enables computers to write in a language and structured data in a way that is readable. Both NLP and NLG have a huge amount of potential in the recruitment of new employees. Therefore, However, to successfully communicate with humans, AI must first fully comprehend human written and spoken communication patterns to successfully include natural language processing. As stated by Faiagka and Ramantas (2012), a person's emotions can be determined by the use of linguistics, but if AI does not have solid algorithms to support its understanding of human spoken and written patterns, its decisions may be untrustworthy. With AI, the biggest positive argument is that it saves money and provides a real-time solution with virtually 100% accuracy. For both candidates and employers, this means that a speedy screening process can be a win-win for both parties. Before the final screening, the AI would have already completed the validation and verification of the criteria.

8.4 Conceptual Model

There is a common consensus worldwide that artificial intelligence has the potential to automate several recruitment processes. Artificial intelligence (AI) has the potential to positively influence the recruitment and selection process, according to many AI specialists.

8.5 Objectives of the Study

- To examine the applicability and range of use of artificial intelligence in the recruiting process.

- To study the Impact of artificial intelligence on recruitment based on case studies of a few select companies.

8.6 Methodology of the Study

This is a conceptual work based on literature reviews. The literature helps us grasp AI's meaning and how it fits into our hiring process. All of the paper's content is based on secondary sources such as websites, journals, reports, books and professional publications. The researcher began searching for relevant keywords to write the paper in the correct format, which led to the discovery of other research articles on AI and recruitment. As a result of employing Google's search engine, the researcher was able to locate other blogs that dealt solely with artificial intelligence, its significance and the commercial implications. The paper's main focus was on AI-aided recruitment.

8.7 Top 14 AI Recruiting Software 2022

8.7.1 Aiola

8.7.1.1 Aiola logo

As demand for its services grows, it is clear that Aiola is succeeding in its goal of bridging the gap between human and machine intelligence. It creates a central hub where recruiters and potential employees can interact easily. Aiola's smart platform processes all collected information, combining it with other sources to produce fresh insights.

8.7.2 Paradox.ai

8.7.2.1 Paradox logo

When job seekers interact with Paradox's chatbot agent, the AI uses natural language processing to gauge how well they understand the questions and ensures they are prepared for their upcoming interviews. Interviews, screenings, and other steps in the hiring process can be scheduled at the company's convenience. There is a self-service portal available for use by both the company and the applicants.

8.7.3 Skillate

8.7.3.1 Skillate logo

To ensure a quick and easy hiring process, Skillate is an AI-powered recruitment software with cutting-edge decision-making tools. Because of this, the candidate experience is enhanced, which in turn helps the company's reputation. Another way in which Skillate helps job seekers is by removing bias from the hiring process by keeping applicants' identities hidden. Instead, it employs deep learning to identify applications that indicate a candidate's suitability for a specific job. Also, JD assistants powered by artificial intelligence craft a compelling job description to help you find and hire the best candidates.

8.7.4 Hiretual

8.7.4.1 Hiretual logo

To build strong pipelines for current and future roles, Hiretual is best suited for large companies. Consequently, you will have a large pool of qualified candidates from which to choose. Hiretual also provides market insights to HR professionals, illuminating the types of candidates most likely to be hired. Faster optimization and complete transparency into the company's data are also assured.

8.7.5 Arya

8.7.5.1 Arya logo

Arya is essential for any recruiter making a good hire, whether they are internal or external. To better engage with candidates, you can use this artificial intelligence recruitment tool to find them across more than 50 social media platforms. The tool will be useful for businesses of all sizes. Since the cost of Arya depends on the number of users and the features they need, all you have to do is choose the best pricing tier for your business.

8.7.6 TurboHire

8.7.6.1 TurboHire logo

This intelligent AI-powered recruiting platform is equipped with tools for structured collaboration and data-driven hiring decisions. The system uses a robust encryption protocol to safeguard sensitive information about businesses and potential employees. By consolidating all of the administrative tasks associated with the hiring process into a single dashboard, it reduces the time and resources normally allocated to the process.

8.7.7 Eva.ai

8.7.7.1 EVA logo

EVA (a modular HR Tech Platform) automates and customises the user experience through the use of conversational AI and predictive ML. By adapting HR 4.0 (the latest iteration of the Human Resources function) to the processes of Talent Acquisition and Talent Management, EVA helps businesses achieve both growth and sustainability.

8.7.8 HiredScore

8.7.8.1 HiredScore logo

Another leading artificial intelligence recruiting tool in 2022, HiredScore streamlines the recruitment process for businesses. The software helps you achieve your workforce goals by providing tailored solutions like diversity and inclusion (D&I) analytics and bias prevention during the hiring process. These methods will help you streamline the hiring process and get more people interested in applying for jobs in the future.

8.7.9 Manatal

8.7.9.1 Manatal logo

Intelligent artificial intelligence (AI) powers Manatal, a recruitment software designed to streamline the hiring process for staffing firms and human resources departments. It has a tonne of cool, cutting-edge features like an AI that makes recommendations and scores candidates, social media enrichment, robust search capabilities, a career page builder and more. Additionally, Manatal's AI aids recruiters in evaluating candidates by identifying and integrating their social media profiles from over 20 different platforms. The Manatal team wants you to try out and benefit from all of these features to improve and streamline your hiring process, so they offer a free 14-day trial.

8.7.10 Humantelligence

8.7.10.1 Humantelligence logo

Humantelligence (HT) is a pioneer in the field of cultural intelligence and a leader in the recruitment technology industry. Humantelligence uses AI and integrates with your applicant tracking system (ATS) to give you access to the information you need to streamline your hiring process. In doing so, you will be able to remove bias, provide better candidates, streamline the onboarding process and increase the representation of different perspectives on your teams. Humantelligence allows managers to build high-performing teams across the company by gauging, managing and hiring for culture fit.

8.7.11 Eightfold.ai

8.7.11.1 Eightfol.ai logo

Eightfold is a great option for hiring managers who need to find and hire a large number of new employees. This is because it quickly and accurately sorts the best candidates for open positions from among millions of resumes. The AI-powered tool also advises users on which jobs they would be best suited for. These capabilities streamline both the talent acquisition procedure and the management of existing employees.

8.7.12 X0PA

8.7.12.1 X0PA logo

X0PA AI is an AI-driven B2B SaaS platform that uses predictive analytics on big data to aid in decision-making (artificial intelligence). X0PA AI makes use of AI, ML and RPA to streamline processes, improve output and cut down on waste on a massive scale. X0PA AI's solutions are highly flexible, allowing them to be adapted to meet the requirements of a wide variety of organizations, including businesses, SMEs, universities and government agencies.

8.7.13 Ceipal

8.7.13.1 Ceipal logo

Ceipal is one of the lowest-priced artificial intelligence (AI) recruitment tools in 2022. It provides competitive pricing packages, from which you can pick based on your needs and the size of your payroll. Ceipal's track record of success is undeniable, as the AI platform has been universally praised by both current and former customers around the world. You will also have access to a cutting-edge platform with a straightforward user interface, both of which will serve to boost efficiency. This is, of course, after the tool has been used to find and hire excellent candidates.

8.7.14 CVViZ

8.7.14.1 CVViZ logo

This cutting-edge artificial intelligence recruiting software finds the best possible jobs for users. During implementation, HR reps can gain insights that boost hire quality. The software is currently used by over 100 businesses of all sizes across the United States. Its ability to work with your current applicant tracking system (ATS) is its greatest strength, as it increases the likelihood that you will find qualified candidates quickly. In addition, all aspects of the hiring procedure, from advertising positions to extending offers, can be managed from a centralized location.

8.8 Role of AI in Recruitment

Every business should be looking forward to 2022 for the use of AI in recruitment, as this will allow them to find the kind of talented workers who will help their company thrive. The best part about AI in HR is how rapidly it is gaining favour with business owners and personnel directors. Although AI has a long way to go before it can replace human intelligence, tools built on the technology do help HR professionals make better judgements. The tools are adaptable and provide a wealth of possibilities, such as automating the hiring process and storing crucial company information for later use. To put it briefly, AI has a positive effect on a business model and allows you to enter markets with more stringent hiring requirements. Additionally, analytics will be better integrated and decisions will be made without bias. You will end up spending less time and money overall.

8.9 AI Applications in Recruitment: Select Case Study

Artificial intelligence (AI), the Internet of Things (IoT), big data analysis, cloud computing and other technologies from the industry 4.0 revolutionized recruiting and other HR processes (Liu et al., 2018), but HRM is still in the early phases of adoption. The employer-applicant relationship has been radically transformed by AI. AI solutions like chatbot give job seekers a fresh perspective on the hiring process. It is also possible to automate the assessment process of the candidate, interview scheduling with the candidate, check references and deliver job offers to the individuals selected. At the moment, just 10% of organizations employ AI in a high context, while 36% of organizations are predicted to fully utilize AI in the future (Harver,

2020). AI applications that have been embraced by giant organizations will be discussed in this section.

Fetcher – Case 1
www.fetcher.ai
As a rapidly growing tech company, Frame.io is constantly hiring, with diversity hiring being a top priority since it is deeply rooted in their values. While the team receives many referrals & inbound applicants, they know that sourcing for each role is necessary to ensure a strong pipeline of diverse, high-quality candidates. Before utilizing Fetcher, Sr. Director of Talent and DE&I, Anna Chalon, and her recruiting team were spread thin and were spending countless hours sourcing for all open roles to build a diverse pipeline. Anna knew that sourcing was essential in building a diverse talent pipeline, but that she and her team were overextended, so she turned to Fetcher for help. Anna and her team utilized Fetcher's combination of human and machine intelligence feature to analyse thousands of profiles for every search, allowing them to build a robust pipeline of diverse, qualified candidates, without needing more time in the day. After identifying great talent, Fetcher made it easy to engage via email, sending automated, personalized messages to prospects. Fetcher gave Frame.io the bandwidth to source for all their open roles and send more outreach than they could ever manage manually. Using Fetcher, Anna and her team were able to build a robust, diverse pipeline in just a few weeks. Best of all, in under 12 months, Fetcher helped Frame.io hire 11 new employees, 9 of which (82%) were women and/or underrepresented minorities. 'With Fetcher, we were able to build a better pipeline with no more effort from our team', said Anna. Furthermore, 'When it came to choosing a platform, pricing was an important consideration for us. With Fetcher, the value we gain compared to its price is huge. We are growing really quickly and Fetcher has become an integral part of our hiring strategy. The return on investment (ROI) we get from it is really high'. 'Fetcher has freed up time and given us the capacity to diversify our pipeline more organically. This has allowed us to make some incredible hires, mostly from underrepresented groups, over the last year'. (Anna Chalon, Sr. Director of Talent and DE&I at Frame.io).

Talkpush – Case 2

www.talkpush.com

Apps like Talkpush have been deployed by Amazon and Walmart to improve communication with job applicants. In other words, it is indeed a CRM-enabled communications channel. the solution that uses chatbot and video screening techniques for an instant, tailored, real-time dialogue. It is apparent from the AI applications listed above that major organizations are utilizing these tools to eliminate human bias while also saving time and resources when it comes to hiring skilled employees. All of these programmes, however, assist humans in their work, thus the human element is not being omitted. Human resources management tasks are becoming more strategic in nature.

Alorica – Case 3

Optimizing the Candidate Experience While Making Connections Easier for Recruiters

Alorica, a global BPO, with offices in every continent, has over 100,000 employees worldwide. With such a huge audience, Alorica uses a regional approach when it comes to its recruitment operations, choosing strategies and solutions that adapt to each of its local markets. It was under this premise that Alorica Central America and the Caribbean (including Panama and Jamaica) began the shift from manual recruitment operations, to an automated process that would provide a fast and easy journey to all of their candidates. With Talkpush as their CRM and chatbot, Alorica is now automating 95% of top-of-funnel recruitment tasks, freeing up their recruiters to focus on top talent while giving every candidate a delightful experience.

HireVue – Case 4

Protective apparel for industrial users is manufactured by National Safety Apparel (NSA). The business was in desperate need of a mechanism to discover and evaluate skilled employees and swiftly fill open positions. When it came to personnel levels at NSA's Ohio production, the company faced a unique dilemma. As a result, the team decided to use HireVue's conversational AI to help them achieve their goals and manage their staffing numbers more effectively. Because of this, HireVue stands apart from the competition because of its simple setup and low cost. Working with the Customer Success team, NSA designed and implemented an interview tracking and scheduling platform. This allowed recruiters to focus on interviewing and hiring the finest prospects without being overwhelmed by the time-consuming tasks that were previously required. Recruiter time savings can make a big strategic difference in a business with a large volume of hiring. NSA was able to make significant improvements to both the hiring process and the results of that procedure. Candidates might use text or a web chatbot on their careers page to find a job, pre-screen for a position and then self-schedule an interview in minutes. Recruiters could conduct interviews with top applicants in less time because NSA no longer relied on recruiters to perform manual screening. For the first time, recruiters and candidates were able to schedule an interview in a matter of days instead of weeks. Candidates no longer had to wait 60 days for an offer because of these shortened limits. Four times as many applicants received offers to join NSA in 15 days as previously. At this point, the NSA's hiring needs are well-managed, the company can respond rapidly to changes, and costs are reduced. When it comes to hiring, they have found that chatbots have saved them 6.5 weeks a year in time and money. When the team is freed up, they can devote their time to onboarding new employees and ensuring that they have an exceptional onboarding experience.

- 2× more than double their usual candidates
- 50% less time than ever before
- Time saver did not have to waste time manually sifting through forms.

"It is quick to implement and there was an instant connection with the sales and support team. Customer service and response rates have been world-class."

8.10 AI in Recruitment: An Impact Assessment

Based on the literature review, the following are the expected outcomes of utilizing AI in the recruitment and selection process.

- Time-saving

- Cost-saving

- Removes bias

- Accuracy

- Increased efficiency

- Better candidate experience

- Reduced workload

8.11 Biasness

Racism, age and ethnicity are all factors that can be influenced by bias. The background of a candidate can be mostly ignored by AI. According to a 2015 Google recruitment tool called qDroid, interviewers are given more reliable questions based on the role for which the candidate is interviewing and over-look the applicant's past. An applicant's likelihood of success in the role he or she is applying for can currently be predicted using data and predictive analytics, Automated algorithms use job-specific and other characteristics linked to an organization's cultural requirements to determine each applicant's match result (Neelie, 2017).Artificial Intelligence (AI) can be used to automate the screening process and combat human bias (Cara Heilmann, 2018;AlexandraLevit, 2017). To put it another way, AI can be taught to disregard a candidate's past. AI can help recruiters see candidates' existing skills that are hidden by unconscious prejudices (Alexandra Levit, 2017). They used AI to organize 'blind auditions', which allowed recruiters to see prior keywords in a candidate's resume to better judge talent (Savar, 2017). Despite their considerable problem-solving capabilities, AIs remain merely tools. A tool's performance will suffer if it is not properly calibrated. Artificial Intelligence bias is a manifestation of this problem. Skewed outcomes will be obtained if you feed an AI-biased data. (Gold, 2019).

8.12 Best Fit Candidate

Automated screening tools can be used once the organizations have a list of potential candidates, allowing humans to decrease the list. According to some techniques, the content of a candidate's CV can be used to identify the best candidates. To select the most potential prospects, other candidates employ a variety of tests and questions. Finding the correct person-to-work fit is more accurate and has a greater success rate when using both strategies. To begin, the readability and other relevant qualities of the source documents will be addressed, and the optimum match for the system will be worked out. Employees that do not fit in with their workplace culture are the most common cause of failure in the workplace. This problem can be solved with AI. An algorithm is already being used by some of the world's biggest businesses to match open positions with those on a company's employment board. You can tell if an applicant is a good fit for a position on LinkedIn by looking at their profile and past employment history. LinkedIn is doing this. This AI will be increasingly accurate at predicting if specific participants or candidates in the workplace fulfil the job description if it is aware that some job descriptions are model fits. There will, however, always be a need for human intervention. Alistair Cox (2018). As the popularity of remote work has grown over the past few years, companies are scrambling to find qualified applicants to fill these positions. Nowadays, AI solutions can really assist, especially if you engage remote personnel. It is hard to believe, but artificial intelligence (AI) can be used to assess a job candidate's honesty and morals. The business is in a position to conduct background checks on applicants and then allocate workers accordingly. Uber, Zomato, and other on-demand companies have found that AI functionality is a tremendous asset (Christopher McFadden, 2019).

8.13 Conclusion

It is important to understand the major benefits the organization will have which will increase the efficiency, and time-saving in the functions of recruitment process. As we all are aware that human resource is one of the most important assets of the organization, through the help of AI we can have the right people in the right place working to their full potential to achieve the goal of the organization. In light of the widespread acceptance of AI and the scarcity of trained workers, AI-based solutions have the potential to fill this gap and revolutionize the workplace. This means that the impact of artificial intelligence on business is substantial, and that AI can establish a better recruitment model. As AI develops further, it will have a profound impact on how businesses conduct themselves in the years to come. By adopting the new demands of technology, both people and businesses can have a better future while reducing their stress.

References

[1] Dashveenjit Kaur (2021). Has artificial intelligence revolutionized recruitment? TechWire Asia. Expert Panel. (2019). 10 Downsides of Using Artificial Intelligence In The Hiring Process. Forbes Coaches Council. Retrieved July 31, 2021, from https://www.forbes.com/sites/forbescoachescouncil/2019/08/14/10- downsides-of-using-artificial-intelligence-in-the-hiring-process/?sh=72f12d2c685e.

[2] Bafna, P., Shirwaikar, S. and Pramod, D. (2019), "Task recommender system using semantic clustering to identify the right personnel", VINE Journal of Information and Knowledge Management Systems, Vol. 49 No. 2.

[3] Eubanks, B. (2018), Artificial Intelligence for HR: use AI to Support and Develop a Successful Workforce, 1 ed., Kogan Page Ltd, London, N.Y.

[4] Bondarouk, T. and Brewster, C. (2016), "Conceptualising the future of HRM and technology research", The International Journal of Human Resource Management, Vol. 27 No. 21, pp. 2652–2671.

[5] Upadhyay, A.K. and Khandelwal, K. (2018), "Applying artificial intelligence: implications for recruitment", Strategic HR Review, Vol. 17 No. 5.

[6] Leong, C. (2018), "Technology and recruiting 101: how it works and where it's going", Strategic HR Review, Vol. 17 No. 1, pp. 50–52.

[7] Dhamija, P. (2012), "E-recruitment: a roadmap towards e-human resource management", Researchers World, Vol. 3 No. 3.

[8] Kim, S. and O'Connor, J.G. (2009), "Assessing electronic recruitment implementation in state governments: issues and challenges", Public Personnel Management, Vol. 38 No. 1.

[9] Parry, E. and Strohmeier, S. (2014), "HRM in the digital age – digital changes and challenges of the HR profession", Employee Relations, Vol. 36 No. 4

[10] Voermans, M. and van Veldhoven, M.J.P.M. (2007), "Attitude towards E-HRM: an empirical study at Philips", Personnel Review, Vol. 36 No. 6, pp. 887–902

9

The Impact of Implementing Artificial Intelligence in Human Resource Management: A Theoretical and Conceptual Framework

S. Gomathi[1], Anjali Sabale[1] and Naveen Chilamkurti[2]

[1]VIT Business School, Vellore Institute of Technology, Vellore, Tamil Nadu, India
[2]La Trobe University, Australia

Email: sgomatthi@vit.ac.in; anjali.sabale2020@vitstudent.ac.in; n.chilamkurti@latrobe.edu.au

Abstract

Artificial intelligence (AI) has evolved the business methodology in public and private organizations. Despite newly developed AI technology, many of the firms still face problems enduring the profits from performance. Also, several studies to date debate improving the capability and resources in an organization. Recruiters are using artificial intelligence software to enhance the value of creating and recruiting more proficient selection and recruitment processes. AI can avail extensive views to exaggerate the function of human resources.

This chapter emphasizes the concept of disruptive artificial intelligence in an organization. We focus on developing a theoretical and conceptual framework for the importance of artificial intelligence (AI) in human resource management (HRM). It also focuses on the impact and consequences of disruptive technologies in the firm. Finally, we plan to identify the essential components that solve the difficulties in adapting artificial intelligence.

Consequently, the primary purpose of this research is to use an artificial neural network (ANN) which helps to learn and recall potential employees.

Furthermore, it eases the workflow pattern of the organization and therefore enhances the performance of the business.

9.1 Introduction

Organizations are widely benefited from the upcoming innovations in technology. Any firm in small or large businesses aims to cope with existing development in the market. Hence, they accomplish enormous growth in their business. Today, the market receives frequent and constant changes in technology. Therefore, it is essential to cross over the challenges faced and grab the opportunities in front to grow the business.

All companies in business could not match the trend of developing progressively. However, many firms had accepted the technological change and are under aim to progress their business with its help. Unfortunately, few companies are struggling to make use of data analytics. However, 56% of CEOs accept the change aggressively and are ready to pursue flexibility and agility with immediate action (IBM 2022).

Human resource management (HRM) plays an essential role in every organization. It is a critical factor that holds the business in the changing environment (Ertel, 2018). Artificial intelligence (AI) is the technology that became essential for learning in every organization. It is the science that mimics intelligent behaviour and human abilities through technology. As the days pass, artificial intelligence is taking over the attention in every field. However, AI is yet to uncover in human resource management.

Researchers distinguished technology into two categories: disruptive technology and sustaining technology. He described disruptive technology as the process which relocates the current technology resulting in fluctuating the pattern of the whole industry. He states that successful organizations may lose leadership in the market if they fail to accept disruptive technology (D.S. Stanley, V.Aggarwal, 2019). Artificial intelligence is one of the categories of disruptive technology.

Artificial intelligence is expanding widely worldwide. Additionally, due to enormous research, AI has developed tools for stretching its value in the market. The launched tools are intelligent resource management, fuzzy sets and neural networks. AI in human resources is involved in various activities like problem-solving, decision-making, repetitive daily workflow, strategy, and innovative work and also monitoring employees' attendance, capability, etc. AI supports managers to avoid repetitive work by maintaining records in its database. However, artificial intelligence has provided vast advantages for the growth of an organization. The flow of work using AI technology saves time and is helpful to provide a valuable and effective output for companies' benefit.

The objective plan is to explore the unique path for HRM that artificial intelligence demands future. This study aims to focus on the technological impact on the organization's business and the employees working in the firm. Furthermore, we aim to create a theoretical framework for the strategic management of human resources, which will be helpful to find out the solution to handle the evolution of technology.

The literature review aims to develop the theoretical and conceptual framework to study the detailed information on artificial intelligence in human resource management. The past literature on this topic supports the flow of this study to achieve its goal. It will emphasize the application of AI in an organization, its impact after implementing AI, and the knowledge to tackle the consequences while implementing AI.

Human resource management is the approach to aims to hold employees who have the capability and skills in a variety of techniques like personnel, culture and structure to bring the organization an inexpensive advantage (Storey, 2004). Several practices are involved in HRM for smooth and efficient workflow, including decision-making, hiring and managing employees, etc. Specifically, HR focus on recruiting new employees by keeping up their level in an organization. It is due to continuous change in technology, requiring the perfect management with proficient employees (Bibi, Pangil & Johari, 2016). The confounding speed of the changes in business growth is shifting the focus on incorporating disruptive technologies like machine learning and artificial intelligence. However, reality and theory are two different approaches. The theory seems to be successful, but the real challenges may hold back the implementation (Hekkala, 2019). So, several organizations are afraid to come forward to implement the new technologies available in the market.

Minbaeva (2020) states that most firms are defying to take up the initial step to developing data analytics abilities. Their analysis showed that 41% of employers were not interested in utilizing their organization's latest data analytic tools. Artificial intelligence classifies a comprehensive class of technologies that require human support for various functions like decision-making, problem-solving, analysing a large set of data, etc.

Furthermore, it is observed that several companies worldwide facing limitless capacity challenges for implementing AI in the HR functions for adopting AI in their work process (Aspan, 2020; Brin and Nehme, 2019). On the other hand, firms like IBM, Amazon, Apple, Tesla, etc., adopted AI in the HR work processes by overcoming all the hurdles of employees and the firm.

It is seen that organizations that are in the business of finance, marketing, etc., are ready to adopt AI-based systems and technology but hesitate to accept artificial intelligence-based processes for their human resource department. Some firms started accepting this new technology but these numbers are very low.

Studies have been done to understand the applicability of technology-based HR systems in the organization and found that the E-HRM and E-business had a major impact on the performance of the organization. The studies have also shown that the contribution of E-HRM to the system is based more on professional HRM practices and activities rather than traditional processes (Sanders, 2007).

The application of AI in HR functions is virtually related to each other that are useful in the field of the recruitment process in the firm. It saves the transactional cost and headcount of the human resource department in the organization. Older and Omotayo (2014) study emphasized that implementing technology in an organization helped business performance by saving other resources.

Studies have focused also on the impact of artificial intelligence on the HR department of an organization. The results from various studies have emphasized that the acceptance of technology in human resource management helps in contributing to a positive attitude in the system and stretching the proficient activities of human resource management (Panos and Bellou, 2016).

El-Dirani et.al. (2019) has also explained the influence of AI on the organization for their growth and future. The study focus was on using AI for all the employees in the organizations. It has shown that AI has significant support for activities like decision-making in a critical situation, handling ambiguity, accurate decision-making without human bias, etc. This study emphasized that the employee plays a significant role in implementing AI. However, humans need to be involved while making a subconscious decision to evaluate the outcome of the decisions. Furthermore, few researchers have identified and used AI-based techniques named artificial neural networks for workforce scheduling, talent selection, employees' personality assessment or stress identification, etc. It is a specific representation of artificial intelligence like system engineering, data processing, clustering, data mining, adaptive control, etc. (Birau, 2014).

Owais Ahmed (2018) explored the ideology of applying artificial intelligence and robotics in business. This study indicates that AI might influence varied processes during the production of the products, planning, research customers, development and performance.

Similarly, several studies in the market are incorporated which indicate that artificial intelligence is crucial in the field of human resources. Therefore, the majority of HR practices will become easy to perform with a complete transformation in the field of human resources. This study will attempt to learn about the application of human resources in various reputed organizations and their outcomes.

9.2 The Theoretical Framework of the Study

In this competitive world, technology has changed the environment of the industry. In this successively running organization, artificial intelligence has given a positive approach to the growth of the business. According to the current survey done by IBM 2022, 52% of members of the organization accept providing excellent business results (IBM, 2022). Artificial intelligence in the organization shows the impact on their increase in performance. Many researchers have emphasized their knowledge of applying artificial intelligence in various sectors.

Initially, computers were designed for numeric calculations. However, the revolution of knowledge and mental activities was used for philosophical problems, data collection and gameplay, which is considered the demand for intelligence (McCarthy et al, 1955).

The theory of artificial intelligence has yet not been solved and accepted by any researcher. The reason is that it is still a process that is misunderstood by many researchers. Hence, artificial intelligence is the collaboration of functions specified in algorithmic and computational terms, which are engrossed in computers and have a solution to all the practical problems (Russell and Norvig, 2010).

Artificial intelligence theory was considered unsuccessful by many researchers. But few of them believed that artificial intelligence is worth investigating. Hence, the initial theory that came into focus was the Unified Theory of Cognition. In this theory, the scientist argued the importance of AI and the link with cognitive science in unified theories. This theory attempts to focus on artificial intelligence and human intelligence (Newell, 1990).

In recent times AGI (artificial general intelligence) came into focus. AGI was adopted by a few researchers who highlighted the general purpose of intelligence as a whole (Bringsjord, 2008).

V. Yashchenko (2014) stated specific general theories of artificial intelligence. Below are those.

- Study of neural-like elements and multidimensional neural growing networks.

- Study the functional organization of the artificial intelligence systems, motor systems, sensor systems, motivation, thinking and behaviour.

- Temporary and long-term memory.

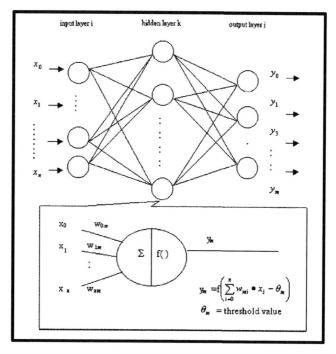

Figure 9.1   A basic structure of neural network.Source: J.Nguyenet al.(2017).

Under human resource management, managers play an essential part in business operations. Hence, there is a need to implement activities to develop managerial skills. All the skills of managers are now equipped with computer technology. The application of information technology in the organization boosted the business with smooth workflow. Artificial intelligence plays a significant role in creating a human resource information system (HRIS). HRIS had played a significant role in organizing the available data, saving time with good output from the employees.

Nguyen et al. (2017), explain the artificial neural network (ANN) in human resource management. It uses the supporting platform of XING for this purpose. It is the career-oriented social network that is helpful to find out the anticipated job and the recruiters. It is helpful to find out the best candidate for a specific job. An artificial Neural network is created with the neural network toolbox in MATLAB to predict the appropriate candidate with the correct users. This research created a two-layer feed-forward network that used an algorithm, namely Levenberg–Marquardt backpropagation algorithm, for good prediction.

Artificial neural networks (ANN) are the basic structure or layer that forms the forecasting system. A neural network is in the form of connected nerves in the human body. It forms a corrective supporting system to align together.

Based on the above theory of artificial neural network (ANN) the theoretical framework of the human resource management are represented in Figure 9.2.

9.3 Conceptual Framework

Artificial intelligence theories are evolving day by day. It is used in many sectors for enhancing performance. AI is the recent trend in the field of human resources. Nevertheless, AI had placed a massive impact on the management of an organization (Inanov and Webster, 2017). With the increasing burden to perform various tasks in an organization implementation of artificial intelligence became a necessity. The market is changing rapidly, hence to match the changes in the business environment funds are being invested by the firms.

The theoretical structure prepared for artificial intelligence in human resource management relates the network to an organization. It explains the basic ideology and the ultimate results of an organization while using artificial intelligence.

Additionally, artificial intelligence expands its impact on various functions involved in human resource management. The functions in human resource management are selection, training, recruitment, performance management and compensation. All these functions stimulated the business with a quality output of the employees (Agrawal et al., 2019).

We prepared a conceptual framework for the functions to elaborate on the impact of artificial intelligence in human resource management.

Based on the above theory of artificial neural network (ANN) the conceptual framework of the study is represented in Figure 9.3.

9.4 Research Methodology

This research is developed based on the data available in the literature. The evaluations of this study support the concept of artificial intelligence in the various functions of human resource management of an organization. Information from various other sources like websites, books, journals, articles and research papers was drafted together to identify the impact of this disruptive technology on the organization. Artificial Intelligence is the dependent variable, whereas human resource management is the independent

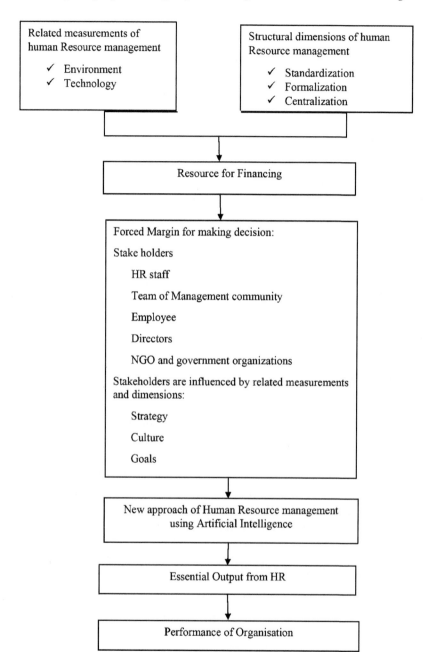

Figure 9.2   Theoretical framework of artificial intelligence in human resource management functions.

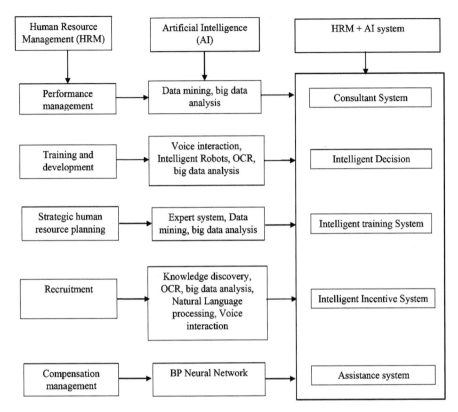

Figure 9.3   Conceptual framework of artificial intelligence in human resource management functions.

variable to prepare the spot-on conceptual framework in the research. The study identified the challenges of the various organization by referring to the data and hence accomplishing the findings or suggestions by applying artificial intelligence in their organization.

9.5 Development and Findings

The application of artificial Intelligence in human resource management is vivid. Various organizations face varied challenges while developing artificial intelligence in their business. We researched the cause of disruption technology in human resource management by referring to various data available and found out the outcome or findings while applying artificial intelligence.

Below are the challenges while implementing artificial intelligence to protect the disruption technology.

9.6 Lack of Proficient Employees and Limitation of Budget

Implementing artificial intelligence in an organization has brought all the board of directors into a complex situation. Recruiting and dismissal of the actual staff numbers may lead to a decrease in product development and a decrease in consumers. Hence, considering the ethics, expenses and behaviour for implementing AI is a must to take the right and immediate decision.

After a review of company cases and studies, it is found that 58.8% of the risk is from the excessive trust in AI systems, 37.3% risk is due to the lack of transparency in the process, and 23.5% risk is due to unemployment and redundancy of traditional occupations. The employee's attitude is increased towards the job and increases in quality of work.

- **The intellectual assumption that AI will solve the problem:**
  AI had become a tremendous impact on several organizations. However, AI needs to apply with proper understanding and training. It should be developed equally.

  Findings: Though AI is in application in several organizations, self-awareness of the system is the most aspirational study.

- **Ignoring the attitude that AI application is not possible in the particular industry:**
  Artificial intelligence is developed to make it useful in all sectors. Every organization works to make their HR team strong for being consistent in their business. The application of AI plays a significant role in many sectors. Therefore, artificial intelligence should be considered before ruling it out for any firm growth.

  Findings: If any firm is not ready to invest its time and money into AI, it is still efficient knowledge because it is impacting many industries worldwide.

- **Attempt to leverage artificial intelligence without sufficient data:**
  Artificial intelligence in human resource management needs to be investigated thoroughly. It is necessary to understand the quality of data that is available in the market. Random information may ruin the upbringing of the business in an organization. Therefore, complete and genuine knowledge such as correct data for conducting analysis, learning and finding patterns play a significant role.

Findings: Missing to acquire all the required and quality data may ruin the company's growth by profit and develop more problems. Hence, reliable data before diving to accomplish the results might be helpful to reach the goal.

- **Deployment issue in artificial intelligence:**
  Deployment in an organization needs a variety of capabilities like upskilling of employees, the approach of organizational management, alteration in the business process, and organizational culture. Therefore, deployment requires a vast investment by an organization. Through substantial investigation, market research globally had reported that deployment challenges are vastly spread with artificial intelligence and big data.

  Findings: Our study reported that 14.6% of the organization had deployed artificial intelligence technologies. Also, 30% of respondents worldwide use artificial intelligence in their process across multiple functions in an organization.

- **Talent issues in AI:**
  HR management in any organization consists of recruiting the right proficient candidate for a certain post. Artificial intelligence intervention improves the hiring process, thereby increasing the effective outcome.

  Findings: Human intelligence, when combined with artificial intelligence enhances the recruiting process seamlessly. The time and effort are streamlined, enabling the focus on interactive and meaningful processes.

All these issues variously impact the organization. The challenges and resolution of the problem is the most necessary result to overcome the disruptive form of artificial intelligence. The above-explained points are on the path of disrupting artificial intelligence. We need to explore more by viewing the platform in a more optimistic and pragmatic view. To improvise the impact of artificial intelligence in an organization, the sustainability formula in human resource management will work.

Disruption problems are massive challenges that need to be overcome by all organizations. However, many organizations have worked on their problems and are into successive businesses. To analyse the impact of artificial intelligence on organizations, a few company processes are reviewed. Table 9.1 presented the outcome and process information of the companies which are using artificial intelligence-based systems.

Table 9.1   Outcome and process information of the companies using artificial intelligence-based Systems.

Company name	Disruption artificial intelligence tackled	Researched data	Successful outcomes
Infosys	Adaptation of new technology and lack of trust was the major concern noticed in the initial stages of implementing artificial intelligence.	To overcome the challenges tall the professionals in the firm were interviewed to discuss about the understanding of the employees on adaptability capacity of the organization with new technologies over artificial intelligence and the value of it after implementation.	Implementation of AI in the organization had made way for making the decision on the recruitment process simpler. Thereby, impacting the turnover of the organization.
Deloitte	Knowledge of artificial intelligence is still not a clear picture to much higher management. This technology was proven to give a massive impact on the performance of the business. Deloitte identified that the human resource department lacks the knowledge of AI which is becoming a barrier to the company's growth.	6000 executives performed well by IBM. It was noticed in the survey of human resource experts in 2017	The data observed that 52% of the organization were doubtful to adopt AI within five years. 22% of organization with high performance adopted AI technology.
Farmer Insurance	Deployment challenges are widely spread among various organization. Farmer insurance has similar concerns to cope with this newly developed technology. This firm has a unique and organized process that had helped the firm to move forward in the pilot phase to full deployment.	54% of the executives were involved to accept that the AI was beneficial to move the prototype into the production process. Also, 52% of the employees developed and implemented a road map for AI in their business.	Artificial intelligence had played a key role in the business of farmer insurance. This approach became a boost for all such organization for getting an artificial intelligence system into deployment.
EY	Artificial intelligence implementation was in the urge to rule out in this organization due to various challenges like a lack of talented professionals, proper equipment maintenance, Integration, privacy and security.	The interviews of all the HR professionals were conducted globally. Also, many privileged members of the firm were also interrogated to learn about the major concern and loopholes for AI implementation.	HR applicants are trained well to contribute to the impending rise of employee knowledge and hence boost the performance of the employee along with the business. Therefore, HR employees are endowed with artificial intelligence to predict, diagnose and analyse with skilled resources.

9.7 Discussion

In current studies, artificial intelligence proves that it is an essential implementation factor in daily life. It had transformed the task of each individual into a task of computers. It has evolved from software smartphone apps to software to track a menstrual cycle. Hence, artificial intelligence plays an essential influencer on a daily basis for all human beings (Sinniah et al., 2020).

Machine learning and artificial intelligence is the latest disruptive technology imposed in human resource management in an organization. Human resources in the firm had impacted the organization efficiently to have skilled talent. Growing numbers of firms worldwide are undertaking digital transformation to aggressively leverage AI and ML in the business journey (Hind et al., 2020).

AI is on the voyage of progress in each field. However, there is far less progress in problems related to the appropriate decision, recruitment process and management of employees. Therefore, artificial intelligence is a dreadful requirement for human resources in terms of efficient impact on the organization's business. This substantial effect on the facilities and the work pattern emphasizes human resource digitization. The application of artificial intelligence is progressively essential to observe the changes within the organization in their activities, and employees must distribute their explicit skills apart from their routine work. Thereby, the human resource management must involve the basic information refined by the computer service, to look into the challenge that all the big companies are experiencing. Furthermore, the organization should explore various approaches to implement AI in its business growth strategies. To make these implementations true, HR professionals must be competent in emphasizing a strategic plan at an organizational level.

Our study focused on developing a theoretical and conceptual framework to identify the significance of artificial intelligence in an organization. The various organization suffered from implementing artificial intelligence in force. Hence, this study investigated the challenges and their successful outcomes after implementing AI in the HR department of various prominent firms in the market.

The implementation of artificial intelligence (AI) in human resource management is relatively new. Many organizations struggle to avail the requirements for implementing AI in their organization. Hence it becomes difficult for the firm to develop the software for proper application. Artificial intelligence was researched without sufficient incorporation of AI in the companies; it limits exploring the implication and effectiveness of AI in the organization's HR department. To make a detailed investigation, this research soothed the process of researching the challenges faced by the organization and its effective outcome in the business.

Additionally, in the future, we need to explore this research by incorporating the quantitative approach to employee management decisions, recruitment process, etc., prepared by artificial intelligence. We need to notice the estimation of the company's turnover in statistical terms. This research could be taken to the next level by studying the impact of AI on organizations in several countries. It should be country-specific research that will be helpful to understand the impact of artificial intelligence in an organization worldwide. To receive a comprehensive perspective on this topic, we aim to explore more organizations for their capacity and ability to implement AI. We also aim to eliminate gender discrimination among applicants in the future.

9.8 Conclusion

The finding is shown in this study exhibit that the implementation of AI and the speedy adaptability approach of the organization have made critical benefits for themselves their business. Similar to this, training to convert their employees brought them technology readiness and helped them overcome the main challenges. The well-defined organizations considered in this study are Infosys, Deloitte, Farmer insurance, and Ernst & Young. These firms identified their limitation in implementing AI in the overall recruitment process, managing employee data, decision-making, low budget, lack of talented professionals, etc. Our study identified the challenges and their successful outcome after implementing AI in their business. This study emphasizes pinpointing the consequences of the implementation of AI in the organizations that guided and helped the recruitment process more authenticating and handful. Similarly, with the use of AI, many more functions like talent management, training, compensation, etc. are made easy, uncomplicated and predictive, which significantly affect the turnover of organizations. This study extended the knowledge of AI in an organization and encouraged other large or small firms to improve their activities, which will intervene in the business outcomes. AI expands the conventional process and helps to be competent for contributing the vast options for both organization and the employees.

References

[1] Ertel, W. (2020). Artificial Intelligence and Society', Education of Artificial Intelligence, pp:1–19, doi: https://doi.org/10.1155/2021/8812542
[2] Stanley, D.S; and Aggarwal.V. (2019) Impact of disruptive technology on human resource management practices', International Journal

of Business Continuity and Risk Management, vol 9. doi:10.1504/IJBCRM.2019.102608

[3] Storey, D.J. (2004). Exploring the link, among small firms, between management training and firm performance: a comparison between the UK and other OECD countries. The international Journal of Human Resource Management, 15(1).https://doi.org/10.1080/0958519032000157375

[4] Bibi, P., Pangil, F., and Johari, J. (2016). HRM practices and employees' retention: the perspective of job embeddedness theory. Asian Journal of multidisciplinary study, 4(5), 41–47. ISSN2348-7186, website:http://repo.uum.edu.my/id/eprint/18284/1/AJMS%20%204%205%20 2016%2041%2047.pdf

[5] Hekkala,S .(2019). Integration of artificial intelligence into recruiting digital natives in Finland: the perceptions of 20–23-year-old students', Aalto University, School of Business. doi:: https://hdl.handle.net/10125/70632

[6] Minbaeva, D. (2020). Disrupted HR? Human Resource Management Rev. Elsevier Inc. doi:https://doi.org/10.1016/j.hrmr.2021.100824

[7] Aspan, H.(2020). Individual characteristics and job characteristics on work effectiveness in the state-owned company: the moderating effect of emotional intelligence. Int J InnovCreatChang (IJICC). 13(6):761–774. https://www.ijicc.net/images/vol_13/Iss_6/13690_Aspan_2020_E_R.pdf

[8] Sanders, N.R. (2007). An empirical study of the impact of e-business technologies on organizational collaboration and performance', Journal of Operations Management, Vol. 25, No. 6, p.1332. doi:10.1016/j.jom.2007.01.008

[9] Oladele, I.O; and Omotayo, O.A. (2014). E-human resource management and organizational performance (E-HRM) in the Nigerian banking industry: an empirical study of guaranty trust bank plc (GTBank). Vol. 7, No. 1, pp.10–20. Doi:10.2139/ssrn.3967550

[10] Panos, S; and Bellou. V. (2016). Maximizing E-HRM outcomes: a moderated mediation path', Management Decision. Vol. 54, No. 5, pp.1088–1109. doi:10.1108/MD-07-2015-0269

[11] Birau, F.R. (2014). Forecasting financial time series based on Artificial Neural Networks, IMPACT: International Journal of Research in Business Management (IMPACT: IJRBM),ISSN(E): 2321-886X; ISSN(P). 2347-4572, Vol. 2, Issue 4, Apr 2014, pp. 63–66. Doi:https://doi.org/10.21919/remef.v15i1.376

[12] El-Dirani, A., Hussein, M. M;&Hejase. H. J. (2019). The Role of Human Resources in Change Management: An Exploratory Study in Lebanon. The Journal of Middle East and North Africa Sciences. 5(6), 1–13]. (P-ISSN 2412- 9763) - (e-ISSN 2412-8937).www.jomenas.org.

[13] Dr. OwaisAhmed.(2018). Artificial Intelligence in HR. International Journal of Research and Analytical Reviews. (IJRAR). Pp 971–978. https://www.ijrar.org/papers/IJRAR1944797.pdf

[14] McCarthy, J., Minsky, M., Rochester, N. and Shannon, C. (1955). A Proposal for the Dartmouth Summer Research Project on Artificial Intelligence. doi:https://doi.org/10.1609/aimag.v27i4.1904

[15] Russell, S; and Norvig, P. (2010). Artificial Intelligence: A Modern Approach, 3rd edn. (Prentice Hall, Upper Saddle River, New Jersey). website:https://zoo.cs.yale.edu/classes/cs470/materials/aima2010.pdf

[16] Newell, A. (1990). Unified Theories of Cognition. Harvard University Press, Cambridge, Massachusetts.

[17] Bringsjord, S. (2008). The logicist manifesto: At long last let logic-based artificial intelligence become a field unto itself. Journal of Applied Logic, 6, 4, pp. 502–525. doi:https://doi.org/10.1016/j.jal.2008.09.001

[18] Yashchenko, V.(2014). Artificial intelligence theory (Basic concepts). Science and Information Conference, pp. 473–480, doi: 10.1109/SAI.2014.6918230.

[19] Nguyen, J; Sanchez-Hemandez, G; Amisen, A; Argell, N; Rovira, X; Angulo, C. (2017). A linguistic multi-criteria decision-aiding system to support university career services. doi: https://doi.org/10.1016/j.asoc.2017.06.052

[20] Inanoy and Webster. (2017). 'Challenges in Adopting Artificial Intelligence (AI) in HRM Practices: A study on Bangladesh Perspective. Vol 1, Issue 1, 2021, pp: 66–73. DOI:10.5281/zenodo.4480245

[21] Agrawal, A., Gans, J., & Goldfarb, A. (2019). Artificial Intelligence, Automation, and Work. The Economics of Artificial Intelligence. 0(1), 197–236. website link:https://economics.mit.edu/files/17109

[22] Huang, L, C;and P.W, Kuo, R,J. Huang, H.C. (2001).A neural network modelling on human resource talent selection. Vol.1, Nos.2, 3, 4. DOI:10.1504/IJHRDM.2001.001006

[23] Sinniah, S., Subramaniam, M. & Seniasamy. R. (2020). Green HRM Practices Towards Sustainable Performance in Facility Management Industry. International Journal of Management, 2020, 137–147. DOI:10.34218/IJM.11.9.2020.015

[24] Benbya, H., Davenport, T.H. and Pachidi, S. (2020). Artificial Intelligence in Organizations: Current State and Future Opportunities,' MIS Quarterly Executive: 19 (4). DOI:10.2139/ssrn.3741983

10

Impact of Artificial Intelligence in Promoting Teaching and Learning Transformations in Education System

Richa Nangia[1], Richa Arora[2], Dimpy Sachar[3] and Abdullah Bin Junaid[4]

[1]K. R. Mangalam University, India
[2]Delhi Metropolitan Education, Noida, India
[3]Maharaja Surajmal Institute of Technology, Janakpuri, Delhi.
[4]American College of Dubai, Dubai, UAE

Email: richa.nangia16@gmail.com; ric.arora85@gmail.com; dimpysachar81@gmail.com; Abdullahbj2015@gmail.com

Abstract

The transformation of the education system to online modes because of COVID-19 has highlighted the huge technological insufficiencies that exist in the educational framework in numerous countries, colleges and primary and secondary schools all over the world. With the advancement of science and technology, artificial intelligence has entered an uncommon period of quick improvement, and it is significantly changing everyday issues. The main purpose of this research paper is to understand the impact of artificial intelligence in promoting transformation in the education system. The purposive sampling technique has been used to collect the data. Both primary and secondary data were used to collect information. A self-structured questionnaire was framed and sent via a Google doc and received a response from 190 respondents. It has been concluded from the study that there is no significant impact of artificial intelligence in promoting the teaching system and there is no positive impact of artificial intelligence on learning transformation. For schools, it is most important to assemble a group of undeniable-level instructors that are adjusted to the advancement of training in the modern era.

10.1 Introduction

Technological advancement has already become a part of our daily lives. The government and schools are paying more attention to the development of artificial intelligence in the education system. Technological advancement has not just promoted changes in schools' showing techniques, learning strategies, ground climate and educational plans, yet the whole education system is likewise going through changes through AI. From essential training to advanced education and grownup schooling, schools are progressively changing with AI innovation. These frameworks can assist individuals with learning better and accomplishing their learning goals. Educators must effectively change their ways of thinking, investigate new types of combinations between artificial reasoning and teaching, advance the profound reconciliation of innovation and teaching, and improve the creative development of education and teaching. The reorganization of instruction and education in schools will break the real limitations of conventional instruction, structure an interstate of data, advance reasonable cycles in training, and make instruction and teaching intriguing and sensible. With the improvement of artificial intelligence, present-day schooling will be enriching and contributing.

In recent years, many technological advances have been made, including robots, modern educational changes, picture recognition, artificial intelligence, educational calculations, quantum calculations and block chains. These advancements are by and large referred to as insightful advances and keep on speeding up the improvement in the education system. The ceaseless presentation of different artificial intelligence showing items will rebuild the schooling business environment. Schooling and learning materials that depend on counterfeit knowledge innovation give artificial intelligence schooling innovation, devices and related administrations to schools and educators. Taking the learners' data information and analysing and critiquing it afterwards, the five areas of learning, i.e., 'teach, learn, test, train, feedback' can then be applied to deliver a customized solution and compelling feedback for students. Innovation in higher education is about upgrading human thinking and expanding the instructional cycle rather than just reducing it to a bunch of methods for content delivery, control and evaluation. As artificial intelligence arrangements expand, it becomes increasingly critical for teaching foundations to stay cautious and check whether the authority over secret calculations that run them is not being consumed by technology masters.

Currently, artificial intelligence innovation has spawned a slew of brilliant demonstrative ventures. In the area of teaching assessment, currently, computerized reasoning, programmed information consolidation, highlighting examinations, profound learning, and demonstrating evidence of patterns of behaviour can make it possible to provide an itemized and precise assessment of an educator's study hall instructing quality. It is evident that in the future, instructors will be assessed through man-made brainpower innovation, rather than by solitary assessment among students and instructors. For a particular examination model, the stage rapidly and instantly frames an analytic assessment report for every understudy's learning and gives customized learning assets and improvement ideas to adequately accomplish 'an understudy with a ruler and a learner with numerous rulers' to elevate studies to their best selves by changing a ruler to assess the current circumstance, everything being equal. This makes the assessment more logical, level-headed and convenient.

10.2 Literature Review

Studies and research are going on to find out the role of artificial intelligence in developing and promoting teaching and learning in the education system. For example, Encalada and Sequera (2017) found in their study that the advancement of virtual reality (VR), augmented reality (AR), and hearing and detecting innovations is helpful for the change in the instructional climate. They further added that the use of pervasive processing innovation helps in figuring out the incorporation of actual space and virtual space to make virtual homerooms and virtual research centres. In 2019, Baker and Smith defined artificial intelligence as 'computers which perform intellectual undertakings, ordinarily connected with human personalities, especially learning and critical thinking'. The field of AI begins with software engineering and design, yet it is unequivocally impacted by different disciplines like a way of thinking, intellectual science, neuroscience and financial matters. Given the interdisciplinary nature of the field, there is little agreement among AI scientists on a typical definition and comprehension of AI and insight overall (Tegmark, 2018).

At the initial stage, artificial intelligence in the education sector frequently refers to smart coaching frameworks to improve the efficiency of administrators (Hwang, 2013). Kwet (2020) in his study mentioned that an information-driven schooling system can be utilized or experienced as a reconnaissance framework. He also added that "what can be achieved with information is typically a code word for what can be achieved with observation". Computer experience research facility alludes to the virtual multiplication of genuine trial scenes through 3D displaying with the assistance of media, reenactment and computer-generated reality advancements; they create related programming and equipment working conditions on the PC that can help, somewhat supplant, or even completely supplant all of the working connections of conventional tests (Want, 2018)

Furthermore, according to Zhou (2020), the utilization of face recognition in schools can break the traditional way educators and students work and live, and can be a significant piece of smart systems. Yang & Zhang (2019) mentioned in their study that mentoring robots are outfitted with an assortment of AI advancements like voice acknowledgement innovation, feeling acknowledgement that investigates articulations and tones, and bionic innovation that can introduce excellent joint innovation like human activities and have human-like tuning in, seeing, thinking and correspondence capacities. Thus, it can be said that adopting these technological changes in the education system would be helpful to enhance the teaching-learning process.

As a result of the advancing and continuously expanding algorithmic separation, an enormous portion of the population faces losing out on numerous political, financial, social, educational, and professional opportunities that AI and man-made reasoning have given (Peter, 2020). According to Min (2020), even if educational institutes' vision, available resources and essential objectives emphasize different ways of motivating, the nonexclusive model laid out in this work for a brilliant foundation remains valid in most circumstances. Tahiru (2022) has added in his study that almost every day the world is getting a novel AI invention, and its application is spreading at an alarming rate. Indeed, AI has altered how individuals learn and has become an integral part of our daily lives. Despite its importance, its reception in the educational system has been troubled by problems and moral issues.

10.2.1 AI in promoting teaching and learning transformation

A change in the resource climate is the establishment of instructing transformation. The progressions in resources and environment will lead to a reorganization of education, which will result in a learning environment that better addresses student concerns and constructs a virtual circle. From a bigger point of view, the effect of present-day science and innovation on instructing and learning is accomplished through changing showing apparatuses, media or the climate (Hill and Hannafin 2001). To start with the advancement of man-made brainpower innovation, an enormous number of organizations have fostered an assortment of smart showing apparatuses and learning devices, and keen assistant learning gear, like shrewd showing stages, showing robots learning programming, and so forth These high-level educating and learning devices have brought a great deal of accommodation to instructors and students, carrying new imperativeness to educating and learning. In the period of AI consciousness, countless insightful gadgets have entered the study hall. Instructors and wise associates will exist together in the homeroom. Students and instructors will each wear different wise machines with sensor gadgets. The whole instruction and showing process are wise. Besides, the improvement of man-made reasoning has brought extraordinary comfort for students and educators to acquire learning assets. During the time spent smart advancement of learning assets, the machine has performed quality control and semantic comment on the assets, and assets are isolated into text, video and other structures. Thusly, when the wise learning climate detects students' requirements, it can adaptively push learning assets that are appropriate for the students, and with the turn of events of web indexes, students can rapidly observe the assets they need without squandering a great deal of time in tracking down materials.

At last, the development of artificial intelligence has given comfort in building an intelligent learning atmosphere, driving the advanced schooling resource atmosphere to an intelligent learning resource climate. Schools can work with artificial consciousness training organizations to utilize computerized reasoning to establish a climate that is favourable for students to do proficient and profound learning. Through astute insight, AI assembles a learning climate that is more helpful for instructor understudy associations. In the time of computerized reasoning, the development of savvy grounds will bring productive and helpful administrations to students learning at school, permitting students to take an interest in learning. The development of demonstrating devices, a streamlining of demonstrating assets, and improvements in demonstrating climates will help educators complete training exercises and enable students to adapt easily.

10.2.2 Major objectives of the present study

- To find out the Impact of artificial intelligence in promoting teaching and learning transformation.

- To determine the requirements of schools in the era of artificial intelligence.

- To describe the opportunities and challenges of artificial intelligence in the higher education system.

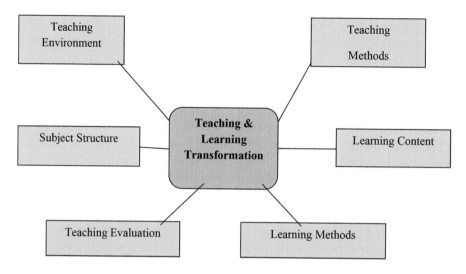

Based on the objectives of the study, the hypotheses of the study are:

H1: There is a significant impact of artificial intelligence in promoting the teaching system.

H2: There is a positive impact of artificial intelligence on learning transformation.

H_{01}*: There is no significant impact of artificial intelligence in promoting the teaching system.*

H_{02}*: There is no positive impact of artificial intelligence on learning transformation.*

10.3 Research Methodology

The purposive sampling technique has been used to collect data. The researcher analysed and interpreted the research findings using quantitative data analysis.

Data collection: The present study is based on both primary and secondary data. A self-structured questionnaire via a Google doc was shared with the respondents to gather the primary data. A total of 190 responses were gathered. The secondary data was collected from various scholarly journals, books, blogs and WebPages of companies, higher education institutes, schools and organizations. The study was conducted in the year 2021.

The study used a 17-item scale related to the artificial intelligence in promoting the teaching-learning and learning transformation for future action.

Responses were taken using a 7-point Likert scale ranging from 'strongly disagree' (1) to 'strongly agree' (7).

10.3.1 Sample variables and scale

There are three main variables selected for the study, and all are related to the advance teaching-learning method with reference artificial intelligence. Thus, the 7-point Likert scale has been used with the ranging from 'strongly disagree' (1) to 'strongly agree' (7).

Sample variables	Dimensions
Performance of structure (POS)	POS 1: Teaching Environment
	POS 2: Subject structure
	POS 3: Learning Methods
	POS 4: Learning Contents
	POS 5: Teaching Evaluation
Differentiated – instruction based (DB)	DB 1: Analysis of teaching strategies
	DB 2: Create a learning station
	DB 3: Use task cards
	DB 4: Use the think-pair-share strategy
Evaluation of active learning based (EAB)	EAB 1: Increase the student engagements
	EAB 2: Reciprocal questioning
	EAB 3: Cooperative learning strategies
	EAB 4: Peer teaching way
	EAB 5: Evaluate the student assessments

10.3.2 Data analysis and interpretation

10.3.2.1 Reliability

The questionnaire has acceptable internal total consistency reliability, and Cronbach's alpha coefficient of scale is 0.800. Similarly, Cronbach's alpha for all selected variables is 0.75 for self-assessment, 0.76 for setting goals and 0.833 for planning for future action. Hence, the variables of the study are acceptable, and all dimensions were used for further analysis as well.

10.4 Results

The first hypothesis for the study is to find out impact of artificial intelligence in promoting the teaching system. The results of the regression explained the variance R Square = 0.361 (36%), $p < 0.001$, whereas β value is 0.56 which is significant at the .001 level. The ANOVA values in the results show a

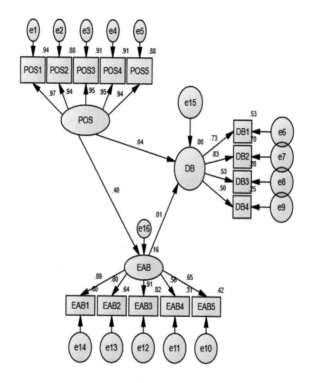

t-value of 3.32 and the standard coefficient is 0.36, significant at 0.001 levels. Hence, a significant impact of artificial intelligence is found in promoting the teaching system. Thus, H_1 is accepted and H_{01} is rejected, that is, there is no significant impact of artificial intelligence in promoting the teaching system.

H2: The results of the regression explained the variance $R^2 = 0.372$ (37%), $p < 0.001$, whereas $\beta = 0.50$, $p < 0.001$. According to ANOVA—the result, there is a positive impact of artificial intelligence on learning transformation. Therefore, H2 is accepted and H_{02} is rejected. (There is no positive impact of artificial intelligence on learning transformation.)

To use the adjusted goodness-of-fit index (AGFI) and the normed chi-square (χ^2/df) to assess the parsimony of the data fit, the fit indices of chi-square of 74.8, degrees of freedom of 41 and Bollen–Stine *p*-value of 0.19 suggest the data set is fit for all the variables of the research. The root mean square error of approximation (RMSEA) is 0.05 with a PCLOSE of 0.29 indicating the test of exact model fit is supported. CFI and TLI are more than 0.97 with AGFI more than 0.92 indicating a good model fit. CMIM/DF is 4.9 (>1.5). Therefore, the total analysis of this model also found an excellent fit and the study is acceptable.

Model fit indices

S. no.	Name	Acceptable level	Model fit indices
1	Chi-square (χ^2/ df)	$1 < \chi^2/df < 2$	74.81(41)1.83
2	Bollen–Stine, p	>.05	0.19
3	CMIM/DF	>1.5	4.9
4	RMSEA	<0.06	0.05
5	PCLOSE	>0.05	0.29
6	CFI	>0.95	0.97
7	AGFI	>0.8	0.92

10.5 Findings

10.5.1 The requirements of schools in the era of AI

Facing the challenges and opportunities of training development in the period of AI, together with the advancement of training and education and the turn of events pattern of computerized innovation, schools will effectively investigate and develop new prerequisites for building a school in the period of insight. For schools, the first step is to assemble a group of undeniable-level instructors who are prepared to advance training in the smart time. Educators are the establishment of instruction and the beginning of educating. For instance, set up an educator instruction advancement base, a creative educator preparing climate, investigate and develop instructors that can adjust to counterfeit knowledge and other new advanced difficulties; complete savvy instruction proficiency improvement activities, and direct shrewd instruction administration preparing and showing capacity preparing for remarkable chiefs and educators. Schools should focus harder on the reasonableness of training and the accomplishment of reasonable training. Instructive advancement objectives will zero in on new norms that are more impartial and, what is more of better calibre. The securing of information will turn out to be more available, the freedom of weak gatherings to acquire instruction will be all the more completely ensured, and the advancement of schooling will make the making of information more widespread. At the same time, schools need to focus on the comprehensiveness of insightful instruction. Insightful innovation ought to turn into a significant strategy to tackle issues of instruction irregularity, and consequently, canny instruction ought not to be made an honour for a small group of individuals. Schools will confront new difficulties and new prerequisites in instruction administration frameworks, social morals and information security. The coming of the wise period will be joined by the age of a lot of information and calculations, and the improvement of low knowledge will additionally obscure the limits between human culture, actual space and data space, subsequently producing a progression of moral, lawful, and security issues. Schools should focus on the security hazard difficulties that man-made brainpower innovation may bring, which is to additionally explain the idea of standards, centre around the friendly worth direction, reinforce forward-looking counteraction and limitation, guarantee information security and calculation reasonableness, and guarantee that the improvement of man-made brainpower is protected, dependable and controllable. At the logical examination level, schools should go to an assortment of lengths to advance the shared advancement of the man-made brainpower industry and school training, support college logical exploration organizations, AI driving endeavours, essential and auxiliary schools, and other gatherings to fortify participation and upgrade the development of one of the smart schooling innovation innovative work frameworks. Likewise, schools should establish a long-term speculation instrument, unite top-tier subject assets and examination power, track the most recent advancements in the artificial consciousness industry, and tap into the genuine development needs of schools. Simultaneously, it is critical to accelerating the internal incorporation and imaginative advancement of computerized reasoning and education, as well as to review the advancement methodologies, guidelines and advancement pathways of canny education.

10.5.2 Opportunities and challenges of artificial intelligence in the education system

A significant challenge of artificial intelligence in education is fusing virtual mentors for every student, which provides unpreventable assistance and support to students with self-heading, self-assessment and collaboration by integrating client demonstration, social reenactment and data depiction. Additionally, at that point, a few people join the gigantic proportions of data about individual learning, group environments, learning settings, and individual interests, increasing the transparency and connectedness of study halls everywhere in the world, taking learning outside of the review lobby and into the life of a student outside of school. Thus, it can be concluded that the work that artificial insight plays in the cutting edge computerized world is brilliant and it is dependent upon to push learning information progressively more quickly. There are certain key points which are to be taken care of and are as follows:

- Ensuring inclusion and equity for AI in education: Developing nations are in danger of experiencing new innovative, financial and social partitions with the advancement of AI. Some fundamental impediments, for example, the essential mechanical framework, should be looked at to set up the fundamental conditions for carrying out new procedures that exploit AI to further develop learning.

- Preparing teachers for AI-powered education: Teachers should master new digital skills to involve AI in an educational and significant manner. AI designers should figure out how instructors work and make arrangements that are practical, in reality, conditions.

- Enhancing research on AI in education: While it may be sensibly expected that research on AI in training will increase shortly, it is nevertheless worth reviewing the challenges that the educational area has had in assessing instructive exploration in a critical way both for training and strategy making.

- Ethics and transparency in data collection, use and dissemination: Artificial intelligence raises numerous concerns in regard to admittance to the instruction framework, proposals to individual students, individual information focus, obligation and sway on work, information protection and responsibility for taking care of calculations. Simulated intelligence guidelines will require public conversation on morals, responsibility, straightforwardness and security.

Numerous research and studies have shown that artificial intelligence is proving to be influential in advanced education for teachers as well as students since the use of these technologies allows for more adaptable learning solutions for students. By using man-made consciousness, colleges from all over the world can pick up a substantial number of students faster. The performance of this application in instructing has also been generally costly, but compared with other manual costs of conducting business, the cost is reasonable. There is no doubt that students who use computerized reasoning over the long term are more financially savvy than students who do physical work and are taught in a more traditional way.

Artificial intelligence is utilized in the schooling framework for evaluation and examination. In this cycle, instructors can automate the review of students for a certain proper arrangement of questions. Simulated intelligence can likewise be applied in versatile and individualized ways to figure out how to satisfy students' necessities.

1. Artificial intelligence-driven tasks give a strong contribution to both students and instructors. It causes the teachers to screen the exhibition

of the understudies and engage them to further develop the direction that they give to the students.

2. Artificial intelligence reinforces their learning and assists in their improvement. Artificial intelligence systems that secure data will change how schools find, teach and reinforce understudies. Truth be told, at certain spots, it may even override instructors in specific circumstances. It has transformed into a learning pal for the aides' understudies in their learning technique.

3. AI establishes a reassuring climate and, in particular, can give a positive setting for understudies' learning attributes and cycle. Artificial intelligence includes all types of electronically created learning, handling and educating.

10.6 Conclusion

This paper focuses on the effect of artificial intelligence in promoting teaching and learning transformation. With the advancement of AI innovation, AI will be increasingly utilized in the schooling field in the future. Individuals have a general understanding of artificial intelligence-based education by dissecting the use of AI in training and the challenges posed by AI innovation in training. Furthermore, it helps educators and students better face and use AI innovation in the educating and learning process, develops educators' and students' learning strategies, and makes students' learning styles more differentiated and customized. In the end, it sums up the requirements for the development of schools in the era of technological advancement, which help the teacher and learner with a better education.

References

[1] Agarwal, P & Yadav, P. (2013). "Research Paper on Artificial Intelligence." Case Studies Journal. 2(6).
[2] Baker, T., & Smith, L. (2019). "Educ-AI-tion rebooted? Exploring the future of artificial intelligence in schools and colleges." Retrieved from Nesta Foundation website.
[3] Bates, T. (2020). "Can artificial intelligence transform higher education?" International Journal of Educational Technology in Higher Education.

[4] Benbya, H. (2021). "Artificial Intelligence in Organizations: Implications for Information Systems Research." Journal of the Association for Information Systems. 22 (2).

[5] Encalada, W. L., & Castillo Sequera, J. L. (2017). "Model to implement virtual computing labs via cloud computing services." Symmetry.

[6] Huang, M. H. & Roland T. R. (2013), "IT-Related Service: A Multidisciplinary Perspective," Journal of Service Research, 16 (3), 251–258.

[7] Huang, J. & Saleh, S. (2021). "A Review on Artificial Intelligence in Education." Academic Journal of Interdisciplinary Studies. 10(3). 206–216.

[8] Jain, S. (2019). "Role of artificial intelligence in higher education – An empirical investigation." International Journal of Research and Analytical Reviews. 6 (2).

[9] Jaiswal, A. (2021). "Potential of Artificial Intelligence for transformation of the education system in India." International Journal of Education and Development using Information and Communication Technology. 17(1). 142–158.

[10] Joshi, S. (2020). "Evaluating Artificial Intelligence in Education for Next Generation." Journal of Physics: Conference Series.

[11] Allah, M. (2020). "Smart Campus: A sketch." Sustainable cities and societies.

[12] M, Kwet. (2020). "The smart classroom, the age of smart university." Teaching in Higher Education. 25(4). 510–526.

[13] Murgai, A. (2018). "Role of Artificial Intelligence in Transforming Human Resource Management in Education System." International Journal of Trend in Scientific Research and Development. 4(3).

[14] Popenici, S. & Kher, S. (2017). "Exploring the impact of artificial intelligence on teaching and learning in higher education." Springer open. 2–13.

[15] Fati, T. (2021). "AI in education: literature review." Journal of cases on information and technology. 23(1).

[16] Tegmark (2018). "Life 3.0: Being Human in the Age of Artificial Intelligence."

[17] Wang, P., Wu, P., Wang, J., Chi, H. L., & Wang, X. (2018). "A critical review of the use of virtual reality in construction engineering education and training." International Journal of Environmental Research and Public Health.

[18] Zhou, X. (2020). "Application Research of Face Recognition Technology in Smart Campus." Journal of Physics: Conference Series.

[19] Yang, J., & Zhang, B. (2019). "Artificial Intelligence in Intelligent Tutoring Robots: A Systematic Review and Design Guidelines." Applied Sciences, 9(10).

[20] Yu, P. (2020). "The algorithm divided and equality in the age of artificial intelligence." Florida Law Review. 72(19).

11

Technology as a Solution for Ensuring Physical, Emotional and Financial Well-being of Employees

Suruchi Pandey[1], Priyadarshini Khaskel[2] and Sumita Misra[3]

[1]Symbiosis Institute of Management Studies (SIMS), Symbiosis International (Deemed University) (SIU), India
[2]SAP Consultant, Infosys, India
[3]Credit Suisse, Singapore

Email: suruchi.p@sims.edu; priyadarshini.khaskel2021@sims.edu
sumita.misra@gmail.com

Abstract

Employee well-being has been the most pressing challenge faced by HR leaders and other business leaders, particularly during the COVID-19 pandemic (2020, Josh Bersin) and post-COVID. There is a considerable amount of stress, fear, anxiety, and a feeling of uncertainty that has contributed to the 'pandemic fatigue'. The paper aims to bring out various aspects of well-being to be considered for employees and address their concerns as well as the available technology solutions that can be utilized to cater to these issues. This research aims to bring out the technology solutions that can be implemented to curb various aspects of well-being, namely, the emotional, mental, physical and financial well-being of employees. The study provides a glance over updated technology solutions that can be adapted by other organizations. This is also a ready reckoner for organizations looking forward to increased use of technology for their employees' well-being.

11.1 Introduction

The HR pulse survey report discussed key concerns of the employees and the HR professionals in the wake of the pandemic (COVID-19). They are mentioned in descending order of importance below:

- Secured job (54%):

- Own health (38%)

- Child-care and schooling (17%)

- Personal finances (15%)

- Remote work (13%)

- Viability of employer (12%)

- Mental health and stress (9%)

- Work-life balance (8%)

- Family health (8%)

- Productivity (7%)

- Social isolation (5%)

Addressing the above concerns has been at the top of the list for all organizations, and in this paper, the technology solutions implemented and adopted by various businesses are discussed. Also, recommendations are made in untouched areas. As conceived from the survey, these concerns are all the causes of emotional, physical and financial ill-being, which brings out the purpose of this study. It provides pragmatic technological solutions to deal with various aspects of well-being, and the literature review elaborates on each section in detail.

11.2 Methodology

Here the authors have extracted data through secondary research, including recent surveys undertaken to measure the impact of COVID-19 on employee well-being. These surveys have been conducted on a sample set of HR leaders from various organizations and their employees. They have been published as white papers. These surveys identified certain problem areas in the employees' physical, emotional and financial well-being that needed an immediate response from the organization's management. Suggestions provided in this study will assist leadership in addressing employee well-being issues remotely. These solutions have been provided based on the available technology in the market to cater to the various requirements of employees, and also feasible solutions have been suggested which can be implemented by any organization remotely.

11.3 Literature Review

11.3.1 What is well-being?

According to the WHO, 'A state of health is not merely the absence of disease or infirmity but a state of complete physical, mental and social well-being'. This raises the question of what is meant by the term 'well-being', which Diener and Suh (1997) believed to consist of three determinants: the pleasant effect, unpleasant affect and life satisfaction. Diener & Suh (1997) further stated, 'Both pleasant and unpleasant effects refer to the respective emotions and moods, wherein life satisfaction reflects the cognizance towards the sense of life satisfaction'. All three components of well-being discussed above are interdependent and cannot exist in discrete forms.

In his work, Ryff (1989a) identified the various constituent aspects of well-being, which are: purpose in life (meaning of one's existence); autonomy (governed by self), positive or healthy relationships with others, environmental mastery, a realization of potential (understanding one's utmost abilities), and self-acceptance. According to some recent studies, well-being can be defined as 'ability to achieve goals' (Foresight Mental Capital and Well-being Project, 2008); 'life satisfaction' (Diener & Suh, 1997) and 'happiness' (Pollard & Lee, 2003). However, this also brings to light the problem that the research documented by academicians is inclined towards descriptions, dimensions, and constituents of well-being instead of defining it in its entirety (Christopher, 1999).

Wellness is also understood as an individual's ability to make choices that lead to successful living. This considered six dimensions namely occupational, emotional, physical, social, spiritual and intellectual (Hettler 2013). Wellness is also considered as activities leading to quality of life overall (Jaring, Pikkarainen, Koivumäki, 2013). This presents a broader view of living that can include physical, psychological and financial well-being. Pope (2015) quoted well-being as 'state of being in good mental and physical health'.

Another interesting development will be how clinical psychology has impacted my well-being. Joseph & Wood (2010) have glorified and called for the adoption and imbibing of positive functioning by clinical psychology.

This stemmed from their belief that psychiatry has embraced a constrained and narrowed view of well-being, by focusing only on the absence of dysfunction and distress. Hence, considering the concept of positive function would organically broaden and expand the horizons. They believed in the possibility of a new bent on measuring technique that would allow for the prediction and healing of distress and dysfunction, allowing treatment for the same. There have been researches undertaken in this area (Keyes, 2002) that perceived and considered mental health to be a 'syndrome of well-being symptoms'. It was previously proposed that well-being be considered a condition of a 'system in which the essential qualities' of a person are relatively stable (Reber, 1995). The 'dynamic equilibrium theory of well-being or the set-point theory' backs up Reber's proposal. Headey and Wearing (1989) proposed this theory 23 years ago, and it delineated relationships between various aspects: a person's life events, personality, well-being and ill-being associated with the person in question. This theory has taken reference from Brickman & Campbell (1971) as its basis and built upon it. They had previously explained, 'Human beings tend to return to the baseline state of happiness despite having undergone or been subjected to major life events (which were difficult and testing'). This can also be called the inertia of happiness, which brings the person back to their natural state even after going through difficult and testing situations.

Headey and Wearing (1991, 1992) concluded through their research that subjective well-being is usually stable for the vast majority of individuals. This was because the stock levels constituting a person's psychic income flow actions and their subjective well-being are seen to be in dynamic equilibrium (Headey and Wearing, 1991). A similar stress and emphasis on equilibrium have been observed in the research work of Herzlich, and the concept is not novel (Herzlich,1973). As per her findings, 'individuals observed equilibrium as a desirable state to attain or be in and not simply as a norm or protocol'. Also, Herzlich's interviewees in her survey showed a deviation from the result of Headey and Wearing's findings and theory of most individuals tending to have a stable state of well-being. However, Herzlich noted the frequency of reference towards equilibrium made by the respondents of the survey that she conducted and found out that it had a varied range of applications. Her results stated that the word in itself induces and reflects a completely unexplored field of individual experience, personal and different for every person. This subjective identification served 'as a distillation of the language of health'. She further explained the 'concept of equilibrium in terms of health'. It encompasses the below-mentioned themes suggested by Herzlich (1973):

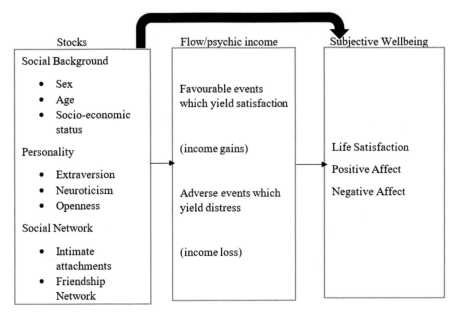

Figure 11.1 Headey & Wearing's (1991) stocks and flows framework.

- Physical health and well-being, and an abundance of physical resources

- Lack of fatigue

- Psychological well-being and temper steadiness

- Movement autonomy and action effectiveness

- Effective interpersonal relationships with others in general (Herzlich, 1973)

In 1992, Headey and Wearing comprehended in their research the actions and strategies of individuals dealing with the change and explained how an individual's well-being is adversely affected by these changes. The authors propose that a person can only find an altar in the state of well-being if, because of external forces, he or she deviates from his or her equilibrium pattern of events. Accordingly, Headey and Wearing proposed that well-being depends on the equilibrium level of happiness and comfort over life and recent activities and occurrences. This leads to their framework to analyse and understand subjective well-being (SWLB), which takes into account the relationship between stocks and flows. Figure 11.1 is representative of the same.

Jackson and Fransman (2018) discussed and elaborated on the inter-relationship between financial well-being and work-life integration making a further impact on job satisfaction as well as productivity.

Financial well-being is interlinked with emotional and physical well-being. The same statement is true with the other two. Emotional well-being links to physical and financial well-being and physical well-being gets linked with the emotional and financial state of the individual. This is deep though to understand. Organizations making any initiative in this direction have to understand the positive implications and impact on the overall well-being of their employees. Rather than only taking these decisions keeping in mind retention or return on investment. These will be short-term perspectives on any technical initiative in this direction. The authors propose technology as an enabler of the well-being of employees. Employees' Health and well-being had started to draw the primary agenda of most corporates over the past two decades. Though the financial angle of employees' well-being is more in discussion for over one decade.

11.3.2 Promoting technology for employee wellness

Henning & Van de Ven (2017) contemplated the use of technology in form of wearable for the well-being of working professionals. The idea proposed is noble and brings in many advantages on one side; however, it has a dark side to its excessive usage. It boosts productivity, performance, health and wellness. Organizations install and track the wearable to promote employee wellness.

Raveendran, Soren and Ramanathan (2021) raised serious concerns about financial well-being in India. Along with a few other studies it also highlighted the lack of financial literacy and how gender, social status, age, employment status, education, and regional differences can have an impact on it Delafrooz and Paim (2011). Nudging and Behaviour based technology can lead to better financial decisions and wellness among people at large. Personalized apps with behaviour analytics can be instrumental in combating financial bottlenecks. Delafrooz and Paim (2011) Going forward technology can definitely help in financial literacy and education, decisions and inclusion hence leading to wellness and reducing financial stress.

Jaring, Pikkarainen, & Koivumäki (2013) highlighted the increasing demand for ICT-based well-being solutions for senior members of society. However, the study project challenges that SMEs face in meeting these, and one of those included investment from people. It will be interesting observation if big corporates come forward and invest in these technologies for ageing employees and their family members. These include some basic apps to order medicines online, consult physicians and socialize when lonely, participate in social events online, attend awareness sessions on mindfulness or mindful eating. It is also relevant that the usage of technology is promoted among the ageing group of people. Innovations in this field are required. A healthy lifestyle is probably the foremost preference where information and communication technology is being considered by end users.

Mobile healthcare has a future keeping in mind the wellness of people. It was the use of the carrot and stick approach to encourage people to use it (Pope 2015). In addition to reducing the cost of healthcare, the benefits of employee well-being have a significant impact on the bottom line. In virtually all studies, improvements in overall wellness, including clinical outcomes, have been attributed to enhancing worksite wellness. A study conducted by Caressi (2014) showed that employers are promoting employee healthcare through mobiles and integrated wearables, and this helps in 24/7/365 services with accountability on investment. The drive for healthcare agenda in the 21st century will be the customization solution for users with location-specific, goal setting and progress tracking, providing feedback for motivation. Mobile, as well as wearables, cater to this agenda. Mobile-related wearable technology not only drives healthcare through walking, running and diet apps but also for chronic care for diseases like diabetes and hypertension. Modern technologies are also helping monitor cystic fibrosis. If employers promote wellness employees' participation increases contrary to no intervention from the employer side (Beaton 2017). As an employer they benefit as a better brand, attracting talent and better retention with less psychological withdrawal from work.

Loeppke et al. (2013) with some other studies on similar lines also depicted positive results of technology-based wellness programmes on de-addiction and on smoking habits along with other healthy habits and routines. Health behaviour in large-scale populations can be successfully bought through engaging technology. The study showed positive results in imbibing healthy habits and healthy eating through the use of several technologies in education and engagement. These are personalized innovative preventive interventions using web base technology, apps, mobile and wearables.

Henniger (2017) contemplated legal issues associated with the usage of wearable technologies by employers for employees' wellness. The increasing usage of any technology leads to data capturing of employees which can be personal and even for family matters. The intentions could be good but implications should be considered. There is a need of defining legal boundaries in this aspect. There is increasing globalization and employees are spread across corners of the world. In such a situation understanding of legal aspects per se wellness and technology is a foreseeable challenge.

Employers survey covering 8000 employers and including 800 healthiest employees conducted by Springbuk ('Springbuk is leading solution provider for employer-based health programmes') and results published by Businesswire 2017. The findings highlighted that 'Fitbit' gazette topped the list of wearables, and ease of usage was the primary factor in this decision-making. Close to 50% of employers are willing to adapt technical solutions for employee wellness over the coming year. Employers describe their matrix for workplace wellness programmes as a health risk, financial impact and clinical outcomes. The data tracked by these wearables also helped make better-informed decisions for wellness programmes in coming years.

The simplest use of these technologies can be in tracking employees' fatigue, spreading awareness for health, and active lifestyles, and curating a culture of flexibility at work. Measuring and improving the wellness initiative becomes a lot easier with the available technology.

Technology updation in this has been a boon for coaching and engaging employee mindset towards mental, physical and financial health at the workplace.

11.3.3 Employee well-being amid COVID-19 pandemic

According to the survey conducted by Josh Bersin (2020), the top issues on the minds of the employees as reported to their HR leaders amid COVID-19 are financial security, their health and well-being, family issues, and the ability to perform their jobs. Similarly, the survey revealed the thematic priority actions taken by the HR leaders in various organizations. It has been found that the pandemic's impact on an employee's health and well-being is the prime trepidation for HR leaders and business leaders.

Although HR technology-proposed solutions geared toward supporting employee well-being have existed for some time now, the industry is expected to innovate quickly to provide technology solutions to address the acute well-being crunch in the majority of workplaces. Furthermore, some non-traditional providers of well-being technology, such as 'Salesforce, PwC and ServiceNow', have rapidly developed a new category of well-being technology known as 'return-to-work' tools.

Since the outbreak of the COVID-19 virus, the most prominent areas for Human Resource functional leaders and business leaders, under their focus lens have been the agility of the business, employees' well-being and the evolution of leadership in times of crisis. Pandey and Pandey (2021) reported perceived stress among employees who were put to work from home immediately after post-pandemic. There was a sort of urgency in the action needed from organizations to initiate actions to deal with the stress levels employees encountered and apparently technology was the only solution. Effective two-way communication still remains instrumental in achieving wellness goals. This research dives into the topic of employee well-being and how HR leaders and organizations can ensure the well-being of their teams in these tested conditions by engaging with them. The three most common aspects of well-being are considered here: physical, mental, and financial (understanding that these do not represent the totality of well-being).

11.3.4 Physical well-being (health)

The leaders of the HR space are focused on the 'challenges of workforce health and safety' particularly, opening the workplaces that are safe for employees, customers and visitors. HR leaders are at the forefront of the many transitioning parts of this challenge:

- **To identify which and how many employees should return to the workplace**
  The major challenge that not only concerned HR leaders but business leaders is to reopen workplaces that are safe for employees and customers. The contamination, poor air circulation, congested sitting spaces, exposure to one another, safe travel and safe place to food with social distancing norms were to be checked. Providing a healthy and safe workplace occupied the top place on the agenda of business leaders.

- **To identify which and how many employees should return to the workplace**
  The Gartner HR Survey found that 88% of organizations encouraged or needed their employees to work from home (WFH) regardless of whether or not they showed the symptoms of COVID-19 viral infection. Nearly all organizations (97%) have cancelled work-related travel.

Also, the reopening strategies primarily rely on the local policies of the state. Organizations also have to keep in mind the guidelines from the Occupational Safety and Health Administration (OSHA), the Center for Disease Control and Protection (CDC), the Environmental Protection Agency (EPA) and more.

Further, organizations are exploring the possibility of centrally managed dashboards to inform key indicators about when it is safe to reopen offices based on changing policies whereas, many organizations have still deferred their joining dates and extended work from home policies.

11.3.4.1 Organizational responses

Initially, all employers had to resolve to work from home however as weeks passed by and clarity over the matter was provided by government officials, Quite a few organizations responded to the crises and communicated the stand they take in calling employees back to work.

- Twitter, one of the world's pioneering technology firms, allowed employees who can or whose job roles permit them to, work remotely to maintain that arrangement indefinitely as a result of the Coronavirus outbreak.

- Facebook Inc. will permit WFH for its employees until July 2021 due to the COVID-19 pandemic and will also grant $1,000 for home office needs. However, the company shall continue reopening its workspaces in a restricted capacity where government guidance permits and where virus mitigation has taken place for about two months.

- Alphabet Inc.'s Google made a statement in late May 2021 that it would consider reopening buildings across more cities with approximately 10% capacity that too in a staggered way over the few months extend the capacity to 30% by September. These companies also called the employees back as was said. It was worth noting that rather than adding to the stress that the pandemic had already created companies tried to support the cause with employees.

Keeping in mind the above responses, it can be concluded that most organizations are trying to limit their employees' returning to the workspace and are allowing WFH unless required. Soon these organizations reverted to various hybrid work models allowing their employees to visit once or a few times a week reporting to the offices.

- **To manage and adjust schedules to support social distancing**
  McKinsey's report on US organizations reflected that 88% of the employees expect to return-to-work by December 2020. The survey also found four interventions to ensure a safe return. One of them is a reduction in person-to-person contact to enhance social distancing. To maintain social distance, many practices are started, like:

  ○ Switching to video-conferencing for large gatherings or meetings

  ○ Reduction of the number of employees sharing the workspace at one time: This can be done by staggered work shifts within the day to avoid contact.

  ○ Restrict non-employee entry to sites.

○ Stagger employee entry to the office premise.

○ Limit capacity on elevators.

To work with 'facilities and operations teams to ensure that necessary physical changes to workplaces are completed and are adequate to support employee safety and health'. According to the McKinsey report, as discussed above, certain measures that organizations have implemented or are planning to implement are:

- Physical separation of workstations by spacing out the desks or installing physical barriers.

- Closing of common areas (to avoid gathering) and removal of communal food and beverage serving equipment such as coffee machines or snack vending machines.

- The changing of surface materials to anti-viral and installing hands-free devices to replace handles and other touch-points

- Reducing operating hours to allow for cleaning and instituting sanitization breaks for employees throughout the day

- Regular temperature checks, implementing contact tracing for infected employees and conducting at-home health surveys.

The most critical HR challenge of top leaders for quite some time was bringing employees back to work with safety precautions. Vaccination drives were conducted by governing bodies, however, that was not at the pace that corporates could resume normal soon. Corporates initiated various programmes to ensure the safety and health of their employees. To begin with, many corporates sponsored vaccination drives for their own employees and family members alongside arranging safe travel and sanitization facilities at work. To achieve these endeavours, technology was the enabler. A variety of technological solutions have been adopted by various companies to improve their employees' physical well-being. Here are certain technology solutions for the physical well-being of employees:

- The emergence of new work, workplace and worker issues lead to the HR and workplace technology market reacting to provide a solution. Many of these were created and redesigned technology solutions to meet these newer requirements. Technology solutions developed by Salesforce, PwC and ServiceNow, among others, ranging from employee health support to contact tracing and return-to-work readiness.

- Oracle started an Employee Care Package linked to its cloud-based human capital management. It is a set of integrated applications based on advanced AI that facilitates employee safety, support and adaptive skills training to help employees adjust to the new norms and ways of working.

These tools among the others still in the development phase are designed to assist HR leaders and line managers. It is to keep employee health, safety and well-being at the core of any transitions back to the workplace including a hybrid workplace.

11.3.5 Mental and emotional well-being

According to the 2019 Mental Health Workplace Study by Teladoc Health, 27% of the respondents, i.e., the employees were diagnosed with mental health conditions, and 38% of those were aged between 18 and 25 years old. This study was conducted by Ipsos Mori on behalf of Teladoc Health. For the research, Mori interviewed 3974 participants online. The study was carried out across four countries, with 1,000 people interviewed in the United States, 1,000 participants in the United Kingdom, 964 participants in Canada and 930 participants in Australia. All participants were adults who were 18–65 years of age and in full or part-time employment.

It might have been easy to ignore mental health-related issues when business conditions were good when many organizations enjoyed inflated growth and high share values, and the 'financial future seemed incredibly bright'. With the outbreak of extraordinary circumstances, the COVID-19 pandemic has added to the plight of this pre-existing employee's emotional and mental well-being crisis. Referring to the global study across more than 10 industries by SAP and Qualtrics in March-April 2020, 75% of the people felt socially isolated, 67% reported a rise in stress levels, 57% of the people felt highly anxious, and 53% of the sample study employees, consisting of 2700 people, felt emotional drain-out.

From the McKinsey report discussed in the previous section, it is clear that employee mental health has been identified as one of the high-priority areas for HR and business leaders. Fortunately, HR leaders have an abundance of tools and technologies at their disposal to assist them in dealing with the situation; these tools will assist leaders in seeing 'how employees are dealing with their own challenges, understanding how they are responding and adapting to workplace changes, and recognizing if they need more help to cope and remain effective at work'. A total of 56% of the respondents from the 2019 Mental Health Workplace Study by Teladoc Health stated that they could be more productive at work with better mental health support.

The following are certain technology-based solutions for mental and emotional well-being:

- **Mood tracker:**
  This is a newly developed solution hand-crafted especially to tackle mental and emotional well-being at the workplace. It is the 'Moodtracker tool from Workhuman'. It is an easy-to-deploy tool that allows HR leaders to take a pulse check on the workforce to identify areas of concern and enables them to make adjustments to create a more supportive and healthy work environment.

- **Health Check 360:**
  HealthCheck360 is an enterprise solution for health management. This platform is tailor-made for employees, which enables them to set personalized health and wellness goals and objectives, and track and score activity and fitness levels across various verticals of well-being. This provides an integrated solution incorporating employee engagement, rewards and benefits, social and emotional health factors, physical health and regular medical checks. This enables HR leaders or employers to capture the employee well-being journey and improve the overall experience. This application also allows the users to socialize about their efforts and achievements within and outside the office by sharing images, healthy recipes, exercise tips, tricks, etc. This results in the harmonious growth of the employees towards well-being.

- **Endomondo:**
  'Endomondo' is created to keep a check over workouts, offering feedback and providing a planned approach towards achieving personal goals. Similar to HealthCheck360, this application also helps to connect and socialize with other motivated and health-conscious people, which pumps up the motivation level and also helps build a healthy lifestyle together.

- **Hotseat:**
  Hotseat is an application specially curated to encourage movement among employees by motivating them to leave their desks more. It has interesting engagement features which allow the employees to organize challenges and face-offs. Such friendly competitions motivate the users to jump up and go for a two-minute activity break. Such activities can be organized by setting up the beginning and end dates and times.

Reminders can also be set, which is integrated with iCal. This makes it easy to catch up on the schedule.

- **MyFitnessPal:**
  This application provides the feature of capturing the calorie intake of a person. This solution is a free application available at the disposal of any user to keep a check on their food intake, which includes the three meals of the day, snacks, beverages, etc. The application has a pre-existing database which serves the purpose of look-up when the user enters the dish or beverage name.

- **TotalBrain:**
  This is a revolutionary application meant to provide employees with a neuroscience-based mental health and fitness solution. This was formulated on the very notion of measurable mental health based on quantifiable parameters, which can be enhanced and further managed similarly to physical health. This application maintains the clause of confidentiality and measures 12 brain capacity metrics to check for the presence of common mental health issues faced by people. Additionally, it creates awareness and increases responsibility and accountability by engaging in mental fitness activities.

- **Meditation Studio:**
  It has been found that meditation can be highly effective in reducing concentration issues as well as de-stemming anxiety. This application offers more than 200 meditation videos under the expert guidance of 27 leading meditation experts to help users get rid of stress, improve their sleeping patterns and gain self-confidence.

- **Headspace:**
  It is a meditation and mindfulness app that provides a workout for the brain. It takes ten minutes a day to listen to it and clear the user's mind, increase attention span, and alertness, and gain instant calm and composure.

- **8fit:**
  It is a custom home workout app that provides an all-encompassing approach to health and fitness–allowing users or employees to personalize their workouts to their strengths and wellness, paired with easy-to-follow healthy and delicious diet recipes. This does not require any gym membership.

- **Streaks:**
  This application provides the employee or the user with a to-do list, which helps to develop good habits and holds one accountable for their

New Year's fitness and other personal development goals. This helps in achieving larger goals by creating smaller or bite-sized targets by allowing the employees to track up to 12 tasks that they want to achieve each day and 'build a streak of consecutive days'. The tasks can range from 'going for a run to reading a chapter of a book or even giving up on smoking'.

- **Sleep++:**
  This application collects all the vital information about the user's sleep pattern while they are sleeping. It tracks the motion of the user to find out how restless the person is during his/her slumber and also checks the timestamp. In addition to providing a deeper understanding of sleep patterns, it also provides solutions and remedies for sleep problems.

- **FIIT:**
  This fitness app brings with it premium boutique-class experiences for the employees, irrespective of their location. Upon signing up, users receive a heart-monitoring chest strap to track their progress during workouts.

  If at all, organizations do not utilize any technology solution, then it is paramount that HR leaders should prioritize checking in, attending to and supporting employee mental health during this period and thereafter.

11.3.6 Financial well-being

Financial stress negatively impacts both the professional and personal life of the employees, which furthermore affects the organization. Financial planning with long-term investments and retirement options are low-rated areas in HR management. According to the Financial Education for Today's Workforce: 2016 quoting a Ssrvey conducted by the International Foundation of Employee Benefit Plans (IFEBP), 'four out of every five employers reported that their employees' financial problems have impacted their job-based performance', which has increased the stress level of employees (76% of the employers reported this effect), employees' being unable to focus on work (reported by 60% of employers), and absenteeism and tardiness (reported by 34% of employers).

Unlike emotional and physical well-being, the US workforce has been facing a much less talked about financial crisis for a long time. The workforce that was living 'paycheck to paycheck' or 'hand to mouth' simply to meet their essential bills and requirements was reported to be close to 40%, and a sizable portion of the workforce did not have a $500 savings to use in the event of a financial emergency. In fact, few also quoted that employees exhaust their monthly salary by 3rd week of the month and thereafter look for petty loans or overdraft facilities. Along with mental health and physical fatigue, the pandemic aggravated the circumstantial crisis. The situation has seen soaring 'job losses, furloughs and reduced work hours caused by the pandemic have been unevenly distributed across the employment continuum'. In addition, such conditions and disruptions of income have disproportionately impacted low-wage workers.

So, the big question that looms is what HR leaders should consider when they look to address the financial crisis of their employees. An immediate option could be 'implementing one of the many immediate access to earned pay solutions in the market. At their core, these tools are all based on the same concept of granting employees access to their earned net pay before the official payday'. These solutions allow employees to better plan their financial requirements. Money is the centre of all activities including well-being. They could align their needs for paying the bills that are due and meeting other necessities apart from the standard payroll calendar. During the pandemic, it was also altered that people did not save enough for bad days. It is then that financial planning becomes important to note present needs and plan for long-term/short-term responsibilities as well as eventualities. Another consideration for long-term goal setting and maintaining pay parity is for 'HR and compensation leaders to conduct a thorough audit of pay and total compensation for equity and fairness'. How employees perceive their pay parity is the primary objective of any good compensation management. Some innovative technological advancements are being made to equip HR with relevant solutions: One of these is the ADP Pay Equity Explorer capability.

Technology-based Solutions for Financial Well-being:

- **LearnLux:**
  It combines personalized digital education with on-demand financial advice. Further, employees are provided access to learning resources and tools around topics like healthcare, benefits, taxes and emerging financial trends. This is elaborative and simple to understand.

- **Your Money Line:**
  A dedicated and confidential financial helpline is provided to individuals for 'access to a team of unbiased financial concierges'. It provides people with pragmatic solutions to day-to-day financial problems faced by employees.

- **Best Money Moves:**
  It is a 'mobile-first financial wellness solution combining technology, information, tools and live money coaching to assist employees' in measuring their level of financial stress across 15 categories. This 'stress assessment' provides them with relevant information and tools to curb their stress levels.

- **My Secure Advantage:**
  This aims at transforming employees' financial well-being through one-on-one money coaching via phone, budgeting software, on-site and web-based education and website resources.

11.4 Conclusion

All business functions are impacted by the available technology and they have to adapt to it sooner or later due to market forces. When it comes to people management function perhaps the adaptation pace is bit slow. However, if the adaptation process of newer technology happens sooner, then it will be good for the wellness of both employees organizations. Wellness Technology will ensure better reach and coverage for all. Gradually, this has to spread awakening in the society. Employers will have to come first in this initiative as well. By ensuring the wellness of one employee they ensure wellness for the entire family. If it is female gender it ensures the spreading of wellness among the family members much faster. Therefore investing in the wellness of employees is anytime worth an investment and proposition beyond money can measure. A spiral effect of this tech-based innovation will also be encouraged.

The discussion provided above is not the only option. However, the authors made effort to collaborate on the available solutions that can be adapted for financial, physical and emotional well-being by employers. The results of the above study can be given by providing a tabulated palette of technology solutions available, which can be left to the employer's discretion and the suitability of the organization to adopt them to cater to the needs of their employees. These are all practical solutions that can be implemented remotely and will benefit employees' emotional, physical, and financial health (Table 11.1).

The complexities in managing human resources functions and challenges in their environment have been increasing in recent times. For sustainable functioning of HR, it is suggested to adopt technology-driven solutions for its modern problems so that organizations can get long-term solutions. To assist employees, HR professionals must be aware of available technology in

Table 11.1   Palette of technology-based solutions to address physical, emotional and financial well-being of employees.

Well-being aspect	Physical	Emotional or mental	Financial
Technology solutions	• Work.com (Collaboration of Salesforce and PwC) • Employee Care Package (Oracle)	• HealthCheck360 • Endomondo • Hotseat • MyFitnessPal • TotalBrain • Meditation Studio • Headspace • 8fits • Streaks • Sleep++ • FIIT	• LearnLux • Your Money Line • Best Money Moves • My Secure Advantage

all areas that surround concerns for employees. There is a need for innovation in all the areas that this research addresses, including the financial, emotional and physical well-being of employees. Technology has changed every walk of life for all over the past two decades and for the past two years it has made life impossible to live without gadgets, apps, wearables, applications, devices, equipment, communication tools, web-based systems. Encouraging constructive use of it can influence wellness in a positive way for employees and their family members. This spreads to society gradually and all forms of social enterprises. This can bring the change all want to be part of.

References

[1] 8fit (2020). The 8fit way Retrieved from https://8fit.com/about/App Store(2020). Sleep++. Retrieved from https://apps.apple.com/us/app/sleep/id1038440371

[2] Assets.ctfassets.net (2020) Retrieved from https://assets.ctfassets.net/l8w1v1tdjd75/2iXva5x7uSdNZm1hREIM0G/bce05d4469b1f-c3acb9332ca2b5af07b/TeladocHealth_2019MentalHealthPerceptionsWorkplace.pdf

[3] Bestmoneymoves.com(2020) Best Money Moves | Money. Career. Life. Retrieved from https://bestmoneymoves.com/

[4] Business-standard.com. (Birla, N., 2020). How Companies Can Maintain Employee Mental Health In The Time Of COVID-19.

Retrieved from https://www.business-standard.com/article/econo-my-policy/how-companies-can-maintain-employee-mental-health-in-the-time-of-covid-19-120061300423_1.html

[5] Brickman, P. (1971). Hedonic relativism and planning the good society. Adaptation level theory, 287–301.

[6] Christopher, J. C. (1999). Situating psychological well-being: Exploring the cultural roots of its theory and research. Journal of Counseling & Development, 77(2), 141–152.

[7] Croman, J., 2020. How Artificial Intelligence Can Improve Your Health And Productivity. Retrieved from https://www.entrepreneur.com/article/317047

[8] Diener, E., & Suh, E. (1997). Measuring quality of life: Economic, social, and subjective indicators. Social indicators research, 40(1–2), 189–216.

[9] Endomondo (2020). Stay active and get motivated by people you know Retrieved from https://www.endomondo.com/features

[10] Fiit (2020). Fiit: Bring The Gym Home | Fiit. Retrieved from https://fiit.tv/

[11] Gambell, Hughes, Thanopoulou (2020, June 26). How US compa-nies are planning for a safe return to the workplace Retrieved from https://www.mckinsey.com/industries/pharmaceuticals-and-medical-products/our-insights/how-us-companies-are-planning-for-a-safe-return-to-the-workplace

[12] Gartner.com (2020). Gartner HR Survey Reveals 88% Of Organizations Have Encouraged Or Required Employees To Work From Home Due To Coronavirus. Retrieved from https://www.gartner.com/en/news-room/press-releases/2020-03-19-gartner-hr-survey-reveals-88-of-organizations-have-e.

[13] Harvard Business Review (2020). How Ceos Can Support Employee Mental Health In A Crisis. Retrieved from https://hbr.org/2020/05/how-ceos-can-support-employee-mental-health-in-a-crisis

[14] Headey, B., & Wearing, A. (1989). Personality, life events, and sub-jective well-being: toward a dynamic equilibrium model. Journal of Personality and Social psychology, 57(4), 731.

[15] Headey, B., & Wearing, A. (1991). Subjective well-being: A stocks and flows framework. Subjective well-being: An interdisciplinary perspec-tive, 21, 49–73.

[16] Headey, B., & Wearing, A. J. (1992). Understanding happiness: A the-ory of subjective well-being. Longman Cheshire.

[17] Headspace (2020). Meditation And Sleep Made Simple - Headspace. Retrieved from https://www.headspace.com/?utm_source=google& utm_medium=cpc&utm_campaign=2041352604&utm_content= 74866873911&utm_term=356461835759&headspace&gclid=EAIaI- QobChMI6-i_-b7f4wIVC5SzCh3b4QdLEAAYASAAEgJ2jfD_BwE

[18] Healthcheck360.com (2020). Healthcheck360 Wellness. Retrieved from https://www.healthcheck360.com/

[19] Herzlich, C. (1973). Health and illness: A social psychological analysis. (Trans. D. Graham).

[20] Hotseat(2020). Hotseat: Don't Just Sit There. Retrieved from https:// www.gethotseatapp.com/

[21] Joseph, S., & Wood, A. (2010). Assessment of positive functioning in clinical psychology: Theoretical and practical issues. Clinical psychology review, 30(7), 830–838.

[22] Josh Bersin (2020). COVID-19: The Pulse Of HR - What Is HR Doing Now? – Josh Bersin. Retrieved from https://joshbersin.com/2020/04/ covid-19-the-pulse-of-hr-what-is-hr-doing-now/

[23] Keyes, C. L. (2002). The mental health continuum: From languishing to flourishing in life. Journal of health and social behavior, 207–222.

[24] Keyes, C. L. (2005). Mental illness and/or mental health? Investigating axioms of the complete state model of health. Journal of consulting and clinical psychology, 73(3), 539.

[25] Forbes.com (Lamkin, P., 2020). Smartwatch Popularity Booms With Fitness Trackers On The Slide. Retrieved from https://www.forbes. com/sites/paullamkin/2018/02/22/smartwatch-popularity-booms-with- fitness-trackers-on-the-slide/#2738d55e7d96

[26] Learnlux.com (2020). Home - Learnlux - Financial Wellness For The Modern Workplace. Retrieved from https://learnlux.com/

[27] Meditationstudioapp.com (2020). Guided Meditation App - Learn To Meditate With The Meditation Studio App.Retrieved from https:// meditationstudioapp.com/

[28] My Secure Advantage. 2020. My Secure Advantage. Retrieved from https://www.mysecureadvantage.com/

[29] Myfitnesspal.com. 2020. Myfitnesspal | Myfitnesspal.Com. Retrieved from https://www.myfitnesspal.com/

[30] Orange Business Services. 2020. How Technology Is Helping Employee Well-Being.Retrieved from https://www.orange-business.com/en/blogs/ how-technology-helping-employee-well-being

[31] Pollard, E. L., & Lee, P. D. (2003). Child well-being: A systematic review of the literature. Social indicators research, 61(1), 59–78.

[32] Reber, A. S. (1995). The Penguin dictionary of psychology. Penguin Press.

[33] Ryff, C. D. (1989). Happiness is everything, or is it? Explorations on the meaning of psychological well-being. Journal of personality and social psychology, 57(6), 1069.

[34] Sanders, W., Zeman, J., Poon, J., & Miller, R. (2015). Child regulation of negative emotions and depressive symptoms: The moderating role of parental emotion socialisation. Journal of Child and Family Studies, 24(2), 402–415.

[35] Stephen Miller, C. and Stephen Miller, C., (2020). Employees' Financial Issues Affect Their Job Performance. Retrieved from https://www.shrm.org/resourcesandtools/hr-topics/benefits/pages/employees-financial-issues-affect-their-job-performance.aspx

[36] Streaksapp.com. 2020. Streaks. The To-Do List That Helps You Form Good Habits. For Ios. Retrieved from https://streaksapp.com/

[37] Tableau Software (2020). Workplaces Are Reopening In The Face Of COVID-19. Here'S Four Areas To Consider In Your Workplace Data Strategy. Retrieved from https://www.tableau.com/about/blog/2020/7/workplaces-are-reopening-face-covid-19-heres-how-data-plays-role

[38] The Economic Times(2020). Coronavirus Outbreak Changes Work Culture, Twitter Allows Employees To WFH 'Forever'. Retrieved from https://economictimes.indiatimes.com/magazines/panache/coronavirus-outbreak-changes-work-culture-twitter-allows-employees-to-wfh-forever/articleshow/75708604.cms

[39] The Economic Times(2020). Google Pushes Office Reopening From July 6 To Sept 7 As Virus Cases Continue To Grow. Retrieved from https://economictimes.indiatimes.com/magazines/panache/google-pushes-office-reopening-from-july-6-to-sept-7-as-virus-cases-continue-to-grow/articleshow/76723515.cms?utm_source=contentofinterest&utm_medium=text&utm_campaign=cppst

[40] The Economic Times (2020). Work From Home: Facebook To Let Employees Work From Home Until July 2021, Will Give $1,000 For Home Offices. Retrieved from https://economictimes.indiatimes.com/magazines/panache/facebook-to-let-employees-work-from-home-until-july-2021-will-give-1000-for-home-offices/articleshow/77406033.cms?utm_source=contentof-interest&utm_medium=text&utm_campaign=cppst

[41] Total Brain(2020). Home - Total Brain. Retrieved from https://www.totalbrain.com/

[42] Your Money Line(2020). Your Money Line - The Financial Wellness Solution. Retrieved from https://yourmoneyline.com/

[43] Henning A & van de Ven K (2017) 'Counting your steps': The use of wearable technology to promote employees' health and wellbeing. Performance Enhancement & Health, 5 (4), 123-124. DOI: https://doi.org/10.1016/j.peh.2017.11.002

[44] Raveendran, J., Soren, J., Ramanathan, V. et al. Behavior science led technology for financial wellness. CSIT **9**, 115–125 (2021). https://doi.org/10.1007/s40012-021-00331-w

[45] Delafrooz, N. PaimL.H, (2011) Determinants of financial wellness among Malaysia workers, African Journal of Business Management Vol. 5(24), 10092-10100, 14 October, 2011 Available online at http://www.academicjournals.org/AJBM DOI: 10.5897/AJBM10.1267 ISSN 1993-8233 ©2011 A

[46] Taft. M.K.,Hosein. Z, Mehrizi.S, Roshan A.(2013) The Relation between Financial Literacy, Financial Wellbeing and Financial Concerns, International Journal of Business and Management; 8 (11) , 63-75 ISSN 1833-3850 E-ISSN 1833-8119

[47] Jackson L. T. B. and Fransman, E. (2018) Flexi work, financial well-being, work–life balance and their effects on subjective experiences of productivity and job satisfaction of females in an institution of higher learning , South African Journal of Economic and Management Sciences 21 (1)

[48] Jaring, P.,Pikkarainen, M.,Koivumäki, T., (2013) Business challenges of SMEs providing ICT-solutions for wellness and healthcare domains, Journal of Business Market Management, FreieUniversität Berlin, Marketing-Department, Berlin, 6 (1) 38–55, https://nbn-resolving.de/urn:nbn:de:0114-jbm-v6i1.427

[49] Hettler, Bill (2013), "The Six Dimensions of Wellness", retrieved from nationalwellness.org/?page=Six_Dimensions&hhSearchTerms=wellness.

[50] Pope, D. (2015) The Wellness Movement .Pharmacy Times Oncology Edition, October 2015,2 (4)

[51] Caressi, G (2014) , Transforming wellness programme: Leveraging mobile technology adoption to drive engagement and outcomes, A Frost & Sullivan White Paper

[52] Loeppke, R. Edington, D. Bender, J. Reynolds, A (2013) , The Association of Technology in a Workplace Wellness Program With Health Risk Factor Reduction, Journal of Occupational and Environmental Medicine. 55 (3), 259–264

[53] Pandey, S. Pandey A. (2021) Study on Perceived Stress and Physical Stress associated with WFH during COVID 19 Pandemic. Indian Journal of Forensic Medicine & Toxicology 15 (3)

[54] Henniger, J. (2017) Wearable Technology And Employer Wellness Programs: Gaps And Solutions. 12 Ohio St. Bus. L.J. 197 (2017-2018)

[55] Beaton , T (2017) Wearable Technology Helps Sustain Employer Wellness Programs

[56] Wearable technology, along with incentives and motivational communications, can help employer wellness programs attract and retain participants. Retrieved from mhealthintelligence.com/news/ wearable-technology-helps-sustain-employer-wellness-programs

[57] Springbuk 2017 accessed from businesswire.com/news/ home/20170425005258/en/Data-From-More-Than-8000-Employers-Finds-that-35-Use-Wearable-Technology-In-Their-Wellness-Program

12

Challenges of Building a Virtual Team in a New Normal

Reena Lenka[1], Suruchi Pandey[1] and Ahmet Yasar Demirkol[2]

[1]Symbiosis Institute of Management Studies, Symbiosis International (Deemed University), India
[2]Educational Management and Planning, Final Educational Institutions (University and Secondary Schools), Turkey

Email: suruchi.p@sims.edu; reena.lenka@sims.edu;
demirkol.a.y@gmail.com

Abstract

Working in virtual teams is almost imperative with the increase of work from home and other flexible working options. As per Gartner's recent survey, by 2023 there will be a 40% increase in people working remotely and in virtual teams.

Because of the tough challenges, building an efficient virtual team is a dream for many organizations worldwide. Many organizations know about the challenges but are not able to overcome them as they do not have a simple solution for the same. Many organizations fail miserably as they are not able to find a proper solution to the same. Many papers and research are being done, but the authors mostly talk about the challenges without giving a suitable solution.

The main objective of writing this chapter is to suggest a simple model with solutions, which has been already explained above. The model is very simple and user-friendly, which when followed as it is, can yield excellent results, leading to a hassle-free virtual team that is as good as an offline team and is equipped to handle any challenges and would be able to contribute to the smooth running and profit maximization in the virtual mode.

12.1 Introduction

The COVID-19 pandemic has forced every organization worldwide to accept and implement certain strategies which were hardly thought of before the outbreak. The pandemic has not only wreaked havoc on the entire human species but also brutally shattered the age-old beliefs and working styles of every organization worldwide.

The pandemic has been instrumental in making the human species realize the value of life. Organizations worldwide have also started seeing and respecting human resources as a valuable asset rather than a commodity. Most organizations worldwide have realized that to sustain and give an economic boost to the country, human resources should be cared for, nurtured and developed in an optimum way so that employees. as well as the organization, get maximum benefit.

For an organization to grow and create a niche, human resources within the organization should be working as a team. Teamwork and team building during this pandemic is a mammoth task, which if not dealt with properly, can create havoc in the organization.

The pandemic has brought along the concept of remote/virtual work. To follow the safety norms associated with the pandemic, it is the need of the hour that organizations worldwide are stressing more on remote work culture.

Virtual work cultures have their challenges of reduced employee engagement, less motivation, mental wellness, reduced performance and limited employee communication. Nowadays, organizations believe that all these problems can easily be addressed through a virtual team-building process where the employees work as a team and, in case of any problem, skilled people from anywhere in the world can be hired and various problems can be sorted out.

This chapter talks about the concept of virtual team building, its necessity, challenges and solutions to overcome the challenges so that organizations worldwide, after implementing it properly, will benefit from the same not only during the pandemic but also in any unpredictable situation that might happen in the future. The COVID-19 pandemic has jeopardised the entire world. The entire world has come to a standstill. It has actually challenged the very existence of human beings. Every human being, rich or poor, has been equally affected by the pandemic, not only physically but also mentally as well.

Organizations worldwide have been badly affected by the pandemic. The economies of every country have been badly shaken. Every country worldwide is planning new strategies for the economic recovery of their country.

The greatest economic support for any country is its organization. The better the performance of organizations the more they contribute towards the economic growth of a country. The pandemic has also affected the organizations in a big way. Every sector of the organization right from human resources, finance, marketing, IT, operations and others, has been badly affected. The growth and smooth functioning of any organization depend on its human resources. The better the human resources are nurtured and developed, the better employee motivation, better performance, better employee engagement, better mental health, better employee communication, and better satisfaction level lead to individual and organization growth and ultimately contribute towards the country's economic growth.

The pandemic has started a new trend on the work front in the form of virtual or remote work. Organizations worldwide have reluctantly or happily accepted the concept as this is the need of the hour. Virtual work has its own set of challenges. The biggest challenge is forming and working in a team. According to world statistics, more than 80% of the organizations agree with the fact that virtual team building is the biggest challenge and it is also affecting the smooth functioning of the organization.

12.2 Virtual Team: Concept

A virtual team means a group of workers who are geographically distributed in different parts of the world who connect to each other and work as a team to finish the organizational task and fulfil organizational objectives through digital tools. Virtual teams are also known as 'geographically dispersed teams' or 'remote teams'.

To work smoothly, the virtual team members should be loyal to each other and develop trust in each other so that the team can work smoothly.

12.3 Examples of Virtual Team

i) **Networked team:** This team is formed based on requirements. The team is a short-term team where people from different parts of the world are collected for the completion of a particular project or job. Once completed, the team is dispersed.

ii) **Parallel teams:** This team is developed by the same organization. This is again a short-term team. The team is formed for recommendation purposes and is on board till the project is not completed and recommendations are not given. Once the project is over, the team is dispersed.

iii) **Product development team:** This team is developed to achieve a specific goal for the organization. This team is highly skilled and they are given the freedom to work independently and also collectively. They are in the team as long as the project is not complete.

iv) **Service teams:** Teams are formed based on different time zones. The team works independently. This team is formed to give respite to fellow team members and they act as a substitute for different time zones. For example, when a team is working in the US and completes the shift, the next shift is filled in by someone working in India so that there is no problem for multinational companies operating due to different time zones.

v) **Management teams:** This team is a collection of managers from the same organization. They come together to develop different managerial strategies for the smooth functioning of the organization. They have the power to work individually as well.

vi) **Action teams:** These teams are formed to address some immediate and urgent problems within the organization. Once the problem is sorted out, the team is dispersed.

12.4 Challenges of Virtual Team Building

Norwich University Online (2020) identified certain challenges unique to virtual teams.

1. **Different communication styles:** *Different* employees prefer different communication styles. Some employees might be comfortable with email, and WhatsApp or some might be comfortable with messages or teleconferencing. Different communication styles make effective virtual communication more difficult. To overcome this, a single communication mode and time should be set so that the team knows the routine and is available at the designated time.

2. **Improper delegation:** Improper delegation of job responsibilities to the team members by the leader is another big challenge in virtual work. The team is mostly confused about what and how to do a particular job, as many employees are not proficient in remote work. Many team leaders try to micro-control the team at every stage. This leads to more frustration and the team loses interest in the job, leading to more employee

disengagement and delayed work. The leader should have trust in his team and also, at times, should give them a free hand.

3. **Delayed response:** Many employees work harder in a physical office when they are with other employees. In virtual work, since employees are disconnected from other employees, they start working at their own pace and do not bother to work or respond faster. This attitude of some employees may create an environment of indiscipline among other employees as well. When employees who are hardworking and sincere come to know that some employees do not bother to finish their work and respond immediately, then other employees also lose interest and they also take the work for granted, leading to delayed job delivery. To overcome this situation, the leaders should take control of the situation and formulate rules to curb this indiscipline from the start.

4. **Disoriented team:** In a virtual team, team members do not meet each other personally, so they start missing each other. The team also starts missing the office. In the case of job-related issues, the issues used to be sorted out in the office itself, but due to remote work, the same issue remains pending as many employees are not comfortable calling up the concerned person at home. This leads to pending work and a disoriented team. The team leader should address this issue by arranging for regular team meetings and also set a time frame for work delivery. This step will lead to team bonding and work engagement.

12.5 Virtual Team-building Process: Role of Managers

There is a key role for managers in building successful virtual teams. Hickman and Ott (2020) have provided certain requirements from managers important for building a successful virtual team:

1. **Daily team monitoring:** This process is very tedious for managers every day. Previously, managers used to monitor employees through messages and emails. Nowadays, the virtual team must be monitored through video conferencing or Google Meet, Zoom, Microsoft Team, WebEx, etc daily. This helps a lot as employees feel connected, and assured and have the feel of a physical office, hence they deliver better.

2. **Increased communication:** To form an effective virtual team, increased communication is essential. Through increased communication, a sense of belonging is inculcated within the employees. In offline mode, normal communication is good enough, but in the case of a virtual team,

increased communication is the key to success for a happy, motivated, engaged and efficient team. Increased communication makes the virtual team understand the requirements of the job, leading to a more focused, efficient and understanding team.

3. **Technologically smart:** The management should be technologically smart so that they can lead the virtual team better. Online mode is sometimes very challenging to deal with. Many team members are not techno-savvy related to the use of virtual platforms like Zoom, WebEx, Microsoft team, Google Meet, etc. This situation creates a lot of problems, leading to inefficiency and lower organizational productivity. The management should not only train the team for the same but also make provision for the proper installation of a virtual platform for the team so that the team is self-sufficient and can work better and deliver results.

4. **Fixed meeting timings:** For the smooth running of the virtual team, a daily fixed meeting time should be arranged so that the team members are aware of and are well prepared for the same. These types of meetings are very important as any work-related problem can be discussed during these meetings and the next step related to a job can also be discussed. Apart from the formal discussion, any other problems faced by the team can be discussed, and any major issues can be discussed and sorted. This leads to a better virtual team connection and bonding, leading to a more charged and efficient team.

5. **Manage hope:** The management's expectations of the virtual team should be clearly communicated to the virtual team so that each member knows what to do. A clear understanding of job expectations and the target should be communicated to each team member from the start so that the virtual team is not confused and they set their priorities correctly so that they can contribute their full effort to the job comfortably and effectively, resulting in a jovial and charged-up team.

6. **Focus on results:** The management should define the job roles for every member of the team so that each member can focus on their own job responsibilities and on the given task. Due to job clarity, the virtual team members can divide their roles and can focus on the job properly, leading to increased understanding, engagement and connection amongst the virtual team members. The management also achieves a lot from this measure as micromanagement for the virtual team is not required and the concerned person can concentrate more on other important issues.

7.   **Emotionally intelligent managers:** Managers should be emotionally intelligent so that they can show empathy towards the virtual team. An empathetic leader is very much needed in this unpredictable time. If the leader is emotionally intelligent, then he can understand the team's situation much better and can be a great support for them. This helps in strengthening the virtual team and the managers' bonding. This professional bonding helps in understanding the work much better and, in this bargain, if there are any obstacles in terms of technology, work–life balance, communication or knowledge, they can be easily sorted out and the individual and the organization can benefit further.

From the above discussion it is clear that to build an effective virtual team during the pandemic, management plays a vital role. Building a virtual team needs a lot of planning and proper implementations of HR policies from the management end as the entire process is full of stiff challenges which if not addressed from the beginning and during the process and lead to various complications like disoriented team, de-motivated and non performing team. The managers have to be extra cautious and build the team keeping all the above-discussed points so that the virtual team becomes the best and is ready for any unprecedented challenges.

Following are a few cases and examples of successful virtual teams (Lepsinger, 2015):

12.6 Case 1: SAP

SAP is the world's largest inter-enterprise software company. It has a total of 30,000 employees in 60 countries. Its global headquarters are in Germany, and it has R & D centres in India, China, Israel and the USA. With such a huge employee base and centres in different countries, a virtual team is needed. In SAP, teams from different centres share their expertise with others, and when there is a need, any team from any centre can collaborate and can complete the task. SAP has an ongoing team development process where teams from different centres collaborate with each other remotely and try to keep each other motivated and develop further through webinars, meetings and training programmes.

In this case, SAP is using two components of a unique virtual team-building model in the form of the latest online technology and proper delegation to motivate, collaborate, and upgrade its employees to increase the organizations' performance and maintain a competitive advantage.

12.7 Case 2: IBM

IBM has 200,000 employees from different countries. The biggest challenge for IBM is managing the time zone. In this case, virtual teams and remote work are the only solutions. Since employees are scattered across different time zones, team leaders make sure that they make a proper plan where employees can connect with each other at their comfortable time and discuss various work-related problems and get a solution for the same. IBM also believes in virtual collaboration, where the best people with different skill sets and who are masters in their domain are hired for consultation and team training so that an exchange of knowledge takes place and the team becomes much more efficient. This helps in the increased performance of the company.

In this case, IBM is using things like open communication, the latest technology and mixing work with knowledge gained from a unique virtual team-building model to improve, motivate and improve the skills of its employees for better organizational performance.

12.8 Case 3: General Electric

General Electric has around 90,000 employees worldwide. To work efficiently, the company follows the method of remote work and believes in virtual team building. At General Electric, the team leaders, to keep the team motivated and upgraded, go to regular meetings and different online training programmes for knowledge enhancement of employees so that the employees are always upgraded and motivated and maintain good relations with the team members.

In this case, General Electric, by using components like proper communication, the latest technology and trusting employees from a unique virtual team-building model, can motivate and upgrade the employees for better organization performance and growth. From the above cases, it is proved that the unique virtual team-building model is the key to overcoming virtual team-building challenges and getting the best results.

12.9 Case 4: Quicklet

12.9.1 Successful virtual teams and why they work by Kevin Senior

Quicklet is a start-up company formed by three partners. The company mainly helps other organizations with reducing employee turnover. The companies' founders are all spread across the globe. Mr. Vivek Kumar, the co-founder of Quicklet, takes care of the seven member companies' activity from India. One of the partners is situated in San Francisco to have immediate access to the investors, and the third partner is in Pittsburgh to take care of the clients. According to Mr. Vivek Kumar, one of the co-founders, the company's success depends entirely on their virtual team, who, irrespective of the fact that they are virtual, are always there to take care of every aspect of business through Zoom and Slack and make it a success.

12.10 Case 5: First Quarter Finance

First Quarter Finance is an independent contract team consisting of 20 members. The company is all about a website consisting of finance-related information for the public. The team consists of 20 independent contractors. The team basically consists of independent people who are mostly editors or writers on a contract basis. The team has very good knowledge regarding financial-related aspects and they mostly develop content for consumers for banking and investments. The entire team is virtual. According to William Lipovsky, the CEO of the company, the company is very successful as people are virtual and they dedicate their time to content creation in their own comfortable time and there is less as no physical office is required. This arrangement saves money and more work is delivered as people are working in their free time.

12.11 Case 6: My BTLR

My BTLR is a US-based virtual company providing hourly services. The founder is Mr. Brad Turner. The company consists of 25 employees. The entire company is virtual, right from the team to the clients. My BTLR provides hourly virtual assistants, a virtual bookkeeper and a social media manager. Mr. Brad explains that the entire success of the company depends upon the virtual mode, where the US-based clients get help through virtual US assistants for their jobs 24 × 7.

12.12 Case 7: Virtual Vocations

The company consists of 40 employees and contractors in the job board industry. The company is purely a telecommuting company. The company provides virtual employee services in the form of job quality specialists, writers, customer service representatives, managers and more. Laura Spawn, the CEO of Virtual Vocations believes that the company's success is totally dependent on virtual team members who are always available and are not restricted to one place of availability. Since the team is virtual and well coordinated, the team can serve various customers throughout the world.

From the above cases, it is clear that to be a successful organization, a physical office is not required. Remote or virtual work is equally successful. A virtual team, with its wider network and wider coverage, is able to cater to many clients at the same time. The work is much faster as they work as a team with ample trust and understanding, leading to a more successful organization and satisfied employees and customers.

12.13 Objectives

The main objectives of this chapter are as follows:

- To understand the main challenges in forming a virtual team.

- To discuss the contribution of management in building an effective virtual team.

- To provide solutions to the difficulties and challenges encountered in forming the perfect virtual team.

The COVID-19 pandemic has inculcated the concept of virtual or remote work. Teamwork is very important for any organization to be successful. The same is true for virtual mode as well. Virtual teams are very important in this competitive age where virtual mode is facing many challenges. Virtual teams have many advantages and disadvantages. In order to be a successful virtual team, certain aspects have to be kept in mind. In order to overcome the challenges and convert any organization into a competitive and successful organization a "Unique model for effective virtual team-building process" has been designed, which if followed can overcome any virtual team challenges and can make an organization very successful. Following are the model for an effective virtual team-building process

12.14 Model Summary of 'Unique Model for Effective Virtual Team-Building Process'

The model is divided into three parts. Each part is represented in the form of a circle.

The first circle represents "challenges" faced by any organization while designing a virtual team. The various challenges faced by any organization while forming a virtual team are as follows:

Figure 12.1   Model for effective virtual team (Yesodharan and Patel, 2021).

- Challenges related to different management communication styles, such as 'assertive communication style, aggressive communication style, passive communication style, passive-aggressive communication style, manipulative communication style'. Different organizations follow different communication styles. In an organization there could be different styles of communication. Different management communication styles actually make the team very confused, leading to delayed work. If the management follows a mostly assertive communication style, which is the best management communication style, it becomes easy for the team to follow and understand. In virtual mode, communication is very important. When the management is using any mode of communication like WhatsApp, Zoom or email, it should be properly conveyed and should be simple for the team to use.

- Challenges related to improper delegation: In teams, there are a lot of issues related to improper delegation, such as 'General or Specific Delegation' which is related to a specific job 'Formal or Informal Delegation' which is related to the type of authority, 'Top to Bottom or Bottom to Top Delegation' which is based on the hierarchy, and 'Lateral Delegation' when a team or a group is working simultaneously. Improper team delegation relates to lots of problems in the virtual team.

- Challenges related to delayed responses from the management and the team members will lead to frustration, disengagement and demotivation among virtual team members.

- Challenges related to disoriented teams: This is one of the worst team challenges where employees are not interested in the given assignment, leading to less organization productivity.

12.15 The Second Circle Represents 'Solution – Unique Virtual Team-Building Model'

Certain solutions, such as the 'unique virtual team-building model', can help overcome the challenges of virtual teams. The solutions are as follows:

- Open communication: Different organizations follow different communication styles. In an organization there could be different styles of communication. Different management communication styles actually make the team very confused, leading to delayed work. If the management follows a mostly assertive communication style, which is the best management communication style, it becomes easy for the team to follow and understand. In virtual mode, communication is very important. When the management is using any mode of communication like WhatsApp, Zoom or email, it should be properly conveyed and should be simple for the team to use.

- Latest online technology: In virtual work and virtual teams, the use of the latest online technology is required so that the virtual team can work, share, learn and be connected with each other. Every organization should take steps to provide the latest online technology in the form of Zoom, Google Meet, Microsoft Team, video conferencing, etc., not only in the office but also to employees as well as give them training so that the team is properly equipped and can work without any hassles.

- Trusting employees: The management should have trust in the virtual team. There should be transparency in employee dealings. The management should discuss everything with the employees. The management should show from their behaviour that they have confidence in each employee's work. This confidence helps the employees to be motivated and energetic, leading to good relationships and profit maximization.

- Proper delegation: Proper delegation of responsibilities to the virtual team is very essential. Without proper delegation and proper segregation of roles, the virtual team gets confused. This situation hurts the work of the employees, which leads to frustration and lack of interest on the team.

- Mixing work with pleasure: Virtual teams are sometimes stressed as they miss the physical work environment. Sometimes this situation leads to less serious work. If the management arranges for certain interactive sessions or some outing or party where the virtual team gets to meet each other, then the team relaxes and starts giving their hundred percent, which leads to increased performance.

12.16 The Third Circle Represents 'Result' After Utilizing the 'Unique Virtual Team-Building Process Model'

By forming an effective virtual team, any organization can achieve a successful outcome. The results are as follows:

- Improved communication: By adopting the 'Unique virtual team-building process model', the management can understand the importance of improved communication and implement it in the form of using the proper online platform, fixing meeting times and adopting an assertive communication style to make the virtual team clearer and more productive.

- By adopting the 'Unique virtual team-building process model', management can improve employee motivation through transparency, daily meetings, work–life balance, realistic targets, immediate problem solving, job flexibility and a regular salary, leading to a motivated, energetic, engaged and productive virtual team.

- Increased trust: Through a 'unique virtual team-building process model'. the management can increase employee trust. The management starts treating the employees better, showing confidence and always being ready to sort out virtual team problems both personal and professional, regular interaction and transparent communication, leading to increased employee trust and productivity.

- Increased employee engagement: Adoption of the 'Unique virtual team-building process model' by the management leads to increased employee engagement. Management that does a good job of delegating tasks, improving communication, building trust in employees, training employees, and making sure they have a good balance between work and life leads to more engaged employees and a productive team.

- Increased performance: The 'Unique virtual team-building process model' helps the management to improve employee performance. The management starts practicing various strategies mentioned in the model, like more communication, the latest online technology, proper job delegation, increased trust, employee upgradation, and daily interaction that lead to a motivated, energetic and efficient virtual team.

12.17 Conclusion

In the present scenario, where the duration of the pandemic is very difficult to guess, it becomes imperative for the entire world to think about a practical approach to tackle this situation. To survive this unprecedented situation and become economically strong, any country must immediately resume normal operations of the organization. The country wants to do it, but a newer variant of COVID-19 is preventing them from doing so. It is the moral responsibility of every country to take care of its citizens' health. In this situation, where social distancing and working remotely are the new norms, there is an all-the-more need to build a strong virtual team.

From the above discussions, it has been seen that many big corporate worldwide, to safeguard their employees' health, are preferring remote work and are building virtual teams for the smooth operation of organizations leading to the economic and social growth of their citizens and the country.

Any organization can do better if the team is working in sync with each other. The same is the case for remote work. There is a greater need for building a strong virtual team as members cannot meet each other personally and, hence, are totally lost and disengaged, leading to a loss in production. A strong virtual team is recommended and required for any organization to stand, prosper and grow globally, leading to an increase in the country's economy.

References

[1] Abarca, V. M. G., Palos-Sanchez, P. R., and Rus-Arias, E. (2020). Working in virtual teams: a systematic literature review and a bibliometric analysis. IEEE Access 8, 168923–168940. doi: 10.1109/access.2020.3023546.

[2] Alsharo, M., Gregg, D., and Ramirez, R. (2017). Virtual team effectiveness: the role of knowledge sharing and trust. Inf. Manage. 54, 479–490. doi: 10.1016/j.im.2016.10.005

[3] Baard, S. K., Rench, T. A., and Kozlowski, S. W. J. (2014). Performance adaptation: a theoretical integration and review. J. Manage. 40, 48–99. doi: 10.1177/0149206313488210

[4] Brahm, T., and Kunze, F. (2012). The role of trust climate in virtual teams. J. Manage. Psychol. 27, 595–614. doi: 10.1108/02683941211252446

[5] Brooks, S. K., Webster, R. K., Smith, L. E., Woodland, L., Wessely, S., Greenberg, N., et al. (2020). The psychological impact of quarantine and how to reduce it: rapid review of the evidence. Lancet 395, 912–920. doi: 10.1016/s0140-6736(20)30460-8

[6] Chen, C., de Rubens, G. Z., Xu, X., and Li, J. (2020). Coronavirus comes home? Energy use, home energy management, and the social-psychological factors of COVID-19. Energy Res. Soc. Sci. 68, 101688. doi: 10.1016/j.erss.2020.101688

[7] Cummings, J. N., and Haas, M. R. (2012). So many teams, so little time: time allocation matters in geographically dispersed teams. J. Organ. Behav. 33, 316–341. doi: 10.1002/job.777

[8] David Strang, K. (2011). Leadership substitutes and personality impact on time and quality in virtual new product development projects. Proj. Manage. J. 42, 73–90. doi: 10.1002/pmj.20208

[9] Dulebohn, J. H., and Hoch, J. E. (2017). Virtual teams in organizations. Hum. Resour. Manage. Rev. 27, 569–574. doi: 10.1016/j.hrmr.2016.12.004

[10] Gilson, L. L., Maynard, M. T., Young, N. C. J., Vartiainen, M., and Hakonen, M. (2015). Virtual teams research: 10 Years, 10 themes, and 10 opportunities. J. Manage. 41, 1313–1337. doi: 10.1177/0149206314559946

[11] Goh, S., and Wasko, M. (2012). The effects of leader-member exchange on member performance in virtual world teams. J. Assoc. Inf. Syst. 13, 861–885. doi: 10.17705/1jais.00308

[12] Hair, J. F., Ringle, C. M., and Sarstedt, M. (2013). Partial least squares structural equation modeling: rigorous applications, better results and higher acceptance. Long Range Plan. 46, 1–12. doi: 10.1016/j.lrp.2013.01.001

[13] Henseler, J. (2017). Bridging design and behavioral research with variance-based structural equation modeling. J. Adv. 46, 178–192. doi: 10.1080/00913367.2017.1281780

[14] Hoch, J. E., and Kozlowski, S. W. J. (2014). Leading virtual teams: hierarchical leadership, structural supports, and shared team leadership. J. Appl. Psychol. 99, 390–403. doi: 10.1037/a0030264

[15] Jarrahi, M. H., and Sawyer, S. (2013). Social technologies, informal knowledge practices, and the enterprise. J. Organ. Comput. Electron. Commer. 23, 110–137. doi: 10.1080/10919392.2013.748613

[16] Kirkman, B. L., Cordery, J. L., Mathieu, J., Rosen, B., and Kukenberger, M. (2013). Global organizational communities of practice: the effects of nationality diversity, psychological safety, and media richness on community performance. Hum. Relations 66, 333–362. doi: 10.1177/0018726712464076

[17] Norwich University online, 2020: Management Benefits of Virtual Team Building Activities for Remote Teams and four challenges of virtual teams and how to address them. https://corporatefinanceinstitute.com/resources/knowledge/other/virtual-team/

[18] Rick, L. (2015). 3 Companies with High-Performing Virtual Teams, LinkedIn

[19] Hickman , A. Ott , B. 2020, The Manager's Role in Improving Teamwork in the Workplace, Gallup

[20] Yesodharan.S, Patel. S 2021, 7 benefits of virtual team building activities for Remote Teams, SAVIOM, https://www.saviom.com/ blog/7-benefits-of-virtual-team-building-activities-for-remote-teams/

[21] https://www.gartner.com/smarterwithgartner/with-coronavirus-in-mind-are-you-ready-for-remote-work

13

Gamification in HR Practices: A Pathway to Sustainable Transformation

Pratibha Pandey[1], Jacintha Menezes[2] and Anamika Pandey[1]

[1]School of Business, Galgotias University, India
[2]Majan University College, Sultanate of Oman

Email: Pratibha.pandey@galgotiasuniversity.edu.in; jacinthamcuc@gmail.com;
Anamika.pandey@galgotiasuniversity.edu.in

Abstract

As business processes have evolved, human resources management has emphasized the concept that positions the human element at the centre of the organization in a modern management style (Guest, 1992). The majority of human resource activities necessitate people-related data for an improved understanding of employee competency, contingencies and organizational performance. It has been shown that when companies use digital, game-based human resources systems, they obtain more data in less time than when they use traditional human resources programmes.

Gamification is a strategy for empowering and motivating employees through the acceptance and use of learning management tools, facilitating employee retention, improving knowledge-sharing prospects, identifying the strongest incentive, highlighting employee preferences, elevating workplace connections, enhancing employee productivity and aiding in the transformation to an agile organization. Gamification can assist both employees and businesses in enhancing their human resource processes. Due to the paucity of research on gamification in the context of human resource management, this study investigates and proposes a conceptual framework of gamification's elements from the perspective of HR practices and their impact on organizations. Utilizing Tranfield et al. (2003) and Crossan and Apaydin (2010) criteria, a systematic literature review was conducted. A thorough examination of the literature contributes to critically assessing, summarizing and mapping the available studies by identifying the significant themes.

Although the amount of literature on gamification has gone up significantly, there is currently no review of the present landscape of HRM-related gamification literature. This study provides a literature review to support and simplify the knowledge of previous research. By evaluating research publications, this study highlights the contribution of gamification in HRM. According to the studies, gamification in human resource practices has a tremendously favourable effect. Gamification in digital media for human resource management helps firms to improve a variety of HR tasks, including Recruitment & Selection, Training & Development, and many more, at a lower cost than traditional approaches.

13.1 Introduction

Human resources management (HRM) is one of the most important aspects of management. Individuals and groups with high competence in terms of knowledge, skills and commitment have the greatest impact on goal attainment. HRM encompasses activities aimed at attracting and maintaining valuable employees. In the literature, many alternative definitions and scopes of HRM can be obtained. The major domain of HRM includes Recruiting and Selecting, onboarding, training, performance evaluation, rewarding and career management. Working conditions including health and safety and the concept of organizational culture are addressed significantly when HRM is approached from a broader perspective. It can be seen that motivating people is a broad term that incorporates many of the tasks listed above.

As stated by Deterding in 2011, the gamification phenomenon, in which game features are applied to non-game contexts, has become massively popular over the past years. The use of game components such as points, badges, and leaderboards has become quintessential in contemporary lifestyle (Rapp et al., 2019). In recent years, countless studies have been done anticipating the development of contexts and taxonomies for gamification and game design components. Few of the research have contributed to the knowledge of systems, design, architecture, and, more recently, the effects of gamified arrangements (Nacke and Deterding, 2017). The conceptualization of game design to innovate and improve human resource management processes and know-how has lately acknowledged a lot of research interests. In this regard, Arajo and Pestana, 2017, and Kumar and Raghavendran, 2015 have brought the focus on understanding the impact of game design concepts on employee behaviour and the modus operandi for embracing gamification in various HR practices.

The study aims to summarize the standpoint of available research on gamification in HRM, together with attributes of meaningful gamification design. In addition to this, the study canvasses the probable hazards of gamifying HRM processes and practices, therefore, aiding to provide a greater understanding of gamification. There are three major objectives of the present study:

- To understand the concept of gamification and its use in the success of the organization

- To understand the applicability of gamification in HR practices

- To identify what impact gamification might have on various HR practices

13.2 Gamification

Gamification, in general, comprises game components, which unlike a game, provide users with an experience and allow them to connect with their surroundings. The concept of gamification was introduced by Nick Pelling in 2002. (Marczewski, 2013). Gamification, on the other hand, can be a valuable and engaging tool for motivating employees, boosting learning, solving problems, and interacting with others (Kapp, 2012). Reward systems, namely partaking points, badges, stages, and leaderboards, are examples of game items utilized in gamification (Deterding, 2011).

Although the caption 'game' and 'gamification' are frequently used synonymously, they are essentially separate ideas. A game is a closed system that describes a set of rules. Games are a process in which individuals connect, have entertainment and engage along with definite aims like winning and losing. In contrast to gamification, gaming is a platform in which game patterns, techniques, and elements are integrated into a real-world activity (Vardarlier P.,2021).

In the arena of the games, participants become players focusing on the tasks they need to perform in the game setting with a substantially high level of motivation. They are essentially instructed to participate in specific activities. As these definitions demonstrate, gaming and gamification are not synonymous (Avolio et al., 2014).

As stated by Şipal in 2015, the gamification theories described in the twentieth century are defined and determined in better detail than those explained in the twenty-first century. Gabe Zichermann (2010) described gamification theory in the twenty-first century as 'communicating with participants to address problems using game-play within the setting of the game'.

The founders of the term 'gamification'. Gabe Zicherman and Christopher Cunningham (2011), define it as 'using the method of thinking as well as the game rules in the game to captivate the user and fix the issues'.

In a nutshell, gamification is the employment of game ideology, game envisaging and game mechanics to archaic organizational functions for enhancing the motivation of the users to solve problems. In other words, Gabe Zichermann contends that motivation tends to make persuasion smoother, and those in-game motivational elements should be planned as per the behaviour of participants (Zichermann and Cunningham, 2011). Miltenoff, Martinova, and Todorova (2015) define gamification as 'implementing ideas and processes to everyday situations to encourage users and solve problems'.

As previously stated, gamification utilizes game features (mechanics) and game design guidelines to subdue obstacles that are not games in the real picture. The concept of a 'meaningful game' can be found in gamification literature and the use of gamification is more closely involved with the application of games to attain significant results.

The following are the basic principles of game mechanics about game dynamics (Cunningham, 2011):

1. **Scores/points**: These serve as a form of reward for making progress and completing tasks with feedback, allowing other players to react quickly. To make a game more enticing, these scores can be given an original name based on the company's name, its products, the game's theme and so on.

2. **Levels**: These indicate the player's current state and rank as compared to peers and others participating in the game.

3. **Awards**

4. **Scoreboards**

5. **Challenges**

Gamification works because it gives employees control over their activities while also providing them with clear indicators of their progress to date, a road map to direct them for future actions, and prizes to clearly show when they have engaged in the appropriate behaviours. It is evident to see why gamification is regarded as an excellent technique when you consider the competitive element that most gamification programmes employ as shown in Figure 13.1.

Gamification market analysis suggests a high-growth area driven by the growing use of mobile devices and the expansion of classic gamification methods across the globe. In 2020, the global gamification industry was

Value of the gamification market worldwide in 2016 and 2021
(in billion U.S. dollars)

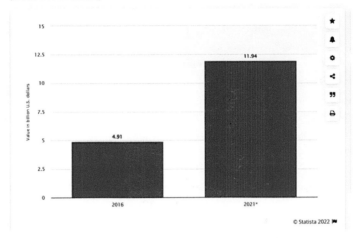

Figure 13.1 Value of gamification market worldwide in 2016 and 2021 (in billion US dollars).

worth $9.1 billion, and by 2025, it is expected to expand at a rate of 27.4 percent, reaching $30.7 billion (Markets and Markets, 2020). According to a survey by Research and Markets, the gamification market will develop at a significant rate between 2020 and 2030, with a CAGR of 24.2% (Prescient & Strategic Intelligence, 2020). The report also states that the HR dept is expected to have the highest growth rate in gamification having a CAGR of 27.8%. This shows how gamification is impacting the business at all corners of the world (Figure 13.2).

There are several significant players in the gamification sector, which is moderately competitive. Few big firms currently lead the market in terms of market share. These main competitors, who hold a significant share of the market, are concentrating on growing their consumer base in other regions of the world. The businesses are relying on strategic collaboration activities to grow their market share and profit margins. The global expansion of gamification deployed in several organizations can be seen in Figure 13.3.

13.3 The Theoretical Framework of the Study

The TTF also known as task-technology fit theory, provides for the study's theoretical basis. The task-technology fit Model was introduced by Goodhue & Thompson in 1995. It explains the utilization of technology by examining

Figure 13.2 Region wise growth rates of gamification market, 2020–25 (Source: Mordor Intelligence).

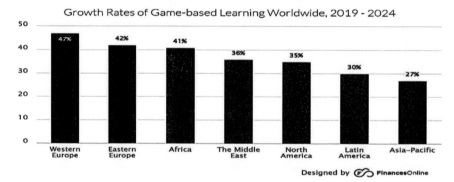

Figure 13.3 Growth rates of game-based learning worldwide, 2019–2024 (source:https://financesonline.com/gamification-statistics/#market).

the fit of technology to the tasks employees perform. The task-technology fit (TTF) idea states that IT is more likely to improve individual efficiency and be used if its mechanisms match the tasks that the user must do (Goodhue and Thompson, 1995). Goodhue and Thompson (1995) found the TTF measure, in combination with an application, to be a significant predictor of enhanced job performance and effectiveness that was connected to their use of the system under investigation.

This theory states that for technology to have a good impact on performance, it must be used and fit with the tasks for which it was developed (Goodhue and Thompson, 1995).

13.4 Research Methodology

A literature review is important for almost every research project. It serves as a foundation for knowledge advancement, facilitating the creation of theories,

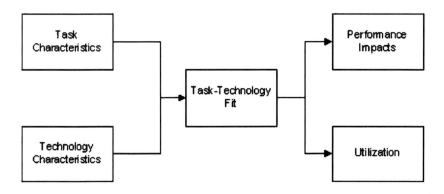

Source: Goodhue and Thompson, (1995)

concluding established studies, and helping in the discovery of new research areas (Webster and Watson 2002).

As the aim of this study is to actualize a unified schema that integrates the different linkages amongst all potential HRM practices and digitalization, a systematic literature analysis is conducted to develop the integrated framework since this approach allows us to analyse all important literature on this domain in depth while also allowing us to identify new untapped aspects. Moreover, engaging a lucid and consistent technique and including a wide-ranging and neutral exploration for recognizing and appraising an eclectic expanse of literature, boosts the worth of the review progression and results (Tranfield et al., 2003; Mulrow, 1994). An inductive research strategy is used applied to analyse the final sample of articles.

The most extensive databases of peer-reviewed journals in the social sciences are Scopus, Web of Science, PubMed ScienceDirect and Google Scholar and they were employed as data sources for this study. The study examined full-length, peer-reviewed articles (Shaheen et al., 2010). Furthermore, all types of studies were reviewed, from empirical to conceptual (Leonidou et al., 2020).

13.5 HR Practices in the Wake of Gamification

Gamification can be used to encourage brand loyalty, employee engagement, and training and development in a variety of management contexts (Tutunea, & Rus, 2015). It can be brought into play for a range of functions, including brand awareness, new technology promotion, research & development, vendor engagement, and supply chain solutions, in addition to internal operations and personnel (Froehlich, 2015). Organizations are utilizing it for recruitment, training, and modifying various HR practices to accomplish organizational goals in the domain of human resource (HR) management (DeWinter et al., 2014).

13.5.1 Gamification in recruitment and selection

The changing workforce dynamics, together with digitalization and shifting job choices require continuous evolution in schemes and procedures. At a time when technology is rapidly evolving, it is a strenuous endeavour for getting exceptional skills from a vast pool of skilled workforce. The crucial necessity of businesses to attract talent makes groundbreaking recruitment strategies, such as gamification, a captivating proposition. Several studies have focused on the critical aspects of recruitment. For example, organizations have set their focus upon the progression as it commences with an attempt to recruit applicants for unoccupied spots (Rynes, 1991), applicant's insights for the organization (Breaugh, 2013), as well as the attitude applicant has towards the organization. These are all factors that are influenced by the way the information is communicated to them (Chow, 2014).

In addition to standard techniques of recruitment, organizations can take the advantage of up-to-the-minute technologies like gamification to try and magnetize prospects. Interlacing work with play is expected to increase engagement and creativity (DeWinter, Kocurek, & Nichols, 2014). Woniak (2015) suggests that gamification can help with employer branding and stimulate the interest of potential candidates.

In the context of recruitment, gamification can be used as a means of not only attracting prospective employees but also altering their behaviour and attitudes about an organization (Chapman & Jones, 2002). Such a design that is in line with the recruitment goals could result in increased engagement and attention to much sought-after organizational information which will influence individuals' decision-making process (Chow & Chapman, 2013). It is observed that when gamification is used in the recruitment process, it usually dilates into several advantages. Organizations can evaluate the abilities and aptitudes of prospects, like time management, creativity and entrepreneurial thinking before making a recruiting choice. This in a way makes the process of eliminating inappropriate individuals considerably faster in the early stages of recruitment. One of the main reasons for gamification's high-time engagement in recruitment is that it piques the interest of the millennial population while also accelerating the recruitment process in the organization. Integrating gamification and related ideas into the recruitment process could help in inviting and captivating applicants' interest on a larger scale, along with traditional recruitment methods (Shree S. & Shekhar A. 2019).

With the influx of millennials and generation Z candidates into the marketplace, as well as their heightened curiosity in technology, gamification has a better chance of turning out to be a lucrative recruitment methodology (Jones, &Katsikitis, 2014). The active participation of today's new generation on social media sites adds to this evidence.

To keep a contemporary approach, many companies are increasingly incorporating gamification into their recruitment processes. Some of the companies that are using it include Google, Formapost, Dominos and Umbel (2015, White). Digital games can promote a candidate's competitive spirit, which can be leveraged to recruit and analyse potential employees, particularly those who are prospects of the new age (Deterding et al., 2011).

Many organizations are discovering that digital games that encompass credits, medals, contests and role-playing may be utilized to efficiently recruit and assess candidates, categorically the millennials. For example, when PricewaterhouseCoopers (PwC), Hungary required a more efficient way to recruit college students, the company created Multipoly, a digital simulation. Students played the game designed for 12 days on a social media site, Facebook, to comprehend how it feels to work for a consulting firm. While receiving feedback from business coaches, students were supposed to reach the quarterly targets and complete projects based on PwC requirements.

Several recruiting games bring in the aspirants to jobs they might not have deemed otherwise, whereas others give them an actual taste of the work. Table 13.1 shows some of the preferred gamification used in recruitment and the features offered by the system along with the array of top customers of these games.

In recruiting, gamification does not refer to only a specific sort of game. To hire the best people, Google employed a public puzzle, but instead, the game might very well be a quiz or a challenge, where the prospective applicants unravel online encoding exercises. In today's organizations, a variety of such platforms are employed to keep their recruitment and selection systems competitive and to keep a grasp on potential applicants (as stated in Table 13.2).

This study emphasizes the advantages of using gamification in the HR recruitment process for organizations. Simultaneously, it also emphasizes the risks connected with 'false' gamification. Organizations must not neglect the design factor backed by research in the effort to stay up with the surge in popularity of gamification owing to shifting demographics within the business environment (Hiltbrand& Burke, 2011). The literature also mentions that the

Table 13.1 The games preferred by the candidates, 2015 (Source: https://www.shrm.org).

System	Customers	Features
Badgeville	Wells Fargo, Wal-Mart, Medtronic	Points, badges and leader-boards Tracks social systems and provides real-time feedback Includes analytics to enable customers to track and characterize users
Bunchball	SAP, Sun LIfe Financial, T-Mobile	Scalable cloud platform Used to motivate employees, test candidate skills and engage customers
Captain Up	Dell, Hewlett-Packard, McAfee	Social and gaming tools with badges, levels, activity feeds, leader-boards and other rewards Customers can add interactive leaderboards to any website or app The Application programming interface adds social layers and competitive elements
Games for Business	PwC, HBO Europe, Huawei	Online simulation models the structure and procedures specified by the customer in a 3-D environment Users follow a work routine: going to meetings, accomplishing tasks, and facing unexpected situations and ethical decisions Measures players based on pre-set variables
Hakcer Rank	Booking.com, Sabre, VMware	Ranks programmers based on coding skills Programmers compete in challenges and code sprints Recruiters move winners through the selection process
mLevel	US Foods, D4, International Hotels Group	Interactive learning missions accessible via mobile app or web Individual and team competitions Scenarios uncover what users know about critical topics and require that they react in real time to responses

Table 13.2   Use of gamification in recruitment by organizations.

Price water house Coopers (PwC)	Multipoly	It lets prospective employees to effectively assess their suitability for a job at the company by collaborative learning to handle real-world business problems.
Hebersham Aboriginal Youth Service (Hays)	Hays Challenge	It gives individuals a realistic impression of a task of recruitment as a fascinating job option.
Marriott Hotel	My Marriott Hotel	In this gamified technique, players are required to virtually run the hotel and do tasks that come up in reality.
Google LLC	Google Code Jam	It is a software-writing competition to identify new talent to work for the firm.
Siemens AG	Siemens PlantVille	This game demonstrates the everyday tasks and responsibilities of the facility manager to the player, who is a prospective applicant, in this game. This offers the candidate an idea of the plant manager's work duties.
Phoenix Technologies	Escape Room	Phoenix software provides prospective candidates a platform where they virtually meet the staff of the firm in a virtual space for a given period of time where they can select the worthy applicant for the vacant position without the other formalities of sending a resume, etc.
U.S. Airforce	Airman Challenge	It was made by the United States Air Force to explain the candidates about the operations and vacant ranks.
LinkedIn	Recruitathon	LINKEDIN partnered Flipkart, India to organize a Recruitment Contest. It started with collecting group members for a project and following up with candidates to fill the vacant position in a limited span.
L'Oreal	Reveal	Graduate recruitment strategy

adoption of gamified settings stimulates the interest of younger, tech-savvy people joining the workforce who are looking for novelty in everything; still, the literature emphasized the significance of constructive discussion among the various stakeholders participating in the process of adopting gamification. The design feature cannot be regarded as suitable until all parties with knowledge of it have been consulted.

Gamification is effective; however, there are certain limitations. It cannot be the all-in-one solution to all recruitment problems. Gamification's effects might only be temporary. Removal from the system, once executed, may have an impact on the most involved players, particularly those with the most points and badges. The context and how users perceive it are also important factors in the gamification process' success. Players might have different approaches towards the game; a few might have a nonchalant approach, whereas some would be very determined and ambitious. This approach might not be suitable for the entire recruitment procedure; therefore, accurate application might oblige the presence of circumstantial necessities as stated by Shree & Shekhar in 2019.

13.6 Gamification in Employee Training

Major human resource operations have unfolded during the last two decades, causing the function's responsibilities to expand to a more strategic level. Human resource management procedures have gradually incorporated the fields of recruitment and selection, training and development, compensation, employee appraisals, work life and learning in the early evolution. More recently, as addressed by Posthumus, Santora and Bozer, this progression has included automation and the application of algorithms for the management of these human resource subsystems (2017).

One of these subsystems is training and development, which is focused on enhancing personal competencies in the workplace. Training is an institutional process that assists an individual in realizing his or her full potential by delivering knowledge to acquire capabilities and competencies meant for day-to-day tasks. It is a short-term assimilation procedure intended at recycling information, abilities, and attitudes directly relevant to work-related tasks (Marras, 2016).

According to Dutra (2016), the process of learning consists of numerous phases in which various activities combine constructively to allow the employee in attaining the goals of their growth. To establish progress and points of development at the end of the training, the search for necessities and the selection of the method are important cornerstones of the training process (Noe, Hollenbeck & Gerhart, 2005).

New trends in organizations have emerged as a result of the advent of new responsibilities in the management of human resources. Meeker (2018) published a report on the trends enabled by increased Internet usage, such as the speed with which disruptive technologies are adopted, the new technologies, such as Internet access and cloud networks, have changed the way we live. The use of game technology in training and development is widely discussed in the existing literatures (Gramigna, 1994; Falcao, 2008). Tichy et al., who examined human resource management in the late 1980s, categorized it into many groups, including training and development.

Khawaja and Nadeem's (2013) defined training as an organized process of understanding that enhances employee and organizational growth (Goldstein & Ford, 2002). Training and development is a sequence of events carried out by the organization that indicates the attainment of knowledge and competencies by the employees for progress at the workplace resulting in the upliftment of the employees, thereby making the organization strong. In response to the growing competition, Manju and Suresh (2011) argue that training helps organizations improve the skillset of employees which in turn enhances the quality. To keep employees and the company successful, firms must conduct employee training and development periodically (Khawaja & Nadeem 2013).

Achieving a competitive advantage requires employee training to unlock employee potential for growth and development (Rama V. & Nagurvali Shaik, 2012). Corporations spend a lot on the skill development of their employees to enhance the output. Understanding, aptitude, and competencies are substantially related to employee accomplishments, and corporations should persistently spend on them to enhance the outcomes. Businesses make significant investments and time in training to help employees gain job-related competencies (Noe, 2006; Dowling & Welch, 2005).

In terms of training learning, it is also vital to mention Knowles' (1980) andragogy assumptions, which include: autonomy, learning readiness, learning application and learning motivation. Autonomy gives the foundation for acquiring new concepts and abilities; in which people feel competent in independent decision-making. Learning readiness is attributed to the reason that people are more interested in learning those aspects which are related to their regular lifestyle. Learning application is geared toward pragmatism, that is, when gaining knowledge is centred on solving issues instead of acquiring facts. Learning inspiration is linked with personal beliefs and aspirations.

Gamification in Training

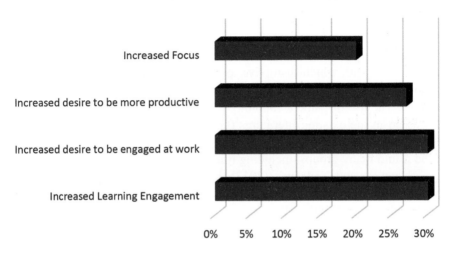

Figure 13.4 Gamification in training (Source: https://financesonline.com, 2021).

The gamification recommendation for the training procedure entails offering a discursive, instinctive and vibrant experience focused on improving problem-solving skills and motivating participants to pursue their succeeding goals, all while receiving dynamically provided feedback, and increasing content retention through experience and engagement (Cherry, 2012; Chou, 2015).

The approach for pursuits using game-based technologies is to provide a distinctive and unambiguous goal that leads to incremental accomplishments over time, with continual feedback. The user should always partake deliberately and have a prior understanding of the activity's guidelines, in which the player is confronted with difficulties in attaining the ultimate objective, similar to a game (Deterding et al., 2011).

While gamification boosts employee productivity, it also enhances employee engagement. For example, a poll of 500 company workers in the United States revealed that gamification increased productivity for 90% of workers, and 30% of respondents stated it enhances their desire to be engaged at work. Furthermore, according to the same report, gamification motivates 27% of workers to be more productive at work and aids 20% of people in staying focused and avoiding distractions as shown in Figure 13.4.

While some may resist the concept of making training appealing, the truth is that most individuals learn effectively when they are engaged in activities and games. Employees are more likely to be engaged and motivated by

Table 13.3 Some of the gamification strategies utilized for corporate training.

Corporate Training Gamification Strategies	
Points and leaderboards	Points are awarded for task completion or achieving milestones.
Scavenger hunts	Required training or assignment in order to obtain a clue and continue on their quest.
Gamified quizzes	To assess employee ability and knowledge on specific issues.
Contests	Encourage personnel to achieve predetermined objectives through incentives.
Role-playing games	Create their own persona and simulate real-life scenarios in a fun and engaging setting.
Gamified learning paths	A set of tasks or challenges must be performed one at a time in a specific order resulting in certification.

gamification since it encourages them to participate actively in their training and development.

There are various ways to incorporate gamification ideas and practices into training, ranging from naming a top performer to holding learning contests. Table 13.3 mentions some of the top business training gamification strategies

In terms of study on applicability and results, the concept of gamification for corporate training still has an enormous possibility for development. As per the available literature, some future directions include: (1) attempting to track the growth of the gamification market and professional sectors that have successfully implemented gamification; (2) better understanding the elements that can cause design failure in terms of corporate training; and (3) investigating the utmost frequent mistake which must be evidence-based on the training process, the organizational activities and the industry.

13.7 Discussion

Although gamification in human resources management is an emerging discipline, the literature shows that gamification in human resources processes has a typically favourable contribution. Gamification in digital media for human resource management allows firms to develop more effective employee communication and receive clear outcomes in terms of assessment, all while spending less money than in previous ways. Gamification has grown more prevalent and preferred by organizations as a result of digital platforms and ubiquitous virtual applications. Human resources have more responsibility as the current generation's demands develop every day, yet businesses limit the options available to those who achieve those standards.

Both practitioners and academics will benefit from this research. Firstly, it outlined the advantages of using gamification in the talent recruitment process for practitioners. Simultaneously, it clearly emphasized the risks connected with 'faux' gamification. Organizations must not neglect the design factor backed by research in the progression to stay ahead with the surge in acceptance of gamification in light of shifting preferences within the industry (Hiltbrand& Burke, 2011).

Using technology for a specific purpose is necessary. Communication clarity and opinion at different steps are the essential factors of an effective roadmap of gamified recruitment. Five specific components of TTF theory mentioned in the study are the nature of the task, the type of the technology, a fit between task and technology, technology consumption within a system, and the influence it has on performance, these components lay the groundwork for successful gamification deployment in HR practices and also help us grasp the consequences of gamification in recruitment.

When properly structured in alignment with the organization's aims and objectives, gamification of recruiting can be an appealing alternative to standard recruitment approaches for attracting a wide range of candidates. If a game is incorporated into a company's career website, for example, a prospective applicant is more likely to engage with it. This may encourage him to spend more time, potentially hours, rather than the typical method of merely moving down the data set to get additional information. If somehow gamified parts are not personalized, the belief that the game environment will only influence select types of persons and therefore be contentious to the organization may be correct. Therefore, Game concepts need to be able to be customized to inspire the candidates.

Since gamified recruitment has made a positive impression on big players in the industry, companies like PricewaterhouseCoopers (PwC), Marriott Hotel, Google LLC, Siemens AG, Phoenix Technologies, and others have developed a system that helps applicants to effectively assess their enthusiasm for contributing in the organization.

The study also talks about the notion of the game from the perspective of employee training, the justification for game-based training approach is discussed, studies on the efficacy of gamification are examined, and a stepwise process of including a game element in training has been presented. In addition, the research literature indicates that the gamification process in training might significantly improve training performance.

Gamification is most effective when combined with instructive learning notions; just incorporating game components into training without carefully considering the psychological implications are unlikely to result in proposed outcomes and may even impair the outcomes. According to the literature, gamification in training improves focus, increases the desire to be more productive, increases work engagement and also improves the learning engagement of the employees. Some of the top strategies in gamified training take into account leaderboards and points, scavenger hunts, interactive quizzes, contests, role-playing, gamified learning paths, etc.

The dimension of gamification is regarded as a success because it benefits both employees and organizations. This study provides directions to researchers who are fascinated by this theme. Future research should look into the usage of gamification in the field of human resource management in greater depth through empirical studies.

13.8 Managerial Implication

Managers can use gamification to improve the efficiency of HR activities in the emerging status quo, consequently improving the quality of the workforce and engagement of employees in learning processes. According to research, gamification in HR procedures is a creative, inventive and cost-effective technique for evaluating individuals, particularly for the recruitment and employee training processes.

Managers must consider how younger generations are becoming more interested in gaming and technology and incorporate this into their HR processes. When complemented by responses, it can be utilized in escorting towards the future, but it can also help managers, and game designers in modifying game components to meet the needs of both employees and the organization. The manager should develop choices with the understanding that users are engaged on several levels in gamified procedures. The procedure should include features such as the organization's aim, rules to follow and feedback to the candidate.

All these initiatives, if implemented, will assist the organization and its people in performing more efficiently, in a more engaging manner, and in less time, resulting in increased productivity and employee well-being, both of which are critical in the modern era.

13.9 Conclusion

Through a comprehensive literature review, this study intended to investigate the seemingly complex study landscape around gamification in HR practices. The review of literature & the findings in the area of gamification and HR revealed two possible application areas for game elements: (1) employee recruitment and the selection and 2) employee training and development. Gamification can make a tedious recruitment process more enjoyable. A simulated work environment represented through gamification, or an examination centreing on gamification, for example, could be a helpful tool. Gamification of real-world goals that are well-designed can link with undiscovered employee capabilities to increase performance and encourage employees to participate in ways that can result in tremendous gains. Suggestion for future research on the use of gamified tools that will help broaden the above-mentioned opportunity to interconnect facets of prolific gamification and the relevance of game-based subsystems in other human resources functions including performance evaluation cycles, employee engagement, employee motivation and psychological well-being, among others.

References

[1] Alcouffe, S., Berland, N., & Levant, Y. (2008). Actor-networks and the diffusion of management accounting innovations: A comparative study. Management Accounting Research, 19(1), 1–17.

[2] Argyris, C. (1986). Reinforcing organizational defensive routines: A unintended human resourcesactivity. Human Resource Management, 25(4), 541–555.

[3] Breaugh, J. A. (2013). Employee recruitment. Annual Review of Psychology, 64, 389–416. doi: 10.1146/annurev-psych-113011-143757

[4] Callon, M. (1984). Some elements of a sociology of translation: Domestication of thescallops and the fishermen of St Brieuc Bay. The Sociological Review, 32(1_suppl), 196–233.

[5] Cardador, T., Northcraft, G.B., &Whicher, J. (2016). A theory of work gamification: Something old, something new, something borrowed, something cool?. Human Resource Management Review,27, 353–365.

[6] Chapman, D. S., & Jones, D. (2002). Recruiting as persuasion: Making the sqaure hole appear round and the round peg feel square. In annual meeting for the Academy ofManagement, Denver, Colorado.

[7] Chen, V. H. H., & Duh, H. B. L. (2007). Understanding social interaction in world of warcraft. In Proceedings of the International Conference on Advances in ComputerEntertainmentTechnology, Salzburg, Austria (pp. 21–24). New York, NY: ACM. doi:10.1145/1255047.1255052

[8] Cherry, M.A. (2012). The gamification of work. Hofstra Law Review, 40(4), 851–858.

[9] Chou, Y. (2015). Actionable gamification: Beyond points, badges and leaderboards. Freemont, CA.

[10] Chow, S. (2014). A novel approach to employee recruitment: Gamification (Doctoral dissertation, University of Calgary). Retrieved from https://prism.ucalgary.ca/bitstream/handle/11023/1916/ucalgary_2014_chow_sam.pdf?sequence=4

[11] Chow, S., & Chapman, D. (2013, October). Gamifying the employee recruitment process. In Proceedings of the First International Conference on Gameful Design, Research,and Applications, Toronto, Ontario, Canada (pp. 91–94). New York, NY: ACM.

[12] Conway, S. (2014). Zombification? gamification, motivation, and the user. Journal of Gaming and Virtual Worlds, 6(2), 129–141.

[13] Cook, D. (2006). What are game mechanics?. lostgarden.com, available online at http://lostgarden.com/2006/10/what-are-game-mechanics.

[14] Cullens, J., & Waters, R. (2014). Hays challenge draws graduates to a career in recruitment: Serious gaming improves the quality of applicants. Human Resource ManagementInternational Digest, 22(2), 4–7.

[15] Dery, K., Tansley, C., &Hafermalz, E. (2014a). Games people play: social media and recruitment. Proceedings of the 25th Australasian Conference on Information Systems, 8th-10th December, Auckland, New Zealand, ACIS.

[16] Dery, K., Tansley, C., &Hafermalz, E. (2014b). Hiring in the age of social media: New rules, new game. University of Auckland Business Review, 17(1), 45–51.

[17] Deterding, S., Dixon, D., Khaled, R. &Nacke, L. (2011a). From game design elements togamefulness: defining gamification. Proceedings of the 15th International Academic MindTrek Conference: Envisioning Future Media Environments, September 28–30, 2011,Tampere, Finland, ACM, pp. 9–15.

[18] Deterding, S., Dixon, D., Khaled, R., &Nacke, L. (2011, September). From game designelements to gamefulness: Defining gamification. In Proceedings of the 15th International Academic MindTrek Conference: Envisioning Future Media Environments (pp. 9–15). New York, NY: ACM. doi:10.1145/2181037.2181040

[19] Deterding, S., Sicart, M., Nacke, L., O'Hara, K., & Dixon, D. (2011). Gamification: Using game designelements in non-gaming contexts. Extended Abstracts on Human Factors in Computing Systems, New York: ACM Press.

[20] DeWinter, J., Kocurek, C. A., & Nichols, R. (2014). Taylorism 2.0: Gamification, scientific management and the capitalist appropriation of play. Journal of Gaming and Virtual Worlds, 6(2), 109–127.

[21] Ezzamel, M. (1994). From problem solving to problematization: Relevance revisited. Critical Perspectives on Accounting, 5(4), 269–280.

[22] Folan, P., & Browne, J. (2005). A review of performance measurement: Towards performance management. Computers in Industry, 56, 663–680.

[23] Froehlich, J. (2014). Gamifying green: gamification and environmental sustainability. In Walz, S. P., &Deterding, S. (Eds.), The gameful world: Approaches, issues, applications, pp. 563–596. Cambridge, MA, USA: MIT Press.

[24] Fullerton, T., Swain, C. & Hoffman. S. (2004). Game DesignWorkshop: Designing, Prototyping, and Playtesting Games. Focal Pr.

[25] Gattulloa, M., Scuratib, G., Fiorentino, M., UVAA, A.E., Ferrise, F., & Bordegonib, M. (2019). TowardsAugmented Reality Manuals for Industry 4.0: A Methodology. Robotics and Computer-integratedManufacturing Review, Elsevier, 56, 276–286.

[26] Hamari, J. (2013). Transforming homo economicus into homo ludens:A field experiment on gamification in a utilitarian peer-to-peer trading service. Electronic Commerce Research and Applications, 12(4), 236–245.

[27] Hamari, J., Koivisto, J., &Sarsa, H. (2014, January). Does gamification work? A literaturereview of empirical studies on gamification. Hawaii International Conference on System Sciences, 14, 3025–3034. doi: 10.1109/HICSS.2014.377

[28] Hamari, J., Koivisto, J., &Sarsa, H. (2014). Does Gamification Work? – A Literature Review of Empirical Studies on Gamification. Proceedings of the 47th Hawaii International Conference on System Sciences, Hawaii, USA, January 6–9, 2014.

[29] Harvey, S. W. (2014). Winning the global talent war: A policy perspective. Journal of Chinese Human Resource Management, 5(1), 62–74.

[30] Herger, M. (2014). Enterprise Gamification: Engaging people by letting they have fun, California:CreateSpace Independent Publishing Platform.

[31] Hiltbrand, T., & Burke, M. (2011). How gamification will change business intelligence. Business Intelligence Journal, 16(2), 8–16.

[32] Hiltrop, J. M. (1999). The quest for the best: Human resource practices to attract and retaintalent. European Management Journal, 17(4), 422–430.

[33] Huotari, K. &Hamari, J. (2012). Defining gamification: a service marketing perspective", Proceedings of the 16th International Academic MindTrek Conference, October 3–5, 2012, Tampere, Finland, ACM, pp. 17–22.

[34] Korn, O., Brenner, F., Börsig, J., Lalli, F., Mattmüller, M., & Müller, A. (2017, July). Defining Recrutainment: A model and a survey on the gamification of recruiting and human resources. In International Conference on Applied Human Factors and Ergonomics (pp. 37–49). Cham: Springer.

[35] Krasulak, M. (2015). Use of gamification in the process of selection of candidates for the position in the opinion of young adults in Poland. Jagiellonian Journal of Management, 1(3), 203–215.

[36] Kücklich, J. (2005). Precarious playbour: Modders and the digital games industry. Fibreculture, 5(1), 1–5.

[37] Kumar, H., & Raghavendran, S. (2015). Gamification, the finer art: Fostering creativityand employee engagement. Journal of Business Strategy, 36(6), 3–12.

[38] Landers, R. N. (2019). Gamification misunderstood: How badly executed and rhetorical gamification obscures its transformative potential. Journal of Management Inquiry, 28(2), 137–140.

[39] Latour, B. (1996). On actor-network theory: A few clarifications. Soziale Welt, 47(4), 369–381.

[40] Lowe, A. (2004). Postsocial relations: Toward a performative view of accounting knowledge. Accounting, Auditing and Accountability Journal, 17(4), 604–628.

[41] Marczewski, A. (2013). Gamification: A Simple Introduction and a Bit More, (self-published on Amazon Digital Services, 2013). Kindle edition, Loc, 1405.

[42] Marczewski, A. (2017). Gamification design framework toolkit: Gamified. Wales.

[43] McGonigal, J. (2011). Reality is Broken: Why games makes us better and how they can change the world, New York, NY: Penguim.

[44] McGonigal, J. (2016). SuperBetter: The power of living gamefully, New York, NY: Penguim.

[45] Meeker, M. (2018). Internet trends report. CA: Kleiner Perkins

[46] Meister, J. (2015). Future of work: Using gamification for human resources. Forbes. Leadership. Retrieved from https://www.forbes.com/sites/jeannemeister/2015/03/30/future-of-work-using-gamification-for-human-resources/#30f1366624b7

[47] Mouritsen, J., Larsen, H. T., & Bukh, P. N. (2001). Intellectual capital and the 'capablefirm': Narrating, visualising and numbering for managing knowledge. Accounting, Organizations and Society, 26(7–8), 735–762.

[48] Nacke, L. E., & Deterding, C. S. (2017). The maturing of gamification research. Computersin Human Behaviour, 71, 450–454.

[49] Negruşa, A. L., Toader, V., Sofică, A., Tutunea, M. F., & Rus, R. V. (2015). Exploring gamification techniques and applications for sustainable tourism. Sustainability, 7(8), 11160–11189.

[50] Oprescu, F., Jones, C., & Katsikitis, M. (2014). I play at work—ten principles for transforming work processes through gamification. Frontiers in Psychology, 5, 1–5. doi: 10.3389/fpsyg.2014.00014

[51] Pavlus, J. (2010). The Game of Life. Scientific American, 303, 43–44.

[52] Pornel, J. B. (2014). Factors that make educational games engaging to students. Philippine Journal of Social Sciences and Humanities, 16(2), 1–9.

[53] Reeves, B., & Read, J. L. (2009). Total engagement: using games and virtual worlds to change the way people work and businesses compete. Boston: Harvard Business School Press.

[54] Robson, K., Plangger, K., Kietzmann, J. H., McCarthy, I., & Pitt, L. (2015). Is it all a game? Understanding the principles of gamification. Business Horizons, 58(4), 411–420.

[55] Rynes, S. L. (1991) Recruitment, job choice, and post-hire consequences: A call for new research directions. In M. D. Dunnette& L. M. Hough (Eds.), Handbook of industrial and organizational psychology (2nd ed., Vol. 2, pp. 399–444). Palo Alto, CA: Consulting Psychologists Press.

[56] Schlechter, A., Thompson, N. C., & Bussin, M. (2015). Attractiveness of non-financial rewards for prospective knowledge workers: An experimental investigation. Employee Relations, 37(3), 274–295.

[57] Shneiderman, B. (2004). Designing for fun: How can we design user interfaces to be morefun? Interactions, 11(5), 48–50.

[58] Taylor, N., Bergstrom, K., Jenson, J., & de Castell, S. (2015). Alienated playbour: Relations of production in EVE online. Games and Culture, 10(4), 365–388.

[59] White, C. (2015). Five companies that are successfully using gamification for recruitment. Retrieved from https://business.linkedin.com/talent-solutions/blog/recruiting-strategy/2015/5-companies-that-are-successfully-using-gamification-for-recruiting

[60] Woźniak, J. (2015). The use of gamification at different levels of e-recruitment. Management Dynamics in the Knowledge Economy, 3(2), 257–278.

[61] Xu, F., Weber, J., & Buhalis, D. (2013). Gamification in tourism. In Information and Communication Technologies in Tourism 2014 (pp. 525–537). Cham: Springer.

[62] Xu, Y. (2011). Literature review on web application gamification and analytics. CSDL Technical report, 11–05.

[63] Zichermann, G. (2013). Gamification: The hard truths. Huff Post. Tech, 32(01)

14

Technology-based Human Resource Practices within Indian IT Industry

Sandeep Kumar Gupta[1], Shikha Kapoor[2], Sebnem Yucel[3], Renu Rana[1], Recep Yusel[4] and Lalit Prasad[5]

[1]AMET University, Chennai, India
[2]Amity University, India
[3]Health Management Department, Selcuk University, Konya, Turkiye
[4]Kirikkale University, Turkiye
[5]"D. Y. Patil Institute of Management Studies, India

Email: skguptabhu@gmail.com; skpoor2@amity.edu;
sebnemasian@selcuk.edu.tr; ims.renurana@gmail.com;
akademikTl @gmail.com; onlylalitprasad@gmail.com

Abstract

This chapter investigates the different human resources practices adopted in the IT sector. To meet present-era demands, IT companies must develop some noticeable HR strategies and eliminate desirable HR activities to gain an advantage in maintaining brand image. The present chapter aims to identify the factors responsible for the bad and good HR practises and their differentiation in the Indian IT industry. It also aims to cover the major implications of the good and bad HR practices for the HRM framework and effectiveness. It is being discovered that IT enterprises having great HR activities and functions have a solid human asset framework and are becoming the forerunners in the help market. Nonetheless, each of these techniques has increased the commitment of human resource professionals. It is self-evident that enterprises that can manage their human resources effectively will reap numerous benefits in terms of the firm's effectiveness and development. This chapter followed a subjective approach to dealing with better comprehending the great and bad human resource practises and comprehending their significance in the Indian IT field.

14.1 Introduction

A plausible procedure between industry standards and imaginative procedures is required for HR work in both small and large companies. The other truth about high-impact institutions is that they are 'essential rights for HR pioneers'. The implementation of the fundamentals of HR components of enlistment, dealing with payroll, compensation, and worker improvement and development should be solid and straightforward, and the association should also be aware of it. The HR experts are given the necessary plan and all rights to carry out the HR functions in an organization. Rights are essential for assuming work-related liability and authority.

However, there is a requirement for consistent improvement at each stage of the task progression. To achieve gradual transition and long-term improvement, the high-impact HR association continues to progress and implement corrective measures. It is assumed that better outcomes necessitate efforts to confine, repair and remake capacities. During the time spent changing, change is essential. High-impact HR associations pioneer unambiguous HR programmes that can be easily embraced by the workforce, the board and the workforce.

Companies must keep in mind that an HR asset is a symbol of life, not a machine or an item. They have feelings, think, see, and decompose and each has its own foundation, experience, culture, age and information. HR pioneers should improve this source in small, manageable steps. Nonetheless, things are moving at breakneck speed. The workplace environment will change in the coming years as a result of recent technological advancements and innovative organizational frameworks.

A viable HR framework necessitates embracing the best HR strategies and eliminating the worst HR strategies. As a result, the firm's IT HR chiefs should be knowledgeable enough to deal with HR policies and arrangements appropriately. HR in IT groups should be regarded as a firm's colleague. Furthermore, HR chiefs now participate in an authoritative dynamic; gone are the days when they were simply viewed as managerial individuals. They have now established themselves as important members of an organization.

14.2 Literature Review

To analyse the perspective which exists between the human resources (HR) strategies and company's performance specifically, the study is conducted to investigate the relationships between a set of network-building HR activities, aspects of top management teams' overt and covert social networks, and firm performance [3–4]. A significant relationship is found between HR strategies and company performance which includes stock growth and sales growth mediated by their top manager's social networking sites in a study of 73 elevated firms [2].

Employees were previously in a position of relative inferiority in comparison to employers. These relationships are evolving today. To be market competitive, a company must compete for the best specialists – for talents. It is especially useful for businesses that rely on the skills of their employees. In today's job markets, one type of competitive environment is employer branding or the development of a brand as a preferred employer. The more expressive and improved the corporate identity, the more appealing the institution is to employees [5–8].

In the current environment, HR function adaptation extends beyond our creative abilities. As a result of these developments, there is a pressing need to advance the fundamentals of human resource management. It is seen that businesses in India can enhance their presence on the global stage by implementing the best and most effective human resources strategies [14, 15].

Best HR strategies assist Indian corporations in developing a brand and leaving an imprint globally. In the field of human resources, the most effective HR drills prepare an establishment for current and future challenges. Businesses (particularly those in the IT industry) face significant pressure from globalization to be serious and empowered. This pressing factor cannot be avoided, and the survival of the business will be dependent on the association's continuous improvement. The current shift in human resource management is beyond one's comprehension. Recognizing these developments, there is an urgent need for advancement in HRM fundamentals since best human resource practices help Indian corporations develop an image and establish themselves in the global league. In addition, these best HR practices also help organizations to deal with current and future organizational and management challenges. Globalization puts a lot of pressure on corporations (particularly in the IT industry) to be competitive and motivated. The impact of this pressure is ubiquitous, and corporate sustainability will be dependent on the organization's ongoing development. To compete in today's extremely competitive business world, corporations must thrive with inventive and innovative HR strategies.

14.3 HR Best Practices

The best HR practice model was suggested by Bersin and Associates in 2013 in which they provided details regarding the process of its implementation,

Figure 14.1 HRM building blocks.

how these practices would work, and contribute to developing the adminis-tration. In addition to it, they also provided the methodology for the measure-ment of the framework's adequacy and productivity. It is shown that many of such HR practices just were not dependent on the size of the company and the business climate but also dependent on the process of the organization and management authority styles [15–17].

'Business development methods' and 'HR systematic governance' are two of the fundamental HR strategies of a high-intensity HR associa-tion. Institutions with a deep insight into their business and that include HR executives in their interactions do better and gain more development in their activities. To develop a business improvement model, HR departments need positive relationships with their co-workers [18–21].

'Business relevant manpower planning' is the next process. The work-force of an alliance would be crucial to the progress of the business. The best companies combine work investigation and workforce by continuously anticipating workforce. Recognizing the best talent in the market is a difficult task for HR pioneers [22–24]. Organizations must interpret the meaning of a talented workforce and investigate the section of the outside workforce. The ability should become more convenient, and there should be measures in place to ensure that the representatives continue to improve. The difficulties for HR directors grow as the work is not just to find the right competitor, but also to develop those up-and-comers with all of the critical abilities required for an organization [25–30].

'The vision mission and the right HR argument' is the third largest HR exercise. An organization that is clear about its vision develops strategies for human resources and establishes a mission statement and vision for its representatives. HR approaches should be focused on fostering advancement and relationships in the workplace. The compelling HR approaches are based on essential planning, a dynamic workplace, a management style and the acquiescence of improvements for the exercises. There should be legitimate rules in place for the HR team to follow and carry out each interaction. Organizations should select articulations that both rouse and motivate their employees [31–33].

Accurately categorizing the HR roles is the fourth strategy being followed. HR executives are working hard to switch from the company level to the governance level. A long time ago, the job of HR was similar to coursework and also was limited to making compensation, checking participation and keeping track of the representative's profile.

HR's role is being refined and retooled as time goes. A high-impact HR company welcomes HR professionals who are dynamic, innovative and creative. HR nowadays has a varied workplace culture. The HR division's concept has been changed and updated to reflect the most recent requirements for the current company [12, 34].

The fifth HR best practice is 'carrying out versatile HR organization structure'. Fruitful associations adhere to a flexible and open hierarchical system. The central component of enhancements is adaptability. Perhaps, just having any model for HR does not ensure the success and effectiveness of HR practices. The ideal blend of arrangements and construction should be planned, and HR executives and managers must embrace every approach in their tasks. HR pioneers should be a part of the context once planning HR arrangements. High-impact association thanks their HR directors for their participation in the significant dynamic interaction between the employees and the company [16, 21].

'Local area constructing HR system' is the sixth HR best practice. When there is a transferable stage for employees, partners and customers, things become simple and nimble. The relationship between businesses and representatives, as well as managers and employees, is almost as important as different capacities. Person-to-person communication is a powerful way to stay connected 24 hours a day, seven days a week and to freely share thoughts and feelings. Executive information gateways, online enrolment, internet preparation and studios enable various HR partners to easily discover their requirements [5, 19, 24].

'HR estimates for workouts and effects' is the seventh HR great method. Estimation techniques are especially important for evaluating functional measures and HR individual measures. Associations developed various estimation methods for business agreement, viability and productivity. HR institutions have become more developed and information-driven as a result of recent HR advancements and new HR abilities. Currently, HR data can be consistently accumulated as well as dissected appropriately. Such estimation methodologies produce reasonable associations between HR work endeavours and the singular man in the organization's creation [26, 31].

'Constructing from within HR clusters' is indeed the eighth HR greatest procedure. Many organizations invest greatly in business development yet neglect investments in their employees, which is not supported. Organizations must devote resources to the development and advancement of disciplines such as information officers, relationship officers, change officers and capability officers. All current HR best strategies should demonstrate the benefits of informal communication and other HR innovation to them [32–34].

'Reconsidering HR activities' is the ninth HR greatest practice. If there is a need to reassess HR presidencies that the company's internal groups cannot perform, the company should put everything on the line. In certain circumstances, we must pay special attention to compelling abilities. Sound institutions are generally re-evaluating their HR central presidencies, for instance, payrolls, benefits and advantages. A few institutions reconsider key administrations, for example, key enlistment, learning and advancement and so on. Association re-appropriates those HR administrations that necessitate skill and global coordination. International firms rethink various HR administrations from central HR associations [4, 14, 36].

'Further developing line-manager skills' is the tenth HR best procedure. Line-manager capabilities influence business execution since they are accountable for the organization's major tasks. The pioneers just on the HR deck should focus on key activities' interaction such as creation, executives and stock management. Cooperation and coordinative power are required for the execution of all tasks in institutions. No office can function effectively on its own. Solidarity is a source of strength, and this guideline should be present in the workplace for powerful administration [17, 24].

14.4 HR Misconduct

Most groups have focused on good human resource strategies; though it is pointless if bad HR strategies continue to exist. It is also necessary to eliminate and identify bad practices when they arise. The following HR practices are considered bad practices:

a) Excessive privacy and confidentiality of individual information: The classification of pay information, considering leaving records, progress subtleties, as well as involvement records creates cynicism and doubt, which affects the business-worker relationship.

b) Imprecise deliverables: Employees and managers should have a clear understanding of the job description and specifications. Otherwise, it will harm their job performance and efficiency.

c) Uncl ear KRAs and objectives: If employees do not understand their key result areas and performance objectives, their performance will be meaningless and they will be unable to contribute to the organizational goals. The representatives should be familiar with the destinations and objectives so that they can set their goals to achieve the organization's goals, which will benefit both the entity and the workers.

d) Employee development in the absence of his/her association: Employees should be aware of the tasks assigned to them, and preparation supervisors should select candidates for various development projects. Otherwise, the advancement programme may not be important to the people, and the results may vary, resulting in spontaneous worker development, and a waste of time, money and effort.

e) Talent rusting: Once a fresher confronts new challenges, enhancements and affords, the task becomes a daily routine, and drudgery takes over. It is the directors' responsibility to reassign and reassign old representatives for workers to advance at each stage and learn new things arbitrarily.

f) Lobby of non-performers: Non-entertainers are consistently glued to their seats. The worst part is that non-performing bosses must survey their subordinates, who are high-energy adolescents and expertly skilled. Such skilled employees either do not stay with the organization or contribute to its deterioration. This will, in some way, allow non-entertainers to enter and eventually obstruct the development of the association.

g) Keeping top performers: Identifying and retaining talented employees are more important than dealing with or getting rid of non-performers. Retention and management of a talent pool of qualified employees must be of great concern for the HR department, as they are one of the most valuable assets for any organizational growth and improvement.

h) Lack of communication and feedback: Employees' performance and actions vary according to the administration in the organization. They know about the jobs and obligations of their working environment. The administration must examine the target input with the goal that usefulness will not ever influence.

i) Technology phobia: The more established representatives refuse to acknowledge that, in the long run, innovation can replace HR staff by providing precise, ideal and quality data in the critical association choice. Perhaps they propose having IT representatives present to supervise technology-based systems and frameworks.

14.5 The Theoretical Framework of the Study

14.5.1 Key terms and definitions

For more explanation, this segment gives the meanings of the above developed in this review.

14.5.1.1 Image building for corporate

'Corporate image' was vitally a publicizing language however by and by it alludes to the organization's notoriety. 'Picture' is the thing that people, in general, see when they heard the organizations name (Eleanor Mckenzie, 2017). The corporate picture currently is the whole of all impressions left on the organization's name. Richard and Zhang (2012) noticed that the corporate picture is interrelated with the association's notoriety and relies on the client's convictions, impressions and thoughts. Likewise, the administration's disposition, reasoning and conduct assume a significant part in building the corporate picture. It is obvious from the realities that the corporate picture is a bunch of convictions and discernments made in the client's brain.

Worcester (1997) delineates that the corporate picture is a general impression of the organization to clients and a picture that the crowd sees about the association. Newman 1989 first utilized the term corporate picture to define the issues that emerge while balancing and looking at the worker character and corporate picture.

HR turned into a powerful capacity in the top associations nowadays thus numerous associations are known for the best HR rehearses that they have for their workers (India Today, 2018). The new HR patterns rethinking the manners, in which staffs are selected, held, compensated and permitted to work. HR rehearses allude to the HR programmes executed by an association for its workers to persuade and to give all necessities to them (Arthur and Boyles, 2007). The current review is expounding the job of HR rehearses in corporate picture building. The need for HR rehearses is diverse for various enterprises relying on their current circumstance, culture, social foundation and sorts of business needs. This review is assigned to the IT area in India explicitly IT Companies-Infosys, TCS, IBM, HCL and Accenture.

14.5.1.2 Manager branding

Manager branding is characterized as a course of understanding the assumptions and impressions of the workers, partners and possible representatives by embracing different practices and projects for drawing in and holding the best ability. In [30, 31], the authors characterize manager marking as the two-way bargain between an association and its kin – 'the explanation they decide to join and the explanation they allowed to remain'. Also, 'it is a picture of the association as an incredible work environment in the personalities of current representatives and key partners in the outer market (dynamic and detached applicants, customers and clients and other key partners)', SHRM, 2008. According to CIPD, 2006 it is a bunch of qualities that make an association differentiation and fascination those individuals who will feel a liking with it and convey their best execution inside it.

14.5.1.3 Social responsibilities of corporate

SRC interest assumes a compelling part in worker organization distinguishing proof. With SRC execution organizations can likewise keep a solid relationship with their workers. The author in [24] analyses and contends that SRC presently become a simultaneous piece of worldwide and current corporate that animates various targets: – assumptions for representatives, social qualities, the strain on officials, changes in purchasers' and providers' attitudes, and adjustment in shopper interest [9, 36] consented to the explanation that 'over the long haul the prosperity of society would be in the possession of socially mindful associations'. In [34–36], the authors characterize SRC as a commitment to update the degree of social, moral, and accepted practices and encourage the connection among proprietors and partners.

Being social not helps the corporate in building a solid picture, yet additionally assists them in keeping a solid relationship with their representatives. The social corporate picture has turned into a resource for the association. The author in [6–8] believes that associations that perform the best and priceless social exercises acquire many benefits like full consumer loyalty and better client assessment. Then again, the significance of SPC and SRC exercises is expanding to partners (workers). SPC drive differs for interior and outside partners. Inner SPC drives for the most part include government assistance exercises for their workers like in-house instruction, professional preparation, at-work and off-the-work preparation [16]. Be that as it may, outer drives incorporate exercises like non-benefit programmes,

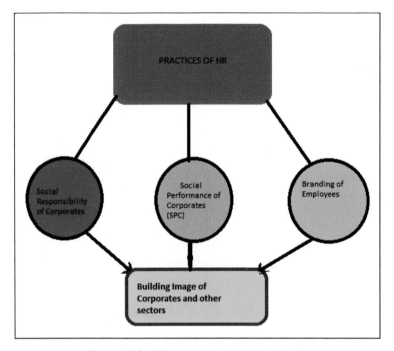

Figure 14.2 The proposed conceptual model.

noble cause gifts, free administrations and so on [15]. SPC helps the HR chiefs in supporting the representative spirit and their presentation and helps in building a positive corporate picture. Rodrigo and Arenas (2008) express that SPC is one of the significant devices for upgrading workers' mentalities that help the HR chiefs in making and fostering the right culture in the association.

14.6 Conceptual Framework

The proposed conceptual model for this research is shown in Figure 14.2.

HR practices go about as an indicator variable that straightforwardly affects the corporate picture building which is the result variable. Business branding, corporate social responsibility and corporate social performance are the interceding factors. These intervening factors are thought of and proposed by a few analysts [17–21, 24]. The review recommends that HR rehearses impact the intervening factors, for example, the branding of organization, social responsibility of corporates and their social performance which then, at that point, impact the image building of the corporates.

14.7 Research Methodology

The advancement of innovation and the cutthroat commercial centre has changed how associations work; there is a significant distinction in the work practices of those organizations who rehearsed picture working throughout the previous few years. Organizations that picked image-building rehearses have begun encountering a significant distinction in their business, like a higher benefit, worker dedication, positive media consideration, fortifying the relationship with clients and investors, and expanded business openings. The corporate picture is tied in with treating individuals' opinions, positive feelings spread good words about the organization and negative feelings spread negative twisting of the organization. The umpteen organizations and gobs of brands have given difficulties as far as manageability in the serious commercial centre. In this way, it becomes important to construct and keep a decent corporate picture to defeat the issues and difficulties of the association. The current research is lacking in portraying the job of HR rehearses in the corporate picture working in IT organizations.

14.8 Development and Findings of the Study

The discoveries of this exploration are obtained from a mix of subjective and quantitative information examination. This current review's exploration method remembers subjective examination for the request to recognize HR rehearses in the IT area that adds to the association's picture building. A topical investigation of semi-organized meetings has been done and it has been observed that subjective examination obviously upholds the assertion and demonstrates that there is a critical connection between HR rehearses and corporate picture building. It likewise thinks that the variables relevant to HR rehearse boss marking, corporate social obligation and corporate social execution truly do add to the picture working of the association. Nonetheless, a large number of the factors of these variables might contribute by implication.

This subjective examination has additionally addressed to answer the development measures/HR rehearses that help IT organizations in building their corporate picture. The imaginative and new HR rehearses that can help IT associations in picture building are remote worker policy, HR confidentiality policy, and education to employee children policy as recommended by the respondents for all the better human assets the executives rehearse. Also, a positive connection between HR rehearses and corporate picture-building has been noticed.

14.9 Conclusion

The review and analysis propose that human resource managers and executives must examine the HR strategies on a regular for the company's growth. Good HR practices to be sustained and employees must also be aware of such practices from time to time. On the other hand, a review of bad practices has to be done and corrective actions are to be taken timely. According to the findings of this evaluation, effective HR procedures should be modified depending on the type of institution. It suggests that HR pioneers' responsibilities must be set including dealing with the workforce with viability, as the job of representatives in IT institutions is a group based in comparison to other associations. The best HR strategies will always be beneficial to the development of the association.

References

[1] Carroll, A. B. (1979). A three-dimensional conceptual model of corporate social performance, Academy of Management Review, 4, 497–505.

[2] Collins, C. J., & Clark, K. D. (2003) the role of human resource practices in creating organizational competitive advantage, Academy of Management Journal, 46(6), 740–751.

[3] Sharma, N. and Tj, Kamalanabhan (2012). Internal corporate communication and its impact on internal branding: Perception of Indian public sector employees. Employees. Corporate Communications: An International Journal, 17(3), 300–322.

[4] Fuentes-García, F. J., Núñez-Tabales, J. M., & Veroz-Herradón, R. (2008). Applicability of corporate social responsibility to human resources management: Perspective from Spain, Journal of Business Ethics, 82(1), 27–44.

[5] Figurska, I., & Matuska, E. (2013). Employer Branding As A Human Resources Management Strategy, Human resources management & Ergonomics, 7(2).

[6] Fombrun, C., & Shanley, M. (1990). What's in a name? Reputation building and corporate strategy. Academy of Management Journal, 33(2), 233–258.

[7] Foster, C., Punjaisri, K., & Cheng, R. (2010). Exploring the relationship between corporate, internal and employer branding. Journal of Product & Brand Management, 19(6), 401–409.

[8] Goyal, R., & Shrivastava, M. (2012). A study of HR practices and their impact on employees job satisfaction and organizational commitment in pharmaceuticals industries, International Journal of Business Trends and Technology, 2(3), 22–28.

[9] Guest, D. (2002). Human resource management, corporate performance and employee wellbeing: Building the worker into HRM. The journal of industrial relations, 44(3), 335–358.

[10] Harel, G. H., &Tzafrir, S. S. (1999). The effect of human resource management practices on the perceptions of organizational and market performance of the firm. Human resource management, 38(3), 185–199.

[11] Hussainy, K., Elsayed, M., &Abdelrazek, M. (2011). Factors affecting corporate social responsibility disclosure in Egypt. Corporate Ownership and Control journal, 1–27.

[12] Jeet, V., & Sayeeduzzafar, D. (2014). A study of HRM practices and its impact on employees job satisfaction in private sector banks: A case study of HDFC Bank. International Journal of Advanced Research in Computer Science and Management Studies, 2(1), 62–68.

[13] Jo Hatch, M., & Schultz, M. (1997). Relations between organizational culture, identity and image. European Journal of Marketing, 31(5/6), 356–365.

[14] Jo Hatch, M., & Schultz, M. (2003). Bringing the corporation into corporate branding. European Journal of Marketing, 37(7/8), 1041–1064.

[15] Kim, D., & Sturman, M. C. (2012). HR branding: How human resources can learn from product and service branding to improve attraction, selection, and retention.

[16] Kim, H. R., Lee, M., Lee, H. T., & Kim, N. M. (2010). Corporate social responsibility and employee–company identification. Journal of Business Ethics, 95(4), 557–569.

[17] Maruf, A. A. (2013). Corporate Social Responsibility and Corporate Image. Transnational Journal of Science and Technology, 29.

[18] Mahadevan, A., & Sn Mohamed, F. A. (2014). Impact Of Human Resource Management (Hrm) Practices on Employee Performance (A Case Of Telekom Malaysia). International Journal of Accounting & Business Management, 2(2).

[19] Mohapatra, S. (2012). Unique HR practices in the Indian IT industry: A research agenda. Delhi Business Review, 13(1), 49–65.

[20] Murthy, B. V. (2015). Innovative HR Practices in its Industry in India-An Empirical Study. UGC sponsored minor research project, University of Mumbai.

[21] Meyers, B. Y. (2005). Analysis: Corporate Case Study—Schering-Plough Looks to Remedy An Ailing Image. PR Week, 12.

[22] Omotayo, A. O., & Adenike, A. A. (2013). Impact of organizational culture on human resource practices: a study of selected Nigerian private universities. Journal of Competitiveness, 5(4).

[23] Rana, R., Kapoor, S & Gupta S. K.. (2021). Impact of HR Practices on Corporate Image Building in Indian IT Sector, Problem and Perspective in Management, 19(2), 528–535.

[24] Shaker, F., & Ahmed, A. S. (2014). Influence of employer brand image on employee identity. Global Disclosure of Economics and Business, 3(3), 51–59.

[25] Sparrow, P., & Otaye, L. (2015). Employer branding: From attraction to a core HR strategy, White Paper, 15(01).

[26] Sharma, N., & Kamalanabhan, T. J. (2012). Internal corporate communication and its impact on internal branding: Perception of Indian public sector.

[27] Tiwari, P., & Saxena, K. (2012). Human resource management practices: A comprehensive review, Pakistan business review, 9(2), 669–705.

[28] Tanković, A. Č. (2015, January). Interrelationship of Corporate Identity, Corporate Image and Corporate Reputation: a New Stakeholder-Time Based Model. In 34th International Conference on Organizational Science Development: Internationalization and Cooperation.

[29] Trehan, S., & Setia, K. (2014). Human resource management practices and organizational performance: an Indian perspective. Global Journal of Finance and Management, 6(8), 789–796.

[30] Tan, C.L., & Nasurdin, A. M. (2011). Human resource management practices and organizational innovation: assessing the mediating role of knowledge management effectiveness. Electronic journal of knowledge management, 9(2), 155–167.

[31] Turban, D. B. (2001). Organizational attractiveness as an employer on college campuses: An examination of the applicant population. Journal of Vocational Behavior, 58(2), 293–312.

[32] Van Heerden, C. H. (1999). Developing a corporate image model. South African Journal of Economic and Management Sciences, 2(3), 492–508.

[33] Virvilaite, R., & Daubaraite, U. (2011). Corporate social responsibility in forming a corporate image. Engineering Economics, 22(5), 534–543.

[34] Wallace, M., Lings, I., Cameron, R., & Sheldon, N. (2014). Attracting and retaining staff: the role of branding and industry image. In Workforce development (pp. 19-36). Springer, Singapore.

[35] Yüksel, M. (2015). Employer Branding and Reputation from a Strategic Human Resource Management Perspective. Communications of the IBIMA, 1.

[36] UYGUN Serdar, Vural, Gupta Sandeep, Kumar (2020). Leadership and Accountability for Social Development: Intellectual Leadership and Rectors, International Journal of Indian Culture and Business Management, 21(02), 171-180.

15

Convergence of Artificial Intelligence in Sustainable Human Resource Management for Modern Organizational Growth

Shimar Mishra[1] and Amit Kishor[2]

[1]Department of Food Technology, S.I.T.E., Swami Vivekanand Subharti University, India
[2]Department of Computer Science & Engineering, S.I.T.E., Swami Vivekanand Subharti University, India

Email: shimarshiatsdt@gmail.com; amit_kishor@rediffmail.com

Abstract

Currently, human resource technology is entering a golden age and the world is interested in human resource management at a completely new level. Human resource technology and modern workforce solutions provide significant opportunities to ensure optimal team member retention and increased long-term success. An area that has been largely steady for decades is seeing significant change due to the growing demand for a high-quality digital human resources experience. However, technology solutions alone will not produce business results unless we invest in other aspects of human resource organizations. Technology alone will not be enough. As a technology, artificial intelligence plays a role in various human resource processes, from recruiting to assessing employee performance. An investigation into the relationships between artificial intelligence and human resource functions, as well as the various activities undertaken by human resources, will be conducted. In the past few years, artificial intelligence technology has enabled the company to improve its performance and conduct daily operations more efficiently. Because of the dynamic and competitive environment, managers at various levels are experiencing increased pressure and recognizing the need for artificial intelligence. A recent survey revealed that approximately 38 percent of organizations are currently using AI for management and day-to-day activities. Over 62 percent of businesses expect to start using it soon. This technology has improved the productivity and innovation of organizations that use it. With the rapidly changing business environment and disruptive technologies, organizations and human resource leaders face tremendous pressure to improve human resource innovation and people management. Due to this, organizations have turned to invest in human resource technologies to improve the human resource impact on business. Disruptive technology is omnipresent in people's daily lives, particularly among millennials. Disruptive technologies can transform conceptual understanding as well as instructional activities. However, if they are not used appropriately, they can be detrimental. Therefore, these technologies should serve as learning facilitators and information disseminators, both locally and globally.

In this chapter, the main aim of the work is to improve the resource management of the organization with the use of the latest artificial intelligence technology. A technology known as artificial intelligence (AI) allows businesses to expand faster while completing their tasks with greater efficiency. In addition to finance, human resources, marketing and production, this technology has found its way into other fields as well. This chapter explores bloggers' perspectives on technological innovations, including disrupting technologies in human resource management through artificial intelligence technology. This study is based on blogger opinions and examines that disruptive technology will not only remain disruptive but will also prove to be an opportunity to achieve maximum impact in HR.

15.1 Introduction

Now, the leaders across a variety of industries need to discuss technology, how artificial intelligence can improve quality, speed and functionality, as well as growth in the top-line revenue. In recent years, artificial intelligence has become a mainstream business concept due to a convergence of forces. Artificial intelligence, networks, and robotics are also disrupting human resource management (HRM) practices. Disruptive technology can be introduced to their organizations to gain commercial advantage. Integrated and complementary management strategies are essential for ensuring the contribution of human resources to organizational goals on an individual and collective basis [1]. The HRM field uses artificial intelligence in a few areas, including recruitment, legal work, performance management, coaching and monitoring employees. As well as controlling harassment, robots are also used in interview and selection processes, learning and communication. In the workplace, in addition, they serve as tools for cobots (collaborative robots). As part of the recruiting process, learning and development, career development and collaboration networks are used. By implementing sustainable practices together with disruptive technology presented by the fourth industrial revolution, new opportunities for professional activities and job creation are created. Currently, disruptive technologies play an ever-growing role in the lives of the population and especially in the lives of the new millennium's youth. On the one hand, their presence is positively affecting knowledge structures and educational activities. Disruptive technologies, however, can have negative effects if they are used inappropriately. It is possible to construct knowledge and stimulate learning with the instruments made by the fourth industrial revolution, but their indiscriminate use, without any educational purpose, should not be encouraged. Therefore, these technologies should be used as a tool for learning and information dissemination both locally and globally.

As social beings, human beings rarely live and work alone. Our relationships, consciously and unconsciously, are constantly shaped, developed and managed. Our relationships are the outcome of our actions and are highly dependent on our ability to manage them. Managing work relations in the workplace is the core concern of human resource management. In Physics, artificial intelligence is the study of how computer programs can mimic human abilities such as reasoning, perception, and critical thinking [17, 53].

An expert in human resources (HR) quoted in 1994 that in the early years, businesses that had access to the most capital or the latest technology had the biggest competitive advantage, and later on, the company with the best technological advantage has the most competitive advantage. The AI does seem able to handle many of the HR functions, but it is still a long way from completely replacing the HR staff because human interaction is still necessary when dealing with employees [21].

Nowadays, artificial intelligence (AI) has become a strategic priority for businesses and is affecting virtually every area of business. As AI crunches vast quantities of big data, it provides decision-makers with meaningful information that alters and enhances the employees', applicants', and candidates' experiences in organizations [18, 19]. Modern tools and AI have been changing the HR game. In the field of artificial intelligence, it is improving the possibility of designing, engaging and developing a robot that behaves like a human with human-like functions. It can be applied to help HR administration to elevate the business's efforts. Today, we are witnessing the emergence of 'high impact digital HR' because of this digital and advanced workforce technology. The latest technological changes have changed the foundation of HR operations, resulting in a need to welcome the latest developments in workforce technology. Organizations are increasingly utilizing HR technology to streamline their workflow and improve capabilities. However, embracing change and adapting to HR technology have been viewed as a stigma [3]. Nevertheless, there will be challenges ahead in transitioning from a manual to a digital system and in updating existing HR systems to transform the employee experience. Because HRs have transformed from simply being a support function in an organization to a strategy-oriented role that helps drive the overall organization, AI's ability to integrate easily into HR and deliver value is crucial for HRs [20]. Human resource management is examined in this chapter in terms of artificial intelligence. Researchers have found that most companies are adopting technology in various HR processes such as recruitment, performance appraisal, and cloud-based employee information systems [30].

15.2 Artificial Intelligence in Human Resource Management: Nature and Function

It is a management function comprising assisting managers in recruiting, selecting, training and developing members of an organization. Human Resource Management encompasses the organization's human resources.

Human Resource Management is based on the following components:

- **Management functions and principles are part of HRM.** Organizations use the functions and principles of compensation to obtain, develop, maintain and reward employees.

- **Integrating employee-related decisions is crucial.** All human resource (HR) decisions must be consistent with other aspects of employee life.

- **Organizational effectiveness is determined by the decisions taken.** As a result of an organization being run effectively, it will provide customers with higher-quality products at a lower cost.

15.2.1 Artificial intelligence in human resources management (HRM): the scope

Human resource management encompasses all major activities that occur in the working life of an employee—from the time he or she enters the

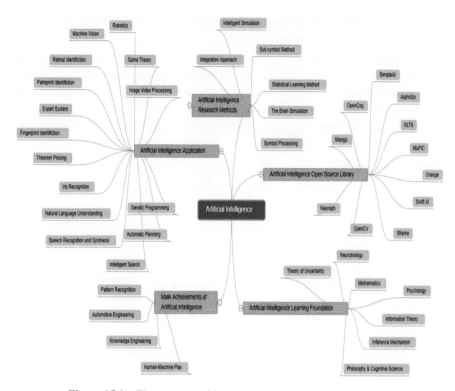

Figure 15.1 The structure of human resource management (HRM).

organization until the time when that employee leaves the organization. Motivating employees, maintaining employees, managing employees, planning, and analysing jobs, creating jobs and hiring employees are among the HRM activities. According to Wang et al. [35], artificial intelligence or the activity of making machines intelligent, contributes to the functionality of intelligent machines in an environment. From Figure 15.1 [48], the structure of HRM starts with recruitment and ends with payroll management.

Human resource management encompasses the following responsibilities:

- Any decision, strategy, factor, principle, operating method, function, activity or method used by an organization to manage people as employees.

- The employment relationships a person has have many dimensions and many dynamics.

15.2.1.2 Conceptual AI application model for human resources management

This 'AI+HRM' model is primarily to assist human resource managers in making better decisions with greater efficiency when confronted with a lot of data on how AI and HRM can be integrated. The article between human resource management, AI technology and the developed Intelligent System is described and explained in this article, as shown in Figure 15.3 [50].

15.3 Human Resource Management's Impact and Innovation with Disruptive Technology

Artificial intelligence, networks and robotics are some of the disruptive technologies that have altered the HRM sector. They are also affecting HRM practices. HR managers use artificial intelligence for recruitment, legal work, performance evaluation, coaching and monitoring of employees. With computers being used for interviewing and selecting candidates, learning, developing, communicating and controlling harassment, networks are widely used for recruitment, learning, development, career planning and collaboration. In computer science, the term 'intelligent agents' refers to a system or systems of devices that make decisions based on perceptions of their environments and the necessary actions to maximize their chances of achieving their goals. Additionally, a system can accurately interpret external data, learn from such data and adapt to that learning to achieve specific goals and tasks. Artificial intelligence is a term used to refer to the performance of machines that mimic human cognitive functions like learning and problem-solving [36]. Figure 15.2 [49] represents the structure of HRM impact and innovation with disruptive technology.

Human Resource Management includes all major activities in the working life of an employee, starting from the time he or she enters an organization to the time when he or she leaves it.

15.3.1 Disruptive HR technology

In the wake of globalization, what was once a domestic market has become Is HR transforming into a global network? As a result, human capital is less predictable, and more opportunities have become available. Therefore, human resources needed to be developed and changed to improve employee recruitment and retention. Usually, disruption is not something that occurs suddenly, and business houses overlook it until the market leaves them behind [45]. By developing an effective human resource management (HRM) system, the HR

Figure 15.2 Basic areas of HR management opened foray implementations.

experts were able to adjust this shift in policy design to meet the needs of today's market and strengthen the company's capabilities. AI, robotics, networking, and advanced manufacturing make up the categories of disruptive technologies [46]. Taking advantage of the emergence of excellence, leadership, and assimilation to the idea of total quality management (TQM) played a pivotal role in the development of HRM. As a result of the TQM movement resulting in conscious cost reduction, strategic application of information and communication technologies for HR operations has emerged in a bid to achieve the goal of the fullest human potential [2]. HR technology continues to simplify organizations' workflows and enhance capabilities, but there is still a stigma associated with adopting modern technology, primarily related to costs, maintenance, lack of knowledge and the costs associated with change. AI stands for artificial intelligence, which is defined differently today, e.g., a system which solves cognitive problems rather than an intelligent being [22].

Management of human resources work days: A quicker and smarter way to manage human resources has just arrived. Now it is easier than ever to keep up with employee performance and compensation. It enables

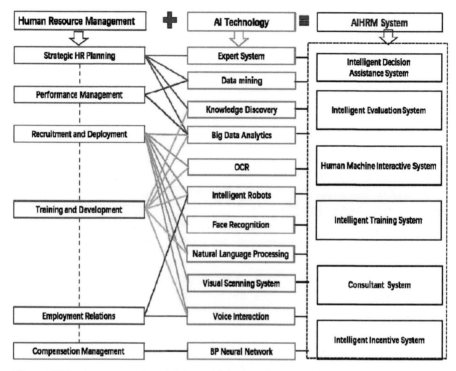

Figure 15.3   A conceptual model for artificial intelligence application in human resource management.

the companies to manage the lifetime global staff, from hire to retirement, with intuitive self-service features. Workday HRM allows them to manage the entire lifecycle of their global workforce effortlessly, from hire to retirement. In addition, the new system will enable businesses to manage compensation programmes effectively and adjust them to meet complex rewards requirements across the globe. Employers and contingent workers can be managed in one place, and contextual decision support features can be used to make better compensation decisions. This implies defining and managing global compensation components, such as allowances, base pay, equity and variable pay.

Newton's application tracking system is an applicant tracking system that is the most efficient among all application tracking systems available, so employers know how to meet the recruiting challenge without overspending. Employers can select hiring platforms to streamline the recruitment process more efficiently and ethically than ever before with this innovative tracking system. There is a mobile candidate tracking system that can be used by small, medium or large employers. All of them can benefit from its features, which are fully featured and will help anyone involved in the hiring process.

Programming software for enterprise resources in addition to offering an unparalleled total cost of ownership, JD Edwards Enterprise One combines essential business values and deep industry expertise with performance-driven HR technology. A group of integrated applications that are included in this unique application suite is designed to provide HR with a comprehensive system for gathering, storing, managing and interpreting data from all the company's business activities.

Through headquarters equipped with performance, recruiting and onboarding modernize recruiting with Cornerstone Rewritings well-organized with applicant management, public sourcing and employee referrals, employers can approach the right candidates very quickly. A recruiting tool can also be used to retrieve data from other talent-management tools, including learning, onboarding and performance. Through Cornerstone Onboarding technology, organizations can easily connect, train and engage new hires into the organization and keep them engaged. This technology connects new recruits to tools and training and gives them a chance to set goals.

By implementing the new system, HR professionals will not only integrate more effectively into organizations but will also be able to find new job opportunities and will also assist in decision-making by the company; HR will leverage technology to manage its human capital. In the era of technology now taking over the role of what is considered a 'core competency' for an organization to grow, HR technology has caused a real disruption to a domain which was relatively stable for many years. The study of the impact of disruption on organizations reveals that they evolve their resources, processes, value systems, and culture in response to this disruption [47]. With technology now becoming the key to an organization's growth, HR technology has become a disruptive force in a sector that has been relatively stable for years [4]. Organizations have therefore switched their focus to investing in HR technology to improve the impact of HR on business as part of enabling high performance through people. Since the digitalization of HR has taken place, the business status has changed since HR technology has evolved with a quantum shift in nature from disruption to disruption. It is the age of 'thinking machines 'applied to HR through the IQ dynamics system.

Cloud applications enable us to apply artificial intelligence to new applications using this technology. Cloud applications have become the 'Next Big Thing' in this era [5]. The need for a machine with intelligence seems to have increased as technology has advanced. As a result, artificial intelligence can perform tasks and reduce human effort. Nowadays, artificial intelligence services are becoming increasingly popular, and most people want such applications to become a part of their daily work lives. Approximately 130 million new jobs will be created with the advent of AI, according to the sources. It is possible to achieve a more sustainable and smarter environment through AI in HR companies' domain, which will improve the skill sets of new and previous employees. AI will take over the mundane and operational tasks of human resources, allowing them to focus on more important things. Adaptive enterprises have become vital to survive and succeed in a changing world due to the development of artificial intelligence (AI) technology [7].

15.3.2 Impact and innovation of HR intelligence

Intelligent computer systems perform human-like functions because of artificial intelligence. Artificial Intelligence makes machines smarter. The Turing test measures how well artificial intelligence can simulate human behaviour. Machine learning aims to develop algorithms and approaches that enable computers to learn. It has been developed for those who are interested in learning more about AI and how it is being applied to HR. It examines the basics of AI and explores how it is being applied to HR. It encompasses both academic and industry sources to present an analysis of artificial intelligence and its application in business. These studies focused on three questions: implementing new tools for AI at a budget-friendly cost; selecting technology that is sufficiently advanced from an ROI perspective; ensuring HR has the technical expertise to implement AI technology; and considering ethical implications. It is the approach used for the development of artificial intelligence. Due to globalization and the rapid development of information technology over the last several decades, human resources (HR) has evolved steadily into much more than an administrative function in the organization [14]. The development of Allo by Google, Messenger by Facebook, Cortana by Microsoft, Alexa by Amazon, and Siri by Apple have led to significant advances in artificial intelligence[13]. Artificial intelligence is being experimented with in various HR functions, including recruiting, onboarding, development, coaching, etc.

In addition, AI tools are used to improve the quality of job interviews and choose the right candidates for positions. We can create, engage and intelligent machines that operate like humans for human-like functions in many industries by utilizing artificial intelligence. Surely, artificial intelligence will continue to change the world of work with extreme promise, deploying AI to help with administrative tasks in HR to elevate the enterprise's efforts throughout the organization. [6]. Many organizational decisions are based on more than just data. Many HR departments in India still think employees can only be handled by human intervention. Resistance may come from focusing on issues such as the ethicality of relying solely on AI and other technology to make decisions [16]. The analytics and intelligence generated by a company are based on the data and information provided by its customers and employees. Using meta-learning, a system can learn through mathematical models. HR intelligence is a proactive, systematic process that gathers, analyzes, and achieves organizational goals by communicating, interpreting and using HR research and analytics results. These findings are used in the development of HR strategies and decision-making in the organization. It is possible to identify candidates for a job using artificial intelligence tools and to evaluate a candidate's performance during a job interview using AI tools. Nonetheless, it also appears that businesses all over the world show a reluctance to invest and adapt AI toward the HR function, in comparison to marketing, finance, etc. [15].

The implementation of AI into the human resource management process reduces bias related to the assessor. Better Works serves as a platform for setting and assessing goals. It provides real-time feedback and performance reviews. As a result, employees are motivated as they can see how their work is contributing to the organization reaching its goals and improving the bottom line. If the employee works hard, he/she is rewarded immediately, and vice versa.

JP Morgan employs a software solution called 'contract intelligence' (COIN) for identifying sources as required by lawyers in cases. AI tools have helped document discovery tools lawyers require for the identification of sources. In the legal field, AI is used to validate background information, predict the outcome of a case, automate document generation and bill clients. A lawyer would spend 360,000 hours reviewing documents, case files and legal briefs without AI.

15.3.3 Impact of robots on human resource management

A robot's use in different industries can differ considerably. Humanoid robots, such as the R2-robonaut, are designed to act like humans and think independently by using software, using tools, and communicating using messages (NASA website). The use of robotics and artificial intelligence in business can be detrimental to an organization's overall functions, as the writer says in his study, 'The Impact of Robotics and artificial intelligence on Business and Economics' [31]. Bernard Schmitt, professor at Columbia

Business School, explains that, whereas previously, robots were used primarily in industrial systems, they are now also used within organizations. He says robots are supercomputers that are human-like and pass the Turing test. Approximately 20 years from now, the author of the article advises managers to prepare for a time when artificial intelligence will be used in concert with human managers to do some of the analysis currently done by humans. It may be true that robots are more efficient at processing information and making decisions than humans, but that is not the whole story; some qualities of humans have still not been replicated by robots, such as emotions and creativity. Even after the digitization of many tasks, people will still be in control of various tasks for which various soft skills are required, including problem-solving, creativity, decision-making, etc. The key finding of our study is that, despite sufficient employment for most scenarios into 2030, a transition will be challenging, exceeding or matching the magnitude of shifts out of agriculture and manufacturing in the past. By 2030, there will be eight hundred million people losing their jobs around the world (one-fifth of the global workforce), as robots replace people [41].

According to Germany's Institute for Occupational Safety and Health (IFA), the new category of industrial robots is called cobots. It is a collaborative industrial robot that collaborates with humans in shared work processes while supporting and relieving the operator (Deligio and Naitove, 2016). In the production arena, cobots work with humans and perform repetitive tasks as collaborators. They are cost-effective and highly adaptable, and they are used by humans as well (Calitz et al., 2017). Using monitoring software, robots are used to curtail workplace harassment in yet another HR function. With the assistance of this technology, human resources professionals can monitor and understand data, and understand the culture and acceptable situations, enabling them to monitor and control workplace harassment. A robot monitors the communication between employees, checking if it is acceptable and congruent with the company's culture.

15.3.4 Disruptions in HRM by AI

In the future, artificial intelligence will undoubtedly disrupt human resources. A future HRM will combine technology focused on humans with people focused on technology. The latter may be viewed by some as a threat to HR as we know it. In the end, however, a pragmatic and optimistic view is that with AI continuing its rapid development, HR will be able to free up more and more time, allowing them to focus on what really matters: human interactions.

15.3.5 Implementing the onboarding procedure

Increasing employee productivity and reducing attrition can be achieved with AI-integrated HR software. Onboarding plays a critical role in reducing attrition. HR teams can use artificial intelligence to tailor the onboarding process to meet the needs of each employee based on their role. Organizations can define and set the algorithm according to their agenda.

15.3.6 Methods for decision analysis

An IBM study conducted in 2017 showed that artificial intelligence facilitates the deployment of data-driven decisions regarding decision-making. The use of data-driven decisions is beneficial for the growth of organizations. Employees' total well-being is the responsibility of the HR department, in addition to their work assignments. It also gauges the anxiety through the employee's voice so that HR can step in at the right time to manage the situation. Through AI integration, the team can analyse the mood of the employees and determine whether they need a break or not.

15.4 Role of AI in the Development of Human Resources

Organizations will be able to train their employees in their respective fields with AI integrated into Human Resource Management Systems (HRMS). Employees will be able to upgrade their skill sets to be at the top of their game.

AI helps HR departments examine their staff skill sets and recommend training modules appropriate for their job roles. The learning path is curated according to the employee's grasping ability to help them learn effectively. It determines the type of training that should be provided in each field. HR leaders can also integrate an artificial intelligence algorithm that defines the career path depending on the employee's skills into training so that they provide the workforce with the skills they need, brush up on existing knowledge, and more at their own pace. A recent article discussed the challenges of AI in human resources, pointing out that AI cannot identify the effectiveness of training costs. The researchers noted in their paper that artificial intelligence technologies can assist humans in performing rapid analysis of data [32]. As well as an array of self-assessment applications for the working individual, utilizing these applications will assist in formulating and judging the individual's career. [42]. HR departments can analyse the data and make concise decisions as a result of AI-based systems.

15.5 The Acquisition of Talent

AI has been successfully applied in the screening, scheduling, and answering of candidate-related questions, in the recruitment and talent acquisition processes. In the recruiting process, candidates frequently complain about the length of time it takes to move from the application stage to the selection stage. With the help of artificial intelligence, companies are not only reducing hiring times but also saving the time used by HR to manage candidate databases and perform other mundane administrative tasks. In most cases, using artificial intelligence to improve talent acquisition produces measurable and significant benefits almost immediately. Thus, it is found that AI and human intelligence are improving the candidate experience as well as the productivity of the process.

15.6 Administration of Human Resources

In human resources, administrative tasks are notorious for being time-consuming. A variety of administrative tasks, such as managing holiday entitlements, absences, performance data and timesheets, can be time-consuming and frustrating, especially when employees repeatedly request information about holiday entitlements. However, HR Management does not stop there—it also includes data collection and reporting on topics ranging from staff monitoring to salary information, as well as individual and team performance rankings. In addition to being able to automate these tasks, artificial intelligence could also contribute to reducing the time it takes to complete these tasks. The leave management, performance management, and shift scheduling functions of Sage HR allow these processes to run smoothly and efficiently without the time-consuming administrative aspects.

Furthermore, there are also approaches to scanning e-resumes by using data mining. Enterprise knowledge management is also solved using expert systems. Also discussed is the controversy about artificial intelligence replacing human resources (Turban & Frenzel, 1992; HRPA, 2017).

15.6.1 Managing human resources in the age of disruptive technology

Automation, digitalization and technological advances are rapidly transforming various sectors, regions and organizations. Human Resources as we know it will not exist in Industry 4.0, as it must evolve along with the industry. According to the PwC report 'Industry 4.0: Building the Digital Enterprise', key industries will see accelerated digitization by 2020. To remain in demand, a person's skills must be constantly updated; soft skills combined with technical and digital expertise are indeed going to be the best combination of human strength in the skills revolution era. Human Resources with universal skills are stagnant, and there is a risk of robots replacing people in the workplace because of technology.

15.6.2 Management of human resources: changing role of HR manager

Currently, companies need to equip their employees with the necessary skills as artificial intelligence has been integrated into human resource departments. However, many employees struggle to gain proficiency in digital technologies as well as to adapt and learn AI tools (Jain S., 2017) [26]. HR professionals can provide administrative services effectively by leveraging technology. It also helps them connect with customers both within and outside their organization. Due to the impact of technology in today's volatile business environment, HR processes and business practices are changing rapidly. Managing technology is a significant role that HR managers play in information, efficiency and relationships. Technology can be accessed and analysed by HR managers for information, efficiency and relationships. Information needs to be shared, HR operations must be improved, people must be connected within and outside of the organization must leverage social media tools, etc., and HR teams need to understand and use technology.

15.6.3 Research areas to be investigated in the future

As disruptive technology gained a lot of attention during the early 2000s which brought significant changes in organizations and people management robots and artificial intelligence technologies may be evaluated in the future for their impact on HRM practises, processes and employee relations, as well as organizational outcomes, as disruptive technologies. It is possible to investigate the impact an HR manager can have on the organization's results and the role's transformation to that of a strategic partner. Furthermore, research on the specific skills and characteristics of HR managers that will improve the uptake of disruptive technologies in organizations shortly can be conducted.

In the HR function around the globe, the digital revolution has brought opportunities, challenges, trends, and rapidly changing competencies across the fields of data science, artificial intelligence, cloud, blockchain and security. An organization's ability to deploy the right human skills efficiently and effectively, within and outside the organization, has become more essential than ever before. The new technology platforms to enhance the employee experience and the shift in expectations of the workforce will receive more attention. Enhancing employee satisfaction, reducing costs, and increasing the quality and accuracy of HR services can be achieved by leveraging existing HR investment in core HR platforms as well as cognitive solutions, including technology. As technology gets integrated into HR, the focus is on productivity, efficiency and effectiveness. HR technology, HR cloud, AI, automation, an agile workforce, flexible working schedules, performance reviews and talent management. We, the authors, have begun to work on a forecast of human resources technology based on the opinions of bloggers. There are numerous implications for conducting extensive research.

A modern augmented workforce is facing challenges due to artificial intelligence, robotics and open talent economies. Technology is likely to transform the future workplace and work over the next few years, disrupting the status quo within the realm of human resources. From the perspective of technology change and change consciousness, this chapter corroborates the shifts in HRM paradigms from the discussion and imagination of technologies and their change.

15.6.4 India's HRM practices using artificial intelligence

The introduction of artificial intelligence to the world has taken it by storm. It continues to grow at a rapid pace and is enhancing the growth of many companies. AI-enabled solutions are being developed for every issue—from sales to management. Employee relationship management encompasses developing corporate human resource strategies, recruiting, and selecting employees, training, and developing employees and managing performance, compensation, and employee mobility [18].

15.6.4.1 Automating repetitive tasks

HR departments are no exception, as they deal with repetitive tasks daily. Automation of this type of work can be achieved using artificial intelligence (AI) in HR applications, allowing your organization to save both time and resources. The advantage of AI is that it can make intelligent decisions, something that other machines cannot do. The management of employee benefits can be automated using AI, for example. The general queries within your team can be handled through it. Additionally, the onboarding of a new employee is an excellent example of automation. If an AI solution could take care of provisioning a device, allocating the space and other relevant tasks, HR teams would not have to worry about them. The scope and potential of AI-based HR applications are great. The saved time and resources can be used by the organization to boost its efficiency and productivity in more critical areas.

15.6.4.2 Experiences that improve employee relations

According to a review conducted by an industry-leading provider of cloud-based applications for the industry, we are already seeing some unique ways in which artificial intelligence is being used creatively to improve workflows. Several companies and organizations are already demonstrating the potential value this technology can bring to improving the quality of care and/ or reducing costs [39]. It is predicted that up to 50% of jobs will no longer be necessary in about 20 years, and healthcare is no exception [40] [55]. Employee engagement is associated with 21% higher profitability for companies. The difference is significant. In summary, companies strive to create a better employee experience for a variety of reasons. Additionally, AI is contributing to their success in this regard. Companies can utilize artificial intelligence (AI) to simplify their HR departments for their employees and provide them with the necessary information with the least amount of hassle. Voice assistants are becoming increasingly popular as a way of assisting employees with business queries. We can use voice assistants such as Amazon's Alexa or Apple's Siri daily to help us through our daily lives [13]. Learning and development are other areas in which AI in HR can be helpful to businesses. Through AI, businesses can automate human resource training. Their team can design effective learning paths with a little help from artificial intelligence. They can also use AI to manage their employees' training. Additionally, AI applications that are HR-based can enhance employees' experiences within an organization in many other ways. Artificial intelligence can be applied in human resource management in a practical and effective manner and provides benefits in the areas of employment, evaluation, and performance measurement [37, 38].

15.6.4.3 Increasing bias awareness

In most cases, bias cannot be removed from humans. Because of this, many recruiting companies are now turning to artificial intelligence for recruiting candidates. This trait makes AI perfect for recruiting since it does not have any biases. It works logically and rationally. A recruiter may have language bias, meaning that they would prefer candidates who speak a different dialect. Recruitment will always be biased, regardless of how subconscious it is.

As a company grows, it must hire people according to merit, and prejudices, such as racial and gender bias, inhibit growth.

There is a solution to this problem through artificial intelligence algorithms. Such algorithms can make an employer aware of their biases and eliminate them. As well as screening rejected candidates, recruiters can use this algorithm to identify those who may have lost their chance because of bias. This algorithm would have a more diverse candidate pool. HR managers who have access to data are better able to act in the interest of employees.

15.6.4.4 Using artificial intelligence to make decisions

HR managers can make better decisions using real-time data provided by modern technologies. Processes for dealing with so much data are cumbersome, but AI is quite fast while delay in decisions negatively impacts the productivity of an organization.

The problem can be solved quickly with artificial intelligence. Data can be transformed into text quicker, and insights gained through NLG software by using AI algorithms. Organizations have been using artificial intelligence when making decisions, dealing with uncertainty and especially when making ambiguous decisions. Even so, when subconscious decisions are crucial to evaluating and facilitating the outcome of decisions in an industry, technologies should rely on human involvement as the role of humans is essential [34]. Many visualization software programs offer quick and accurate results by utilizing artificial intelligence. If companies make faster decisions, they will be able to become more productive.

15.6.4.5 Reshaping skills

Based on a recent study conducted by Oracle and Future Workplace, human resource professionals believe that AI offers a chance to acquire new skills and lets employees enjoy more free time. By expanding their current responsibilities, human resources professionals can increase their strategic roles within their organizations. However, 81% of HR leaders who participated in the survey said that keeping up with technological changes is challenging at work. It has never been more important for human resources professionals to understand how AI is reshaping their industry.

15.7 Conclusion

This chapter addresses how technology can be deployed in the context of contemporary management and organizing technology to impact HR by systematically positing a global opinion. The study concludes with a perspective on disruptive technology that avoids the negativistic approach but emphasizes its positive impact on the application. Technology-driven HRM can harm people by disrupting the way they operate their human resources. On the other hand, such technology can have many positive outcomes for individuals as well as the organization.

HR functions have been transformed by disruptive technology and there is a gap in research between the application of AI in HRM and the AI application study observed. Employees and employers alike have benefitted from it. As a result of disruptive technology, HR functions are more effective and employee-friendly. Organizations need to embrace it as it is critical to their survival. The use of new emerging technologies by organizations lets them enter new markets, grow and create a learning culture based on their benefits, such as reduced costs and increased profitability.

References

[1] Rotich. K. J. (2015), History, Evolution and Development of Human Resource Management: A Contemporary Perspective; Global Journal of Human Resource Management; Vol. 3, No. 3, pp 58 – 73, May 2015; Published by European Centre forResearch Training and Development UK (www.ejournals.com), (browsed on 15th Dec2017).
[2] Barman. A, & Postangbam. C, (2018), Marriage of Human Resource to Data Science- A Narrative (an unpublished article submitted to IJMOS), (browsed on18 Dec 2017).
[3] Lovina (2017), — Breaking top 5 Myths about HR Technology, http://bloghiringplug.com/post/134/breaking-top-5-myths-about-hr-technology, (Browsed on 19th Dec 2017).
[4] Mazor. A., Kaushik. K., Magill J., Parthasarathy M., (2017),. Learning – The next frontier of digital HR, Hr technology, Talent, and Learning.
[5] Chinnuswamy. Y., (2017); HR in the age of technology; hrmasia, www.hrmasia.com (browsed on 12 Dec 2017).
[6] Darji S., (2016), Why do business require artificial intelligence (AI) in a HR Software?,; in http://blog.informa-mea.com/businesses-requireartificial-intelligence-ai-hr-software/ (browsedon 13th Jan 2018.
[7] Ertel, W. (2018). Introduction to artificial intelligence. NewYork, MA: Springer International Publishing.
[8] Sheila L.M., Steven G., Chad M. & Mayank G. (2018). The new age: artificial intelligence for human resource opportunities and functions. Ernst & Young LLP. 1–8.

[9] Noe, R., Hollenbeck, J., Gerhart, B., & Wright, P. (2006). Human Resources Management:Gaining a Competitive Advantage, Tenth Global Edition. New York, MA: McGraw-HillEducatio

[10] Kovach, K. A., & Cathcart Jr, C. E. (1999). Human resource information systems (HRIS):Providing business with rapid data access, information exchange and strategic advantage. Public Personnel Management, 28(2), 275–282.

[11] Lippert, S. K., & Michael Swiercz, P. (2005). Human resource information systems (HRIS) and technology trust. Journal of information science, 31(5), 340–353.

[12] Richard D. Johnson, Hal G. Gueutal (2011). Transforming HR Through Technology: The Use of E-HR and HRIS in Organizations. Retrieved from https://www.shrm.org/hr-today/trends-and-forecasting/.

[13] Maria Aspan. (2020, January 20). A.I. is transforming the job interview— and everything after. Retrieved from https://fortune.com/longform/hr-technology-ai-hiring-recruitment/.

[14] Mellam, A. C., Rao, P. S., & Mellam, B. T. (2015). The Effects of Traditional and Modern Human Resource Management Practiceson Employee Performance in Business Organisations in Papua New Guinea. Universal Journal of Management, 3(10), 389–394. doi: 10.13189/ujm.2015.031002.

[15] Wisenberg Brin. (2019, March 19). Employers Embrace Artificial Intelligence for HR. Retrieved from https://www.shrm.org/resourcesandtools/hr-topics/global-hr/pages/employers-embraceartificial-intelligence-for-hr.aspx.

[16] Vaishnavi J. Desai. (2019, 5). AI not gaining ground in HR functions: Arvind Gupta ofKPMG explains. Retrieved from https://cio.economictimes.indiatimes.com/news/strategy-and-management/ai-notgaining-ground-in-hr-functions-arvind-gupta-of-kpmg-explains/69659723.

[17] Cedric Villani.(2018,March).What is Artificial Intelligence? Villani mission on artificial intelligence. https://www.aiforhumanity.fr/pdfs/MissionVillani_WhatisAI_ENG(1)VF.pdf

[18] Jyoti Kapoor. (2020). Understand the Role of AI in HR in 2020.Retrieved from https://www.cutehr.io/ai-in-hr/.

[19] Meister, J. (2019, January 9). Ten HR Trends in The Age of Artificial Intelligence. Retrieved from https://www.forbes.com/sites/jeannemeister/2019/01/08/ten-hr-trends-in-tartificialintelligence/#3993dcec3219.

[20] V. K. Jain. (2014). Impact of Technology on HR Practices. International Journal of Informative & Futuristic Research, 1(10), 25–37. Retrieved from http://www.ijifr.com/pdfsave/13-062014621 JUNEV10-E15.pdf.

[21] Davenport, T. (2019, February 11). AI And HR: A Match Made in Many Companies. Retrieved from https://www.forbes.com/sites/tomdavenport/2019/02/10/ai-and-hr-a-match-made-in-manycompanies/#71bcdc983cd3.

[22] Marr, B. (2018). The Key Definitions of Artificial Intelligence (AI) That Explain Its Importance. Retrieved from https://www.forbes.com/sites/bernardmarr2018/02/14/the-key-definitions-of-artificial-intelligence-ai-that-explain-itsimportance/#766cc5bf4f5d.

[23] Alriza. (2018). 15 AI Applications / Use cases in Healthcare [2018 update]. Retrieved from https://blog.appliedai.com/healthcare-ai/ Applications, N. (2018). Blog. Retrieved from https://www.newgenapps.com/blog.

[24] Bharadwaj, R. (2018). AI in Transportation-Current and Future Business Use Applications. Retrieved from https://www.techemergence.com/ai-in-transportation-current-and-future-business-use-applications.

[25] Hooda, S. (2018). People Matters - Interstitial Site — People Matters. Retrievedfromhttps://www.peoplematters.in/article/employee-relations/5-ways-hr-will-be-affected-by-artificial-intelligence-18113.

[26] Jain, S. (2017). Is Artificial Intelligence –The Next Big Thing in HR? International Conference on Innovation Research in Scinece, Techonology and Management (pp. 220–224). Rajasthan: Modi Institute of Management & Technology.

[27] Riebli, J. (2018, January 25). bthe change. Retrieved from bthe change website:https://bthechange.com/3-ways-artificial-intelligence-can-improve-workplace-learning-40b1185bc0d3

[28] Amla, M., & Malhotra, P. M. (2017). Digital Transformation in HR. International Journal of Interdisciplinary and Multidisciplinary Studies (IJIMS), 4(3), 536–544. Retrieved from http://www.ijims.com.

[29] Kapoor, B. (2010, December). Business Intelligence and Its Use for Human Resource Management. The Journal of Human Resource and Adult Learning, 6(2), 21–30.

[30] Jain, D. S. (2018, March). Human Resource Management and Artificial Intelligence. International Journal of Management and Social Sciences Research (IJMSSR), 7(3), 56–59.

[31] Dirican, C. (2015). The Impacts of Robotics, Artificial Intelligence on Business and Economics. Procedia-Social and Behavioral Sciences, 564–573.

[32] Buzko, I., Dyachenko, Y., Petrova, M., Nenkov, N., Tuleninova, D., & Koeva, K. (2016). Artificial Intelligence technologies in human resource development. Computer Modelling & New Technologies, 26–29.

[33] R,G., & D,B.S. (2018, July). Recruitment through artificial Intelligence: A conceptual study. International Journal of Mechanical Engineering and Technology (IJMET), 9(7), 63–70. Retrieved from http://www. iaeme.com/ijmet/issues.asp?JType=IJMET&VType=9&IType=7

[34] Jarrahi, M. H. (2018). Artificial Intelligence and the Future of Work: Human-AI Symbiosis in Organizational Decision Making. Business Horizons, 61(4), 1–10. doi: 10.1016/j.bushor.2018.03.007.

[35] Wang D. et al.(2015). A problem solving oriented intelligent tutoring system to improve students 'acquisitionofbasic computerskills // Comput. Educ

[36] Kaplan, A., & Haenlein, M. (2019). Siri, Siri, in my hand: Who's the fairest in the land? On the interpretations, illustrations, and implications of artificial intelligence. Business Horizons, 62(1), 15–25.

[37] Aldulaimi, Saeed Hameed, and Obeidat Abdul Qadir (2016). Human Resources Performance Measurement Approaches Compared to Measures Used in Master's Theses inApplied Science University. International Review of Management and Marketing, 6(4), 958–963.

[38] Abdeldayem, M.M., and S.H. Aldulaimi, 2019. How Changes in Leadership Behaviour and Management Influence Sustainable Higher Education in Bahrain. International Journal of Scientific and Technology Research, 8(11): 1926–1934.

[39] Mesko B. The role of artificial intelligence in precision medicine. Expert Rev Precis MedDrugDev. 2017:1–3.

[40] Frey C.B., Osborne. M. (2013). The future of employment: how susceptible are jobs to computerisation?

[41] McKinsey & Company. (2013). Disruptive technologies: Advances that will transform life, business, and the global economy. NewYork City, NY: McKinsey Global Institute. https://www.mckinsey.com/quarterly/the-magazine.

[42] Schermerhorn, S.G. Hunt & R. N. Osborn (2012) Comportement Humain et Organisation, (Village mondiale, 2emeédition, Paris, France, impriméau Canada,), PP 75–80.

[43] Wire Piazza, L.N. (2018). How Can Artificial Intelligence Work for HR? SHRM.

[44] Abdeldayem, M.M., and S.H. Aldulaimi, 2018. The economic islamicity index, between islami city and universality: Critical review and discussion. International Business Management, 12(1): 46–52.

[45] Christensen, C.M., Johnson, M.W. and Rigby, D.K. (2002). Foundations for growth: howto identify and build disruptive new businesses, MIT Sloan Management Review, Vol. 43,No. 3,pp.22–31.

[46] Evans, G.L. (2017). Disruptive technology and the board: the tip of the iceberg1, Economics and Business Review, Vol. 3, No. 1, pp. 205–223.

[47] Karimi, J. and Walter, Z. (2015). The role of dynamic capabilities in responding to digital disruption: a factor-based study of the newspaper industry, Journal of Management Information Systems, Vol. 32, No. 1, p.39.

[48] Nalina Ganapathi & Dr. N. Panchanatham 'The Role of Human Resource Management in Cross-Cultural Environment' - The Way to Managerial Communication. https://www.researchgate.net/publication/259998636_ The_Role_of_Human_Resource_Management_in_Cross-Cultural_ Environment_-_The_Way_to_Managerial_Communication.

[49] Qiong Jia (2018). A Conceptual Artificial Intelligence Application Framework in Human Resource Management.

[50] Charbel José Chiappetta Jabbour* and Fernando César Almada Santos. The central role of human resource management in the search for sustainable organizations. The International Journal of Human Resource Management, Vol. 19, No. 12, December 2008, 2133–2154.

[51] Martín-Alcázar, F., Romero-Fernandez, P.M. & Sanchez-Gardey, G. (2005). Strategic human resource management: integrating universalistic, contingent, configurational, and contextual perspectives. International Journal of Human Resource Managament, Vol. 16, No. 5, Pp 633–659. Retrieved March 7, 2010, from: http://molar.crb.ucp.pt/cursos/ 2%C2%BA%20Ciclo%20%20Mestrados/Gest%C3%A3o/200709/ DGRH/Papers/Alcaz%C3%A1r_revis%C3%A3o%20de%20litera-tura%20sobre%20GERH.pdf

[52] Kishor, A., Chakraborty, C. Artificial Intelligence, and Internet of Things Based Healthcare 4.0 Monitoring System. Wireless PersCommun (2021). https://doi.org/10.1007/s11277-021-08708-5

[53] Kishor, A., Chakraborty, C. & Jeberson, W. Reinforcement learning for medical information processing over heterogeneous networks. Multimed Tools Appl 80, 23983–24004 (2021). https://doi.org/10.1007/ s11042-021-10840-0

[54] Kishor, A., Chakraborty, C., & Jeberson, W. (2020). A novel fog computing approach for minimization of latency in healthcare using machine learning. Int J Interact MultimedArtif Intell, 1(1).

Index

About the Editors

Anamika Pandey is presently working as an Associate Dean in School of Business, Galgotias University, Delhi-NCR, India. Her area of specialization is human resource development and organizational change and development. She has more than 16 years of academic and industry experiences. Her bachelors, masters and D.Phil. degrees are from the Central University of India. She has more than 30 research papers in high indexed journals in the area of organizational assessment and techniques, assessment of intangible assets and stress management. She has also authored two books in the area of HR. She is also on the editorial board of one ABDC journal. In addition to her academic experience, she has also conducted more than 30 management development programs for the armed forces, banking and manufacturing sector employees on soft and behavioral skills.

Balamurugan Balusamy is currently working as an Associate Dean Student in Shiv Nadar University, Delhi-NCR. Prior to this assignment he was Professor, School of Computing Sciences & Engineering and Director International Relations at Galgotias University, Greater Noida, India. His contributions focus on engineering education, Blockchain and data sciences.His academic degrees and twelve years of experience working as a Faculty in a global University like VIT University, Vellore has made him more receptive and prominent in his domain. He has 200 plus high impact factor papers published with Springer, Elsevier and IEEE. He has contributed to more than 80 edited and authored books and collaborated with eminent professors across the world from top QS ranked universities. Dr. Balusamy has served up to the position of Associate Professor in his stint of 12 years of experience with VIT University, Vellore. He completed his Bachelors, Masters and Ph.D.degrees with top premier institutions in India. His passion is teaching and adapts different design thinking principles while delivering his lectures. He has published 80+ books on various technologies and visited 15 plus countries for his technical course. He has several top-notch conferences in his resume and has published over 200 of quality journal, conference and book chapters combined. He serves in the advisory committee for several startups and forums and does consultancy work for industry on Industrial IOT. He has given over 195 talks in various events and symposium.

 **Naveen Chilamkurti** is currently Acting Head of Department, Computer Science and Computer Engineering, La Trobe University, Melbourne, VIC, Australia. He obtained his Ph.D. degree from La Trobe University. He is also the Inaugural Editor-in-Chief for International Journal of Wireless Networks and Broadband Technologies launched in July 2011. He has published about 165 Journal and conference papers. His current research areas include intelligent transport systems (ITS), wireless multimedia, wireless sensor networks, and so on. He currently serves on the editorial boards of several international journals. He is a Senior Member of IEEE. He is also an Associate editor for Wiley IJCS, SCN, Inderscience JETWI, and IJIPT.

For Product Safety Concerns and Information please contact our
EU representative GPSR@taylorandfrancis.com Taylor & Francis
Verlag GmbH, Kaufingerstraße 24, 80331 München, Germany